the intuitive parent

CURRENT

STEPHEN CAMARATA

the intuitive parent

WITHDRAWN

Why the Best Thing for Your Child Is You

Current

CURRENT
An imprint of Penguin Random House LLC
375 Hudson Street
New York, New York 10014
penguin.com

ISBN 978-1-59184-613-0

Printed in the United States of America
10   9   8   7   6   5   4   3   2   1

Set in Janson Text
Designed by Spring Hoteling

To intuitive parents everywhere—and
to their fortunate children!

contents

CONTENTS

the
intuitive
parent

introduction
What Is Intuitive Parenting?

During more than twenty-five years as a researcher studying child development at Vanderbilt University, and as a practicing clinician working with ASD, Down syndrome, and other developmental conditions, I have never met a parent who did not want to give his or her child the best possible start in life, or to raise that child to become a healthy, happy, successful, independent adult. But over the last decade, I have noticed a marked increase in the anxiety—and guilt—parents feel about how exactly to go about it. The glut of information, accurate and inaccurate; an ever more competitive, global economy; and the burgeoning market of books, shows, products, programs, "experts," apps, and devices marketed as essential aids in raising the smartest, healthiest, best baby ever have many parents feeling either overwhelmed, insecure, or intensely driven to succeed at this most important job.

Recently, the *Guardian* newspaper in London publicly wondered why modern parents are so anxious about raising their children—especially at a time when the likelihood of a child dying young is

1

at an all-time low:[1] "Why is it that at the very time in western history when humans have finally been freed from the probability that our children will die young, that anxiety about children has become [so] rampant?"[2] Best-selling author Jennifer Senior talks about how children radically alter their parents' lives in the book *All Joy and No Fun*, and discusses the never-ending anxiety parents have about raising their children, from the moment of birth through high school. In my own work as a child development specialist, I have talked with hundreds and hundreds of parents and most seem worried—if not downright petrified—by the short- and long-term consequences of their everyday parenting choices. One mother recently told me that if her son didn't learn to read by the time he reached his third birthday, he wouldn't be admitted to the competitive preschool they were applying for. This in turn would mean that he wouldn't be selected for an academic magnet grade school. The poor little fellow was only eighteen months old at the time! A father insisted that his toddler shouldn't waste time playing with blocks because it was crucial that her developing brain be "wired" to learn vocabulary—while insisting that his wife pound flash cards rather than play with their daughter because it was vital that they take advantage of a "critical period" for "neural plasticity" as soon as possible. This couple believed that they had only another year or two to get their daughter's brain properly constructed for lifelong learning. If they didn't, they mistakenly believed the opportunity would be lost forever and she would be doomed to a life of intellectual mediocrity. This kind of anxiety is a major obstacle to living in the moment with your baby or child and creates pressure to accelerate development and micromanage learning in a way that actually derails healthy intellectual and emotional growth and undermines a child's self-confidence.

I feel for these caring, conscientious, concerned parents. The world can be a difficult place to navigate these days; they want to give their children every possible advantage, and a vast industry leverages their fears, hopes, and love for their child in order to "get eyeballs" or simply to sell them unnecessary stuff. But what the information glut and relentless marketing obscures is this: Focusing on—and unleashing—your natural personal parental intuition is *exactly* what it takes to raise intelligent, confident, curious, and talented children who will develop into equally talented adults. A surprisingly large body of scientific literature supports this conclusion; and I can vouch for it personally, having raised seven children—three daughters and four sons—in light of its principles. But too many parents these days have lost confidence in themselves and in the genius of Mother Nature.

That's why I wrote this book: to show parents that they are already equipped with all the "state-of-the-art" know-how necessary to "wire" their child's brain and instill in him or her a love of discovery and of learning that will last a lifetime; and that they can best prepare their child to thrive in school and in adult life through a natural process I call intuitive parenting.

What is intuitive parenting? Simply stated, intuitive parenting emphasizes focusing on your child, enjoying the moment, and reacting naturally to whatever the baby is doing. It's a style of parenting that allows you to concentrate on being a learning partner rather than a taskmaster or über-teacher, and helps you resist the panic that comes with thinking that there are other things or more things you should be teaching your child at a given moment. It is a way of parenting that supports clearing your mind of all the noise, worry, guilt, and anxiety that are part and parcel of parenting in the modern world and living in the moment with your baby and, later, with your toddler and young child. It even works great with teenagers!

By reacting—and acting—intuitively, you will actually become the very best teacher (and parent) your child could possibly have. As your child grows from baby to toddler and then preschooler, he or she will be naturally and continually *signaling* you as to what they currently know, what they need to learn next, and precisely the right input needed from you for them to learn and to wire their brain. An intuitive parent's main job is to *pay attention* to your child and then *respond* normally. And fortunately, this intuitive parenting is seamlessly integrated into the daily caregiving that babies and young children require. Feeding, diaper changing, bedtimes, wake-up routines, bath time, and quiet moments together all yield extremely powerful learning opportunities for your child's developing—and plastic—brain. Whenever you are engaging in any of these everyday tasks and *following your baby's developmental lead*, you're doing the right thing for your baby's brain.

By giving parents a greater awareness of their intuitive parenting powers, I hope to inoculate them against feelings of inadequacy preyed upon by self-styled experts and manufacturers of educational products claiming to accelerate "brain development." In addition, I hope that the information herein helps reduce the overwhelming stress parents feel raising a child in what has become a highly competitive and peer-pressure-driven culture. That stress not only produces undesired outcomes in child rearing but it also all too often robs parents, especially mothers, of the natural enjoyment of interacting with their infants, toddlers, and preschoolers.

One of the most striking things about children—and human beings generally—is just how variable we are in personality, temperament, and learning style. How can any book on parenting possibly provide accurate and relevant advice for all parents and all their children? Even a cursory survey of current how-to books on parenting illustrates this problem. There are books that advocate "laissez-faire" parenting wherein children are essentially allowed to roam free in the belief—and hope—that nature will automatically teach them what they need to learn. At the other extreme are books that exhort parents essentially to micromanage their children beyond what even the most exuberant "helicopter mom" could possibly imagine. The truth is that there is no one-size-fits-all parenting approach just as there is no one-size-fits-all child.

But wait a minute! Isn't *this* book advocating a particular parenting style? Actually, intuitive parenting is not a one-size-fits-all or one-dimensional approach. The fundamental principles—paying attention to your child and responding intuitively and naturally—can and should be done within the context of an individual child's traits and any parent's normal way of responding. Indeed, the foundational basis for intuitive parenting—following your child's lead and responding to him or her—*automatically* coordinates their temperament, current knowledge level, and stage of brain development with your individual parenting style. You can find your child's—and your very own—learning "sweet spot." Free-range parents, "tiger mothers," and everyone in between can readily implement the basic principles of intuitive parenting within the rubric of their own personal parenting style and comfort level.

Every parent who has more than one child understands, no, *lives* the fundamental truth that no two children are alike. In my own personal experience raising seven children, some were cautious, others were daring. Some were introspective, others were outgoing and gregarious. Although all had—and still have—a love of learning and an ample supply of curiosity, the way that each one learned and their individual patterns of strengths and weaknesses were—and still are—strikingly different. Another universal appears to be that each has a strong, positive self-image, a well-developed sense of humor, and a high degree of confidence in their abilities. No doubt these positive traits were inherited directly from their mother, who needed an ample supply of both to raise them and to be married to me!

Some of our children preferred a relatively high degree of

independence and wanted to learn things on their own. Others seemed to prefer learning in groups and enjoyed receiving relatively frequent feedback. Some were self-starters, others benefited from having us provide incentives and supervision as a way of supporting their development and learning. All had vivid imaginations growing up, but some were more imaginative than others. In short, our parenting required not only the inevitable adjustments that every child requires as he or she grows up, but sensitivity to each of our children's *individual* temperaments, learning styles, and needs.

To be sure, there are certain common elements in parenting, especially intuitive parenting, that benefit all children regardless of their individual traits. Independence, resilience, creativity, confidence, and thinking ability should be nurtured in *all* children. But how these are nurtured can vary greatly, depending on the individual child. And these common elements can be readily adapted to your own, individual parenting style and comfort level. A "tiger mother"[3] could never be a "free-range"[4] mother, and vice versa. Yet, in the end, both want the same things for their children, and each is trying to foster the foundational traits described above. Given all this variability in children—and their parents—which parenting elements could possibly be readily adopted by all? More important, which of these elements would nurture their children, facilitate brain development, and harness brain plasticity while also meeting their individual child's needs—and also readily be incorporated into their own parenting style?

The breathtaking diversity in human abilities and capabilities is a direct reflection of the flexibility and resilience of the human brain. Like snowflakes, no two human brains are wired precisely alike.[5] But the good news is that this remarkable organ comes well prepared to efficiently develop in a wide variety of environments offering a myriad of learning opportunities.

Parents: Take a breath, slow down, and experience the sheer joy—and fun—that infants, toddlers, and preschoolers bring to the learning experience. In doing so you will lay the foundation for the school years, adolescence, and beyond. Your precious baby will learn what you teach, and so much more, if he or she is simply given the opportunity. And you will be forming a lifelong positive relationship with your child. As a parent, your challenge is to filter out the nonsense and concentrate on responding naturally, confidently, lovingly, and *intuitively* to your baby's needs. Trust Mother Nature—and trust your own intuition. Your parenting mantra will be to do what comes naturally and focus on nurturing and enhancing your child's natural curiosity and problem-solving abilities.

HERE ARE THE BASIC PRINCIPLES OF INTUITIVE PARENTING:
- An intuitive parent is devoted to raising a confident, smart, emotionally healthy child.
- An intuitive parent *knows* that all children are inherently curious—and can become highly intelligent—and that their goal as parents is to nurture and encourage these traits.
- An intuitive parent is positive, **confident**, and in tune with his or her own inner "parenting voice."
- An intuitive parent knows there is no one-size-fits-all parenting or teaching style. Even children within the same family have different temperaments and needs; an intuitive parent can stick to his or her values but also provide individualized responses to a child.
- Intuitive parents are patient, knowing that they have eighteen years—or more—to guide their child's development and can therefore resist the anxiety and pressure to rush development or cram "knowledge" into their child's head before the child is ready.
- An intuitive parent knows that he or she is laying the foundation for an adult brain and resists "get-rich-quick" schemes that shortchange them—and their child. Their child's brain becomes wired to reason and problem-solve, traits that can

be adapted to whatever knowledge and challenges the future holds.

- An intuitive parent is a guide—but also a *partner* in his or her child's development.
- Intuitive parents teach *in response to* their child's interests and initiations and nurture their child's own innate curiosity and love of learning.
- An intuitive parent knows that a developing child—and their brain—needs to try, and to make mistakes, in order to learn.
- An intuitive parent understands that he or she must foster a child's sense of self by helping them discover how to regulate their emotions and how to overcome adversity.
- An intuitive parent enjoys and takes pride in his or her child and maintains positive and optimistic interactions with that child regardless of temperament or learning style. Girls and boys learn early on that their parents are interested and engaged mothers and fathers who will help them when they need help, but that they are also empowered—and expected—to seek knowledge and solutions to their problems on their own.

You already have everything you need to properly raise and teach your child and ensure optimal development of his or her neural architecture for lifelong learning: love and affection, common sense, and a positive outlook. Everything else will arise naturally in the process of caring for, nurturing, and naturally interacting with your baby—and your growing child. No special tools or software or apps are required.

Now let me show you why and how intuitive parenting works.

chapter 1

Mother Nature's Instruction Manual

Whenever you purchase a complex product such as an automobile or a computer, it comes with an instruction manual that describes its operation. While you often can buy a more detailed technical manual that will delineate the intricacies of how each element in an automobile engine works or how the motherboard in the computer is configured, most manuals that come with your product are designed to simply and efficiently teach you how to operate it.

But a baby—a much more complicated "device" than any automobile or computer—does not come packaged with a technical manual explaining how to simply and efficiently parent her nor detailing the intricacies of her brain and how to wire it for future use as she grows into a toddler, preschooler, primary student, middle school student, high schooler, college student, or perhaps even graduate student on her way to becoming an independent adult.

Human beings have by far, at least by animal standards, the

longest childhoods and require the most parental nurturing of any species.[1] Single-cell creatures such as amoebae receive no parenting whatsoever; their "parent," which is both mother and father, simply divides and the "babies" go on their merry way.[2] Many species, including alligators, fish, and spiders, protect their eggs or nests but do not parent their offspring after they hatch. Their "babies" are smaller versions of the adults and enter into the Darwinian "survival of the fittest" without the benefit of parental guidance.

Mammals parent their offspring—at least to some extent—before the young strike out on their own. Sometimes, this parenting means simply feeding their babies. All mammals nurse their young, but some take care of their offspring even after the babies are no longer nursing; humans and other primates do so for a much longer period than other species. Mice and other rodents bid their offspring *vaya con dios* shortly after weaning them, which only takes a few weeks.[3] Canine babies such as foxes, coyotes, and wolves will stay with their mothers and learn to hunt during their first year before striking off on their own.[4] Whales also tend their young for about a year.[5] Lion cubs stay with their mothers for about two years and polar bear cubs stay with their mothers for about two and a half years[6]—and of these, whales, wolves, and lions stay in family groups even after the young have been weaned and have learned to obtain food.

In contrast, humans and other primates have much more parental investment in their offspring, extending to nearly a decade in chimpanzees and often nearly two decades in humans.[7] Of course, human parenting never really "ends," but if we define the boundary as the moment a child is capable of living independently, the norm in modern human societies would be approximately two decades. As a human parent, you may sometimes envy insects, fish, reptiles, and other species that essentially provide no parenting whatsoever, so that no instruction manual or decision making in the absence of such a manual is required. One can speculate that no insect has ever felt any remorse or guilt about being an ineffective parent or has lost sleep worrying about its child's future!

But for humans in an increasingly complex modern world, the problem of child-rearing is much more difficult. Parents face difficult choices and serious information overload. The Internet is replete with all kinds of conflicting advice from self-styled parenting "experts" whose only credentials may be a computer and access to WiFi (and, perhaps, an ax to grind). Thanks to advances in medical science, neuropsychology, brain imaging, and other fields, there is also a lot of genuine new data and information available about how babies grow, how brains learn, and how people stay healthy and thrive in the social world. But there is also a wealth of different interpretations about what the new information means, what findings are—or aren't—definitive or important, and what, if anything, we should do with what we have discovered.

To make matters worse, there is the burgeoning child development educational industry offering a myriad of products claiming to properly "wire" children's brains so that they can grow into adults who are well prepared to thrive in a rapidly changing world, to utilize modern technology, to multitask, and to gain a competitive advantage over the neighbors'—or a faraway country's—kids.

How can a parent possibly know what to do without having an extensive database on child-rearing practices stored in his or her own brain? Thankfully, Mother Nature did provide her own version of a training manual: She provided parents and babies with a DNA map—and a plastic brain that predisposes them to interact in ways that ensures necessary parental input is provided at the time it is most needed.[8]

A child is born with the uncanny ability to elicit appropriate teaching responses from her parents. And parents' normal, nurturing responses to their baby's needs and their responses to the social contact the baby initiates give the baby *everything* its developing brain requires. Even more important, this feedback loop effectively wires children's brains for problem solving and reasoning, the very skills that will be increasingly important to them in the future. And because this learning occurs in the context of natural, normal social interaction, these skills, unlike computerized learning or flash cards, readily transfer to other people and other social contexts, such as school. Moreover, building "people skills" in addition to intelligence will serve your child very well indeed, both in school and in adult life.

But because this interactive process is automatic and ubiquitous, it is all too easy to overlook how powerful and amazing Mother Nature's implicit instruction manual really is. Parents do not need to be child development experts with PhDs in developmental psychology in order to be terrific mothers and fathers! Indeed, if a parent sets out to micromanage a baby's brain development and learning by consciously seeking to teach everything the baby needs to know, that parent would inevitably fail miserably. Worse, that parent could even inadvertently derail the proper process for ensuring that their child develops a facile, intelligent brain and a healthy mind, especially if they push things before their child—and the child's developing brain—is ready to learn that information.

Early on in infancy and toddlerhood, a child's brain is biased toward learning through the experiences of interacting with the environment in natural ways. Problem solving is built upon trying *and failing*, and using the input—and experience from these successes and failures to develop more sophisticated approaches to solving problems—and learning to persist while regulating his or her emotions when things don't go as planned. The time spent playing with blocks, exploring objects, learning about the different sounds that occur when their parents speak, and the literally thousands of pieces of information that are integrated in their developing minds is more than ample to get the job done.[9] An extensive scientific literature supports the importance of intuitive play on shaping the brain—and on developing reasoning ability essential to problem solving.

My own research—and that of many other scientists—has indicated that play-based interactive learning is a key foundation for language development and many other aspects of reasoning and social skills. Studies also show that intuitive play also has a vital role in shaping the foundations for a child's understanding of science and math as well as learning to read.

Intuitive Parenting in Action

Several years ago I experienced one of the most spectacular events anyone can have in their life: I become a grandfather to a beautiful granddaughter. It has been wonderful watching my oldest daughter, Katie, and my son-in-law Brent raise their precious baby Nina, and it is a real treat to see them and her whenever possible.

When they were visiting several years ago, I happened to witness the following scene: Katie was holding baby Nina, who was about three months old at the time and had just finished her milk "dinner" in a rocking chair in their living room, rocking gently back and forth. Nina started cooing (making contented baby noises), which got her mother's attention. Immediately, Katie lifted baby Nina while turning her so that the baby was now facing her. Katie smiled and began speaking in a happy, high-pitched singsong voice to her baby: "Oh, you are so cute. Now you have a full tummy and are soooo happy. Mommy thinks you are the best baby ever!" Nina looked into her mother's face and smiled back. Naturally, this resulted in an even bigger smile from Katie and more happy chatter from her and reciprocal happy sounds from baby Nina. The back-and-forth went on for more than ten minutes. It was simply wonderful to watch the sheer joy of a mother and her baby discovering each other.

Fast-forward eight months: Now Nina is a toddler nearing her first birthday. She is not yet walking but can crawl quite rapidly and is into everything she can reach. Her father, Brent, is playing a game with her that he calls "Smash Boom!" He stacks a set of four or five foam blocks into a minitower and says "Smash boom!" Nina looks up at Brent from across the family room and smiles and then looks at the blocks he has stacked. She crawls as fast as she can to the tower and swipes with her hand, knocking over the blocks. This is evidently wildly funny: Brent and Nina (and Grandpa too) all laugh and laugh after she knocks the blocks over. Then Brent starts stacking the blocks once again. What could be better than watching a father play with his daughter while they have so much fun together? This seemingly mundane activity is laying the foundations for important father-daughter emotional bonds[10] as well as teaching Nina about cause and effect—and she is learning about humor too.

Another year passes and now Nina has a baby sister. Like most two-year-olds, Nina has difficultly pronouncing some words. Her sister's name is Gwen, so Nina does the best she can, calling her sister "Gong-Gong." Mom, Dad, Grandma, and Grandpa all think this is hilarious and immediately start calling baby Gwen "Gong-Gong" too. But we also call her Gwen, especially after Nina has said "Gong-Gong." A conversation between Brent and Nina went something like this. *Nina*: "Gong-Gong eat." *Brent*: "Yes, Gwen is eating! You are eating too." *Nina*: "Gong-Gong night-night." Now Brent says "Yes, Gwen is sleeping. I will read you a book before you go night-night too." Nina grabs a stuffed animal and a book and snuggles into Daddy's lap.

This scene may seem mundane, but the power of these parent-child interactions is immense. Nina is learning how to pronounce "Gwen" while also learning new vocabulary, the grammar of English, and setting the stage for a lifelong love of reading and learning. Even better, Nina is forming strong, positive emotional bonds with her mother and her father that will empower and sustain her as she meets the inevitable challenges she will encounter growing up.

These are just a few simple examples of intuitive parenting in action. Intuitive parenting means simply *responding* naturally to a baby or a young child after he or she *initiates*, in what brain and behavior scientists call a "feedback loop." In essence, a baby or a child's behavior elicits a response from the parent—which in turn elicits another, perhaps different response from the child—with yet another parent response, and so on. The back-and-forth interaction between parent (or any caregiver) and child is every bit as important to a child's development as the particular "educational content" of the activity they are engaging in.

The main scientific elements in this parent-child feedback loop were described by psychologist Arnold Sameroff more than thirty years ago.[11] Technically, Sameroff named this parent-child feedback loop the "transactional model" of development. He was most interested in how parent responses fostered positive social development in children. But in subsequent years, scientists studying language development, math learning, problem solving, learning to draw, learning to read and to play music, and many other aspects of development have also come to recognize the power of the transactional model of development. Study after study over the last half century has shown that a parent's intuitive response to their child's initiations is one of the most powerful and positive learning experiences a child can possibly have.[12]

Research continues to support the importance of intuitive parenting—and transactional learning. For example, the October 16, 2014, Science section of the *New York Times* proclaimed: "Quality of Words, Not Quantity, Is Crucial to Language Skills, Study Finds." Those of us studying typical—and atypical—child development have long known that simply throwing mass quantities of words, or letters, or numbers, or anything else at children—and at their developing brains—simply doesn't work. The lead author of the study discussed in the *Times* article, Dr. Kathy Hirsh-Pasek from Temple University in Philadelphia, sums up the results: "It's not just about shoving words in, it's about having these fluid conversations around shared rituals and objects, like pretending to have morning coffee together or using the banana as a phone. That is the stuff from which language is made."[13]

Of course, the importance of parent-child interaction is not limited to language development alone, nor to early child development. Laying the right foundation is important, but so is building on that foundation as your child—and his or her brain—grows up. The relationship you build with your young child will blossom and help both parent and child navigate difficult school years that morph into even more daunting and turbulent teenage trials and tribulations. The intuitive parent is well equipped to handle—and actually enjoy (as I did)—not only early childhood, but all stages of their child's growth and maturation, including the teenage years.

The Marketer's Myth of "Enhanced" Parenting

A combination of factors has coalesced to cast doubt on the value of intuitive, transactional learning in favor of technology and artificially enhanced learning programs touted as a way to accelerate development and provide shortcuts to wiring the brain. Commonsense, intuitive parenting is continually being undermined, and it often comes under direct assault.

How has this happened? First, parents are working longer hours, live increasingly complex lives, and seemingly have less time to spend with their baby, toddler, or preschool child.[14] A recent study by the Pew Research Center found "roughly equal shares of working mothers and fathers report in a new Pew Research Center survey feeling stressed about juggling work and family life: 56% of working moms and 50% of working dads say they find it very or somewhat difficult to balance these responsibilities."[15] This report also suggested that parents, and mothers in particular, feel guilty about not spending enough time with their babies and young children. In short, they are primed to fall prey to clever marketing pitches urging them to "make up for lost time" by buying educational products.

Another factor undermining intuitive parenting is that schools and preschools, especially in the United States, are becoming increasingly competitive, and the amount of information a child is expected to learn seems to get bigger and bigger every year. Worse, children are expected to accumulate this knowledge, and take tests, at younger and younger ages.[16] No wonder parents mistakenly believe that every moment they get to spend with their baby, toddler, or preschooler must be designed for artificially accelerated learning and brain development—and that the "old-fashioned" way of relaxed, intuitive parenting dooms a child, and his or her brain, to failure.

This guilt and anxiety about whether we, as parents, are doing what's best for our babies, toddlers, and preschoolers is leveraged and amplified by manufacturers pushing DVDs, educational toys, computer software, and other products purported to accelerate, enhance, and maximize learning. *Forbes* magazine recently reported that sales of Baby Einstein videos and DVDs and multimedia products aimed at preschoolers aged birth to four grew from $1 million in annual revenue to more than $10 million in just a few years, and the brand was rumored to be valued at more than $400 million.[17] Another product, Your Baby Can Read, reportedly raked in more than $185 million in total sales at the peak of its popularity.[18] In essence, these products emphasize a particular skill—in isolation—and repeat it over and over. In Your Baby Can Read, the target skill is memorizing letters and recognizing simple words. But this drill is akin to teaching a parrot to talk. A young child can be induced to recognize and parrot the names of letters and words using a DVD or set of flash cards, but this comes at the cost of bypassing the actual knowledge he or she needs—what the words *mean* in the real world and how words are assembled

into sentences as a means of communicating ideas—to truly master reading. A more accurate name for the product could be My
Baby Can Parrot!

Such programs claim to bypass (or do better than) intuitive
parenting and often base their claims on new discoveries in "brain
science" and how babies learn.[19] The appeal of these products, and
the kind of marketing used to sell them, is very powerful indeed.
They target the premise that the time my daughter Katie spent
gurgling, smiling, and simply doing what comes naturally could
be far better spent by preparing baby Nina for what she will be
expected to do in school and "preparing" her brain to excel in that
learning environment. Modern technology and brain science
must be able to do far better than Mother Nature and mom and
dad's intuition! Right? Wrong!

Actually, a look at the data from hundreds of studies on child
development and the developing brain increasingly shows that
Mother Nature, and mom and dad, are doing a fantastic job. If
powerful, natural learning opportunities are replaced by plopping
your child in front of a Baby Genius or Baby Einstein or Smart
Baby DVD,[20] playing them classical music CDs, or engaging them
in educational games like Railway Line or Baby Flash Cards or
ABC Alphabet Phonics on the latest tablet technology, the natural
foundations for harnessing all aspects of brainpower for problem
solving in the real environment will not be properly developed.[21]
The most important result from a study directly comparing
DVDs to natural learning was that "children who viewed the
DVD did not learn any more words from their month-long exposure to it than did a control group." The highest level of learning
occurred in a no-video condition in which parents tried to teach
their children the target words during everyday activities. Interestingly, when the researchers interviewed the parents about what
they *thought* their child had learned they found that "parents who
liked the DVD tended to overestimate how much their children

had learned from it."[22] This is a powerful finding, because it shows that parents *assumed* that the "science-based" DVD instruction was more effective than the naturally occurring learning and may, in part, explain the positive testimonials endorsing these products despite what research tells us.

The demise of the My Baby Can Read program is instructive in illustrating the advantages of intuitive parenting and the disadvantages of slick, prepackaged, rote parroting schemes that only *appear* to accelerate learning. This product was heavily marketed as a teaching package that would give kids a head start on learning to read. A kit including flash cards, books, and DVDs costing around $200 was widely marketed. The advertisements claimed that toddlers could be taught to read and that these gains would be a key to future success in school. Like all "too good to be true" products and get-rich-quick schemes for artificially accelerating development, the product did not deliver on its promises, and some parents complained to the U.S. Federal Trade Commission (FTC) that the manufacturer of Your Baby Can Read used misleading claims to sell the program.[23] The FTC reported: "The amended complaint alleged the defendants failed to have competent and reliable scientific evidence that babies can learn to read using the Your Baby Can Read Program." After reviewing the complaint, on August 22, 2014, the U.S. Federal Trade Commission announced that "Your Baby Can Read creator, Dr. Robert Titzer, and his company, Infant Learning, Inc. d/b/a The Infant Learning Company have settled charges that they made *baseless claims* about the effectiveness of Your Baby Can Read program and *misrepresented that scientific studies proved the claims*" (emphasis added).[24] The defendants are now prohibited from using the term "Your Baby Can Read" in future marketing. But be forewarned, although the FTC has taken action for this particular product, there are plenty of other products being marketed to unsuspecting parents that are quite similar to "Your Baby Can Read" but are not included in the FTC action. Even the defendants in this case continue to advertise—and sell—educational products with titles such as "Your Baby Can Learn" and "Your Baby Can Discover."[25]

Despite the results of the FTC's "Your Baby Can Read" review, there had been many claims and testimonials about how wonderful this product was. Advertisements included mothers talking about how their little babies learned to read and were subsequently successful in school. These children's developing brains may have been artificially induced to parrot letter names and visually recognize words but perhaps without learning to actually *comprehend* the meaning of these words. One can only speculate about how these children ultimately fared in later school years, when reading comprehension and thinking ability become much more important than simply parroting letter names and memorized words.[26]

The truth is that intuitive parenting techniques are far better than DVDs for teaching babies and young children: A review of the impact of media-based learning in infants and toddlers revealed that "young children may better understand and learn from real-life experiences than they do from video. Moreover, some research suggests that exposure to television during the *first few years of life may be associated with poorer cognitive development*" (emphasis added). Stated simply, the claims that learning through media is faster or better than learning through real-life interactions with the environment—and with intuitive parents—are directly contradicted by the results of scientific studies.[27]

Artificially breaking learning into small parts and attempting to teach babies that way is an impossible task. The natural environment provides multiple learning cues that babies' brains can "grab" when they are ready to learn the information. For example, consider how a child learns to talk.[28] There is no possible way that any parent could set out consciously to school a child on everything about language using either direct instruction or "baby genius" programs.[29] Speech and language development includes understanding and identifying the speech sounds or phonemes in a language; learning specific words and syntactic and grammatical rules for generating (and understanding) sentences; and a knowledge of the nuances of social interaction wherein humans use speech and language to communicate and exchange ideas. There are very few humans on the planet who even know the details of each of these elements for any given language—and virtually no parents possess in-depth knowledge of specific language components. Yet with very few exceptions, nearly everybody learns to talk and communicate in at least one, and in many societies more than one, native language.[30] How could this possibly happen without special step-by-step instructions?

Talking involves multiple centers in the brain that must be properly wired and coordinated to generate speech and language. Motor control centers must move the lips and tongue and the other structures in the oral cavity that produce speech sounds. Reasoning centers generate ideas and then must translate these into meaningful words, organize the words into coherent sentences, and then tell the mouth how to say the sentences. Further, people also have to be able to understand what is being said to them, so the brain must also coordinate the auditory regions with the areas responsible for decoding meaning and translating the speech sounds back into meaningful ideas. In short, language and speech development is a highly complex "whole brain" process that can't possibly be broken down into component parts and taught explicitly. Instead, the developing brain is designed to pick the component next needed from the ample language "data" it receives in everyday interactions.[31]

So babies come to the world prewired to receive information on speech and language and, by receiving naturally occurring input from their parents, learn to talk. That is, learning and neural development are a natural outgrowth of the responses the baby elicits from her parents and from the information she naturally hears from others in the environment. This process is described in detail in Steven Pinker's excellent books *The Language Instinct* and *Words and Rules*. As Pinker explains, there is very little "formal" language instruction during development. Indeed, most children do not learn even the rudimentary aspects of grammar via direct instruction until they've been in school for several years, yet they learn to talk just fine. Naturally occurring input is all that's needed for the baby's brain to "turn on" the language wiring. Even better, there is a relatively wide learning window for this, so parents do not have to precisely time their delivery of this input to their child.

Many other aspects of brain development are similarly biased toward being activated by natural, ubiquitous (available in lots of settings with a high occurrence) responses that are broadly available during development. This means that the ever-increasing stress that many parents currently experience and the sense that they are somehow shortchanging their children with regard to "wiring the brain" within a very short "critical period" to optimize their development is unfounded. The "learning enhancement" tools they are encouraged to buy are a complete waste of time and money. Worse, attempts to circumvent natural processes or unnaturally accelerate learning may actually backfire and have unintended consequences because they may end up reducing—or even displacing—the beneficial parent-child interactions that are the authentic foundation of early learning and the source of brain activation.

When educational products are marketed to parents, there is always the explicit, or at least implicit, promise that teaching a limited, specific skill will somehow "unlock" a baby's potential. For example, there has long been a myth that playing classical music to a baby will make him or her more intelligent. The movie *The Incredibles* made a joke about this and, in the 1990s, Governor Zell Miller of Georgia proposed providing a classical music tape or CD to mothers of babies born in his state in the hopes of "stimulating brain development." The *New York Times* article on this story included the following observation from Professor Sandra

Trehub, a psychology professor at the University of Toronto: "I don't think we have the evidence to make that statement unambiguously. If we really think you can swallow a pill, buy a record or a particular book or have any one experience and that that's going to be the thing that gets you into Harvard or Princeton, then that's an illusion." Playing classical music to babies wires their brains for listening to classical music. Nothing more and nothing less. Although parents may want their baby to appreciate classical music as a desired outcome, this will not make their baby generally more intelligent.

Study after study has shown that *children will learn what you teach them*. Showing them letters when they are babies will wire their brains for seeing and recognizing letters, it will not teach them to read or to comprehend what they read. Showing them numbers will introduce their brains to seeing numbers, it will not turn them into math geniuses. Conversely, if you want a child to read, he or she must be taught to read. This entails not only showing them letters and introducing them to the sounds that go with these letters but also learning the real-life meanings the written words represent. Both decoding, the ability to recognize the letters in written words, and comprehension of what these written words mean must be taught. And, reading comprehension requires engaging the mind by tapping reasoning ability. Teaching a child phonics is important, and doing so will help him or her learn to sound out words. But learning phonics will not teach a child to understand what he or she is reading.

The same is true in math. Recognizing the number symbols is not enough. Children also need to learn the concepts that the numbers represent. Recently developed "brain games" also explicitly or implicitly promise generalized boosts in a child's intelligence. But learning to solve Sudoku puzzles will teach a child (or an adult, for that matter) how to solve number puzzles of the same nature as Sudoku. It cannot teach algebra, calculus, or trigonometry. Nor does it generate the thinking ability to become a Sherlock Holmes or an Albert Einstein.

There is a computer game currently being marketed that teaches how to clap your hands and tap your feet to a particular rhythm (like following a metronome). The makers of this product claim that it will improve timing and rhythm, which is a credible claim, but they also claim that it will improve concentration, balance, memory, language, and general motor skills—and that it will improve clinical conditions such as ADHD. But both neuroscience and learning studies tell us that a person trained to clap their hands and tap their feet will learn to clap their hands and tap their feet—nothing more and nothing less. Now this may be a desirable outcome, but it is not the key to unlocking untapped brainpower and intelligence. Nor is there credible evidence it will "cure" ADHD, autism, or any other clinical condition.[32]

Consider the claim that computerized training for foot tapping and hand clapping improves motor skills in more detail with the idea that children will learn what is taught. Of course, it will improve the motor skills directly associated with foot tapping and hand clapping. But who cares about that unless they are only trying to improve hand clapping and foot tapping? The point of buying this computer training is to improve lots of other, more useful motor skills. I like to play basketball, but I'm not very good at it. I can't jump very high, and I am not especially well coordinated. If I wanted to become a better basketball player, would it be better for me to play a computer game that taught me how to clap my hands and tap my feet in rhythm or would it be a better use of my valuable learning time to practice shooting and dribbling a basketball? If I became extremely proficient at the computer game for clapping and tapping, would I then be able to dunk a basketball with greater skill? Of course not! The same is true for golf, running, baseball, volleyball, swimming, or any other sport you care to name. The way to improve motor abilities for these sports is to practice the motor skills that directly impact performance. Common sense also tells us that not all people with well-developed timing and rhythm, such as dancers and professional athletes, are automatically highly intelligent, nor are Nobel Prize–winning geniuses necessarily good dancers or skilled athletes.

Parents should apply the same skepticism to get-rich-quick schemes for increasing their child's intelligence or magically wiring their brains. There are no shortcuts. If a child watches an educational Baby Genius DVD that essentially presents pictures and the names of these pictures, they will learn to name these pictures as they appear in the video. Nothing more and nothing less. But, it will not make them into either a baby Einstein or, later, an adult Einstein. The take-home message here is to view these products and think through *exactly* what the child is experiencing. That is, what they are actually learning and what their brains are actually being wired to do.

Intuitive Parenting versus Preprogrammed Parenting

Because simple, relational interactions occur every day between parents and babies all over the world, it is all too easy to overlook the significance and *sheer teaching power* of intuitive parenting. Because it is *intuitive* and *instinctive* for mothers and fathers to respond to their babies by holding them in their arms, talking to them gently, and smiling at them, no one steps back and thinks about how important such activity is for developing the child's mind in the proper way while also nurturing their physical and emotional well-being. The magic of those moments and the *millions* of times they occur in a child's life, from birth until he enters school, is crucial not only for a baby's emotional development but for ensuring that his or her developing brain is properly wired for a lifetime of thinking, learning, and social interaction. And because there is nothing "special" required to raise your children this way—no special gadgets, technology, or advanced degrees required—I worry that parents like Katie and Brent may not be giving themselves sufficient credit for the wonderful job they are doing in providing Nina—and now Gwen too—with *exactly* the right teaching each girl needs at that particular moment in her life.

Indeed, if a developmental specialist like me, who studies how children learn, attempted to design and deliver the absolute optimal early education program for my granddaughters Nina and Gwen, I would recommend exactly what my daughter Katie and son-in-law Brent are already doing. In fact, if I tried to design an "accelerated" learning program for baby Nina by attempting to teach a young mother like Katie specific, "preprogrammed" incremental steps she could take to deliver input to Nina's developing brain, I would, in all probability, derail the intuitive process so essential for properly developing my granddaughters' growing minds.

To illustrate this point, let's pretend that I am a football announcer dissecting the intuitive parenting examples from my own family that I described above, using instant replay. I would probably start by identifying the various players on offense and defense and discussing the role each had on the play under discussion. Scientists do something similar, breaking down interactions like the ones between my daughter and granddaughter into a series of key steps using a process called "event coding."[33] Scientists then track these events as a way of understanding how the mind develops.[34]

Let's start with the first example, of Katie and baby Nina cuddling and communicating in the rocking chair, and examining their relative physical positions in that chair. Katie is holding Nina in her arms while rocking. Nina's head is being supported by Katie's arm, and Nina's face is oriented upward but not directly focused on her mother's face. The next key event is my granddaughter making a cooing noise. As a young baby, Nina is simply responding reflexively to the situation: She has a tummy full of mother's milk, she is dry and warm, she is being held in her mother's arms, and she is being rocked gently in a soothing manner. What could be better than that? Naturally, Nina makes contented sounds. These sounds trigger a whole series of interactive events between mother and baby.

The next event is Katie's response to these contented sounds. She holds Nina in both arms and raises her face so that mother and daughter are now looking at each other from approximately one foot apart. Katie probably doesn't even know this is the optimal distance for a baby's eyes to focus on an object.[35] Then, Katie smiles and starts talking to Nina in a happy, singsong tone of voice. Little do they know that all babies' ears are specially tuned to the frequencies that their mother's voice produces and that by exaggerating the suprasegmental envelope, that is, the intonation contours, Katie is providing Nina with input that draws attention to the specific acoustic characteristics of her speech. This will lay the foundation for Nina's speech perception and help wire her developing brain to notice the key features of what her mother is saying, including the speech sounds, words, and intonation of spoken language. Not only that, Katie's singsong words are tuning Nina's developing brain to the specific features of English, the language her mother speaks, and the one that, since she's growing up in the United States, will be her primary language as well. (If my granddaughter were growing up in Thailand and subject to the same kind of interaction, but with her mother speaking Thai, her little brain would be automatically exposed to the key features of that language, which has even more intonation contours than English.)

Scientists studying the development of perception in babies have concluded that

> infants 18 to 20 weeks old recognize [that] the correspondence between visually presented speed sounds and the spectral [auditory] information contained in the sounds is *critical* to the detection of these correspondences. Some

infants [verbally] imitated the sounds presented during the experiment. Both the ability to detect the auditory-visual correspondence and the tendency to imitate may reflect the infant's knowledge of the relationship between audition [listening] and articulation [watching her mother's mouth pronounce speech sounds while she is talking].[36]

In plain English, this study shows that my daughter Katie is teaching Nina's brain about English phonemes (speech sounds) and what these phonemes sound like—and how to pronounce them. Their interaction is also laying the groundwork for reading, because baby Nina is learning about the speech sounds that later she will use in phonics. How fantastic is that? Isn't my daughter an amazing mother? And equally cool is that *all* mothers and fathers doing this are equally amazing! Who knew?

The next event in our instant replay is Nina smiling back at Katie. Now, new sets of brain circuits are being activated. Instead of the listening (auditory) centers in the brain, which are unconsciously paying attention to the singsong patterns of Katie's speech, baby Nina's visual centers are now being activated. Not only that, Nina's brain is automatically coordinating this visual input with the emotional regulation centers in her brain. That is, Nina's initial reflexive vocalization arising from contentment has now become associated with positive social engagement with her mother. In effect, baby Nina's internal happiness is being transferred to her mother, who in response is transferring her own happiness back to the baby. The visual signal for this in humans and in some other primates is smiling.[37]

Of course, baby Nina's face is not very coordinated and the smile looks a bit like a grimace. But because my daughter is actually (and intuitively) exaggerating her own smile—it's as big as it can possibly be—she is helping baby Nina notice the key features of the smile and to learn how to replicate these by coordinating motor movements in her own cute little face.[38] In fact, Katie is actually training Nina's visual cortex to link up to and synchronize with the movement (motor) centers in her developing brain. And this is simultaneously being integrated with the auditory information and the emotional aspects of the moment. Because this interaction and social engagement is rewarding to both mother and baby, they seek to repeat the process over and over again. Indeed, this kind of engagement is one of the most sustained kinds of focus a baby is capable of producing.[39] Stated simply, my daughter Katie's intuitive actions are precisely in Nina's sweet spot for learning *and* brain development.

Perhaps even more amazing, Nina is also incidentally wiring her mother's brain to recognize and respond to her facial expressions. A paper entitled "What Is in a Smile? Maternal Brain Responses to Infant Facial Cues" that recently appeared in the journal *Pediatrics* concluded that "when first-time mothers see their own infant's face, an extensive brain network seems to be activated, wherein affective and cognitive information may be integrated and directed toward motor/behavioral outputs. . . . Understanding how a mother responds uniquely to her own infant, when smiling or crying, may be the first step in understanding the neural basis of mother-infant attachment."[40] In other words, baby Nina's smiles activate special circuits in Katie's brain that tune in to her baby's initiations. And this includes nerve pathways and special chemicals in every mother's brain that are responsible for pleasure and reward. Who could have imagined that such a natural and intuitive interaction could be so powerful?

Now, imagine that I produced a DVD or tablet app designed to replace or, in the height of hubris, "enhance" baby Nina's learning by outdoing mother Katie and, by proxy, Mother Nature. I could record video of people smiling and talking in singsong voices and play this DVD using a monitor placed inside Nina's crib. I could even tell my daughter Katie to wait for Nina to coo and then play the DVD. After all, science tells us that smiling at babies triggers brain activation and so does using a singsong voice.[41] And I could artificially boost the frequency with which baby Nina hears these speech signals. A ten-minute mother-baby intuitive teaching episode could morph into an hour-long auditory bombardment via DVD or app.

I could use animation and music editing software to artificially augment the visual features and the acoustic features of the DVD so that they are even more salient. I could also coach Katie to artificially replicate the steps that are already occurring intuitively using the computer and DVD. But because I am essentially breaking the interaction down into microsteps of events that my daughter has to learn, recognize, and respond to, in all probability she would be unable to execute these nearly as well and as effortlessly as she does naturally. This "improvement" of the natural interactions would make the process even better, right? Unfortunately, attempting to "enhance" this process artificially using DVD and computer technology ends up failing to trigger the special circuits in a parent's brain that respond to her baby's facial expressions.[42] Worse, computers, apps, and DVDs cannot respond *flexibly* (nor intuitively) to baby Nina's moment to moment initiations, nor can they intuitively replicate mother Katie's responses. In short, it is impossible for me to improve on what was intuitively and naturally occurring between Katie and Nina. And any attempts to do so would risk leaving out crucial elements and potentially *derail* brain development and social attachment in both baby and mother.

In addition to a lack of flexibility and moment by moment individualized responses to baby Nina, my scientifically designed DVD even with augmented visual and auditory enhancements would still be seen via a two-dimensional delivery system rather than a three-dimensional one, which neuroscientists have long known the brain processes quite differently.[43] Even the best 3-D and virtual reality videos fall far short of the texture and nuances of the real world—and the developing brain notices these differences. Also, the natural process of holding baby Nina in front of her face would be derailed so that the visual attention my daughter is naturally enhancing would be lost completely. Worse, because my daughter is smiling in response to baby Nina's own efforts to smile, the timing in the DVD would not be synchronous with the baby's attempts. And so on.

The first and foremost element in the interaction between Katie and Nina—*the* crucial key for Nina's future mental development—is that her own behavior, in this case cooing, *triggered* a response in her mother: in this case, holding baby Nina close to her face, smiling, and speaking to her in a singsong voice. This interaction produces positive feelings for both mother and baby while also helping Nina take that next "baby step" toward acquiring an adult brain that fulfills its amazing destiny. And this pattern of interaction will be repeated millions of times before my granddaughter enters kindergarten.[44]

The beauty of this is that a baby's *initiations* directly tell the parents what she knows and what she is ready to learn next. In this manner, my granddaughter's coo unconsciously signaled Katie that her developing brain was ready to receive input on how to smile, how to process features of the English language, and how to integrate visual, motor, acoustic, and emotional centers in her developing brain. Talk about a whole-brain experience!

The Limits of "Scientific Improvement": Lessons from the Infant Formula Feeding Fad

As a scientist, I am thrilled and fascinated by all the new information about child development, neuropsychology, and learning that scientific progress has made possible in recent years. But it is important to distinguish between what we are learning and the potential pitfalls—and adverse consequences—of attempts to apply it to the creation of products or techniques aimed at "scientific improvement" of the natural parenting process. The history of the controversy surrounding breast-feeding and infant formula provides a good reminder of what can happen when we lose perspective.

It may seem hard to believe today, but when my children were babies, proponents of modern technology and food science were busy assuring young parents that scientists had developed infant formula that was superior to breast milk. They claimed that many aspects of development, including physical growth and, yes, even "brain development," would be far better if babies were fed "technologically advanced" and "scientifically" engineered formula with all those added vitamins and nutrients that no "mere mother" acting naturally could ever hope to rival.

As a result, breast-feeding got a bad reputation as something that poor or otherwise disadvantaged mothers who could not afford this "super-food" formula would have to do to feed their babies. "Everybody" knew breast milk was inferior to the manufactured product.

As we well know now, it turns out that breast milk is every bit as good as, if not superior to, even the highest-quality manufactured infant formula. As an article in the *Journal of Urban Health* proclaimed in 2008: "Breast milk is the gold standard for infant nutrition and the only necessary food for the first 6 months of an infant's life. . . . Infant formula is deficient and inferior to breast milk in meeting infants' nutritional needs."[45]

This example is in no way meant to induce guilt or suggest that anyone is somehow harming their child by feeding her or him formula instead of breast-feeding. In fact, infant formula is a wonderful invention, a great choice for some parents, and perfectly fine for a developing baby to drink. But using it is not *superior* to breast-feeding, as was originally claimed; and all things being equal, there are some advantages to breast-feeding. Mothers who *instinctively* let nature take its course and provide nourishment for their children, as women have done throughout human history, are in no way behind the times or somehow putting their precious child—or their child's developing brain—at a disadvantage.

The same is true for intuitive parenting: You have everything your baby needs, it is simply a matter of unlocking your natural abilities. When deciding what to feed your baby or how to wire his or her brain, don't forget to take into consideration the influence marketing can have. No company has an incentive to help you parent intuitively—in fact, just the opposite. Formula manufacturers funded advertising campaigns designed to persuade mothers that formula was superior to breast-feeding, in part by creating anxiety as to whether doing the natural, intuitive thing—breast-feeding—is what's best for baby. These companies couldn't profit from breast-feeding; they could only profit from people buying their formula. Similarly, companies producing "better parenting" and "smarter baby" products, along with the marketers they hire, are working to persuade parents they need to purchase these products to "wire their baby's brain" and to do so more rapidly and more efficiently than they could on their own. They can't cash in on what parents normally, naturally, and intuitively do, so they benefit from stoking parents' anxieties that technology is somehow smarter than they are.

The reality is that all adults, including grandparents, nannies, day-care workers, and preschool teachers generally—and fathers and mothers specifically—will provide precisely the right learning opportunities at precisely the right moment to ensure a baby's, a toddler's, or a preschooler's maximum brain development if they *instinctively* and *intuitively* respond to initiations from the child. As with everyday "old-fashioned" breast milk, it is all too easy to overlook how powerful these microlearning events really are and to fall victim to marketing schemes designed to prey upon parental insecurity about whether they are doing everything possible to enhance their child's development. Tune in to your baby—and tune out the marketing nonsense.

Technology and the Intuitive Parent

After reading the warnings in this chapter about using DVDs, tablets, or computer programs to take the place of intuitive parenting, you might expect that intuitive parenting is incompatible with technology. Actually, nothing could be further from the truth. Human beings have been inventing technology and incorporating it into society for centuries. And the pace of technological development is increasing. It would be downright foolish to withhold technology completely while raising children. The aforementioned caveats for technology are focused on *substituting* technology for intuitive parenting; for example, expecting a baby to learn to read using the My Baby Can Read educational program *instead of* encouraging and facilitating natural language development and then teaching reading when the child—and his or her brain—is ready for it.

An intuitive parent can readily incorporate technology into their everyday interactions with their child. The operative words here are ***incorporate into everyday interactions***. Intuitive parents do not leave their babies or toddlers alone with a tablet or other technology for long periods of time. Rather, they play with—and interact with—their preschool and older children while activating the technology. Parents should not feel guilty if their children occasionally play alone with technology. After all, there are times when parents need to do things without their children. But it should not be for very long and should not be an everyday occurrence.

Also, quite a number of experts recommend withholding or at least strictly limiting 2-D technology for the first two or even three years of life. This is sound advice because early exposure to technology may displace natural bonding and attention to parental input. In short, exposure to too much 2-D technology too soon risks irreversibly "imprinting" a baby's mind on technology rather than on parents. The scientific literature on imprinting is relevant here. More than one hundred years ago, biologist Douglas Spalding discovered that baby chickens, from the time they first emerged from their egg, imitated the other animals around them, a phenomenon he called imprinting. For the chicks, all is well and good if the first animals they encounter after hatching are other chickens. But what happens when the chick imprints on a different animal? Scientist Konrad Lorenz studied this problem and found that imprinting was far more powerful than originally thought. He showed, for example, that baby geese could be taught many humanlike behaviors when they became imprinted to him! And these improperly imprinted geese paid more attention to him than to their biological parents—papa gander and mother goose.

My brother-in-law worked at the San Diego Zoo and brought home eggs he found in the foliage to his little sister, who later became my wife. She delighted in hatching these eggs and finding out what bird each egg contained. The hatchlings included ducks, peacocks, and guinea hens. All went well until some of the guinea hens became imprinted on some of the ducks that had hatched a few days earlier. They imitated the ducks, which was fine for waddling around but not so great when the guinea hens tried to swim like the ducks. My wife still gets a sad look in her eyes when she talks about what happened to those poor guinea hens.

The point here is that you want your baby to imprint to humans generally—and her parents specifically—*not* to a tablet, smartphone, computer, television, DVD player, or other form of technology. Technology is fine *after* imprinting, and after multiple neural connections have been laid down and strong emotional bonds have formed and become well established through interactions with parents. And after the child's brain has been properly wired to interpret and utilize 3-D real-world information so that the brain can interpret 2-D information relative to the real-world experiences stored in long-term memory. Technology should be gradually introduced after a child has passed the toddler years *and* parents should actively interact with their children while using technology after it has been introduced.

As adults, we all can obtain useful information by accessing tablets, television, computers, smartphones, and so on. We can also waste a considerable amount of time using these devices in mindless ways. The same is true for children! Intuitive parents make sure that their children learn to use the technology properly and productively and know not to rely on it as a surrogate parent, teacher, or "intelligence-creation device."

Tune In to Your Child

The first step in the journey of intuitive parenting is learning to pay attention to your particular, utterly unique child. Of course this is both natural and intuitive and shouldn't be difficult at all— most parents already do it quite well. It has just become too easy to be persuaded that because you're not a child-development expert and (therefore) don't know what you're doing, prepackaged or preprogrammed educational products are needed. They aren't. Nor do you need to carve time out of a busy schedule specifically to engage in "intuitive learning" sessions. Indeed, the beauty of intuitive parenting is that *every* moment you spend with your child is potentially a *teachable* moment. Intuitive parenting is seamlessly integrated into the daily caregiving that babies and young children require. Feeding, diaper changing, bedtimes, wake-up routines, bath time, and quiet moments all together yield extremely powerful learning opportunities for your child's developing mind. Whenever and wherever you are engaging in any of these everyday tasks and following your baby's developmental lead, you're doing exactly the right thing for your baby's brain.

By reacting intuitively, you will become the very best parent— and teacher—your child could possibly have. As they grow, your baby, toddler, and then preschooler will be naturally and continually signaling you precisely what they currently know, what they need to learn next, and precisely the right input needed from you to learn and to wire their brain. As an added bonus, you and your child will both have a lot of fun along the way.

- Intuitive parenting means paying attention—and responding naturally—to your child.
- Be prepared for the onslaught of marketing and the never-ending number of parenting "products" that undermine intuitive parenting. Pressure may also come from well-meaning but misguided fellow parents who believe the products they are buying are better for their babies than intuitive parenting. The fact is, playing with your child—and talking to him or her—is far more powerful than the latest "baby genius" product being pushed on anxious parents.
- Intuitive parenting *automatically* individualizes the "lessons" your baby needs to learn at precisely the right time in his or her development and nurtures social development and a positive sense of self at the same time. After all, the baby is learning that you are genuinely interested in him or her, and in what they are doing.
- Intuitive parenting seamlessly *incorporates* technology into a child's world—as a tool for accessing information, communication, and entertainment. But electronic technology is not a substitute for intuitive parenting or a proper means for accelerating brain development. Indeed, access to electronic technology should await proper imprinting on people (after the age of two or even three) and should *never* be a mindless waste of time for a child. Be sure to limit your own technology usage when paying attention to and interacting with your child. Don't let Netflix, Facebook, Twitter, or texting cause you to miss opportunities to respond to your baby!

- Early exposure to electronic technology should, like books, be a catalyst or starting point for parent-child interaction rather than a solo activity.

- Because intuitive parenting, like mother's milk, is both natural and generally available at no cost does *not* mean that it is somehow inferior. Indeed, intuitive parenting naturally provides *exactly* the teaching your child needs from you. The instruction manual is in your brain and your child's—and in your very own DNA.

chapter 2

Brain Science for the Intuitive Parent

Scientists have been studying the brain for more than two thousand years. The Greek philosopher Plato hypothesized that the brain is the source of thinking ability.[1] In the second century AD, the Roman physician-scientist Galen made many discoveries about the structural traits of the brain that have stood the test of time; that is, a modern brain is pretty much identical to what Galen described. You and I have the same basic brain architecture that humans have always had in terms of general neural anatomy—and in terms of brain circuits.

What has changed in the last several hundred years is not how the brain works or its overall capacity to learn—these aspects are essentially the same as what Plato and Galen studied (and used themselves while thinking about the brain!)—but our understanding of how the brain is organized and what happens when we learn. In just the last few decades, researchers in the field of neuroscience have made quantum leaps in our knowledge.

But the human brain is an incredibly complex organ. There's

a lot we don't yet know, a lot of research yet to do, and many discoveries still to be made. The inherently complex and often confusing nature of brain science can lead people to misunderstand, misinterpret, or oversimplify findings—including marketers who want to sell new products that seem to have "scientifically proven" value. Parents who want to ensure their child receives the latest, most up-to-date learning opportunities can be vulnerable to claims that this or that product has been developed in light of new neuroscientific findings. In this chapter I hope to describe what scientists know and how this translates to what intuitive parents should do with that information. I also want to highlight the extensive brain science supporting intuitive parenting in order to encourage parents to cultivate a healthy skepticism about marketers' and others' claims that products and practices that actually undermine intuitive parenting are "scientifically based" to "wire the brain."

In the late 1970s and early 1980s I was a teaching assistant for graduate students learning about the brain. In those days, much of what scientists knew focused on the structure of the brain, the various nerves connecting the parts to one another, and the overall geography of this remarkable organ.[2] It is hard to imagine today, but much of what we knew about how the brain worked was based on observing and reporting on the behavior of patients who had received some form of brain injury in an accident or stroke, just as doctors and researchers had done for more than a century.[3]

For example, the speech centers in the brain were discovered in 1864 when Dr. Paul Broca described two cases of patients with head injuries who had lost their ability to speak.[4] It is amazing that Broca's original discovery has withstood the test of time and is now a widely accepted principle of brain science. After Broca's discovery, when patients died, doctors could see by examining the surface of the brain directly what regions had been damaged. X-ray technology yielded significant improvements in the ability to pinpoint brain damage and had the advantage of being viable while the patient was still alive. But even X-rays could not tell doctors and scientists *how* the brain was functioning, it could only tell them *where* the damage was. Observation and neuropsychological testing could then yield reasonable guesses about the duties these damaged brain areas were supposed to be carrying out, but the whole process was quite crude by today's standards and yielded some profound misunderstandings. One of those misunderstandings was the notion that brain development was primarily predetermined and that genes (nature) were more important than parenting (nurture). Thankfully, it is now quite clear that input from parents—as well as from other sources in the environment—plays a crucial role in wiring a baby's brain.[5]

Since my days as a TA, advances in science, medicine, and technology have exploded our understanding of how the brain works. A recent BBC news story entitled "A Golden Age of Discovery in Neuroscience" proudly proclaimed, "Developments in imaging technology, genetics, brain chemistry and computing are promising fresh insights into the workings of the mind and mental illness."[6] And who could disagree? Amazing advances in our ability to "image," that is, take pictures of the brain while it is working, have generated a revolution in discovering how neural systems in the brain take in and process information, and how the brain heals itself after injuries.

Naturally, parents hope to utilize these discoveries to help their children learn more efficiently. However, there are still important limitations in neuroscience and in the very methods we use to study the brain—namely, attempting to isolate and classify individual neural circuits. While the way we are studying the brain is certainly valid in terms of the scientific method, findings may also lose something in translation to a manufactured system or educational product intended to enhance the wiring of a baby's brain. Or be completely misinterpreted.

Much of brain science is focused on clever experiments designed to isolate individual pathways and circuits that tell us how various components of the brain work. But never forget that the brain is an organ that functions as a *whole unit* and that the goal of wiring a brain is for it to function effectively not just in a lab but in the real and very complex world. Because your goal as a parent is to wire your child's brain for real-life thinking, the latest findings from neuroscience, based on the narrow bits of behavior scientists use to isolate minute brain circuits in the lab, may not be very useful to you.

For example, studies of how the visual centers in the brain recognize letters show that there are specialized centers within the visual centers—and that the development of these centers is influenced by when and how a person sees the letters.[7] Scientists interested in learning more about how these letter recognition circuits actually work develop and then conduct even more refined experiments designed to systematically isolate the particular systems and circuits used in letter recognition. One recent study, for example, examined the effects of relatively intense computer-based exercises on letter recognition. The study found that "subjects who performed eye exercises were more accurate in responding to target letters," and concluded that "eye exercises may prove useful in enhancing cognitive performance on tasks related to attention and memory over a very brief course of training." This should come as no surprise, because the brain will learn what you teach it, in this case recognizing letters using "eye exercises" that teach letter recognition.

But, a problem arises when this relatively narrow finding is overgeneralized to suggest that such eye training on letter recognition actually improves reading skill—or any other practical skill outside of the experimental conditions. Other studies show that, in terms of the ability to read and actually *understand* the words—and the sentences that the letters represent—it is far better for children's overall brain development to learn to recognize letters by having parents read to them. Letter recognition is then supported by the positive emotional context of parent-child interaction and the meaning of the letters is properly placed in the context of reading words and phrases within an actual story. And—in early reading—attractive pictures and a simple, engaging narrative activate multiple areas of a child's brain and not just the letter recognition circuits. Plus there is the emotional attachment of sitting with mom or dad and reading together. Some of my favorite memories are acting out the stories I read to my children when they were young, and now with my grandchildren. Trust me, I read—and act out—an unforgettable "Goldilocks and the Three Bears" that is every bit as appealing to my grandchildren as it was to my own toddlers thirty years ago.

What would you rather do? And what do you think your child prefers: to drill letter recognition on a computer screen or read an interesting story with his or her parents? And which activity actually wires the whole brain for not only recognizing letters but also for understanding what these letters mean while enjoying the entire reading experience?

Scientists have long known that "dialogic" reading, wherein a parent actively engages the child while reading by asking questions and having the child recall and retell story elements, is strongly correlated with higher levels of reading comprehension and later language development.[8] As Professor Grover (Russ) Whitehurst at SUNY Stony Brook in Long Island, New York, and his colleagues have noted: "Research we have conducted as well as the work of others suggests that the particular way in which preschoolers are read to is related to the language gains they obtained from picture book reading experience. When adults give children opportunities to become active participants in the reading experience by using evocative techniques during the reading (e.g., asking the child questions about the pictures or the story, encouraging the child to tell the story along with the adult), children showed greater gains than when adults simply read the book to the child." In short, the children's brains are better wired for reading—and for language—if the parent uses a transactional, intuitive approach. Simply reading to the child without shared transactions has much less of a positive impact. And taking this a step further and drilling a child on letter recognition or "eye tracking" is even further divorced from the real transactional process the child—and his or her developing brain—needs.

What's in a Baby's Brain?

Brains are made of cells called neurons, which have an intriguing, unique structure. While most cells in other parts of the human body look just like an egg in a pan, brain cells and other nerve cells look more like a squid, but with tentacles at both ends instead of just one end.[9] That is, the "heads" of nerve cells have tentacled cell structures called dendrites, which also contain the nerve cell nucleus. And there is a long "tail," called an axon, with a smaller set of tentacles at the end of the axon called the axon terminus. The axon is coated in a fatty sheath called myelin.[10] The "head" part of the cell looks gray and is creatively called "gray matter" whereas the tail, covered with the fatty myelin, looks whitish yellow and is called "white matter." Pictures of the brain show regions of cell bodies that look gray and groups of axons that appear white.

Nerve cells can communicate with one another. They do this by transferring an electrical impulse from one nerve cell to the next. Neurons are connected to one another, head to tail, with the areas of gray matter connected by white-matter "cables." Electrical messages travel from the head to the tail and are transferred to the next cell in the cable across the small space between the axon tail and the dendrites of the next nerve cell in the chain. This small

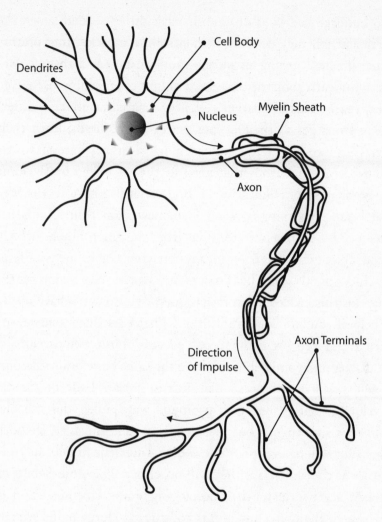

Figure 1. Depiction of a neuron (nerve cell).

space between neurons is called a synapse. To help direct message travel, the brain uses special chemicals—neurotransmitters—to vary the amount of electricity needed for messages to "jump" the space in the synapses. Messages can be prioritized and altered using these different neurotransmitters.

The brain is quite complex: Although all neurons are nerve cells and have these same basic components, there are more than two hundred subtypes of neurons that differ depending on the particular job they do, such as controlling muscles, interpreting visual images, storing memories, and so on. (And there is still plenty to learn about neurons; new subtypes are being discovered every year.)[11] Part of a parent's job is to ensure that all these different neurons get to their proper places in the brain, learn their duties, and work together. Indeed, a newborn may have up to one hundred *billion* neurons that need to get organized by the time she graduates from high school.[12] Brain scientists have also learned that brain cells migrate—and form new axon connections between cells—in response to input from the environment, which, when it comes to your baby, means you, your home, and your family's life. Sounds scary, but don't panic. Mother Nature has set the stage for this process to work out quite well, so you'll have plenty of help, if you follow your intuition. Thank goodness one doesn't have to be a neuroscientist to be a successful intuitive parent!

Babies and young children have the same basic brain anatomy as adults, but their brains—like the rest of their bodies—are still developing and changing in profound ways. Like adults, babies have toes and fingers, but these are not quite the same shape as what they will be eventually. And their cute little fingers and toes are not as coordinated as they will be, either. The same is true, on a much larger scale, for their developing brains. Of course, as with the rest of the body, our brains continue to develop and change during our entire lifetime. But infancy and childhood is when the foundations for this development are laid down.

In order to understand how a baby's brain grows and develops, it may be helpful to describe the basic regions—and functions—of the human brain. Although there is considerable individual variability in the details of brain architecture, there are broad basics that apply to all humans, both baby and adult. The top region of the brain—where thinking occurs—is called the cortex, which has four lobes. The front part of the cortex is called the frontal

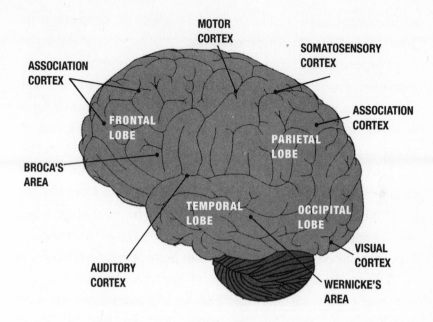

Figure 2. Brain regions and their functions.

lobe. The sides, next to where your baby's ears are, comprise the temporal lobe. The region at the back of the head is called the occipital lobe, and the area immediately behind the frontal lobe and above the temporal lobe is called the parietal lobe.

Each of these regions has a specific job. The *frontal lobe* in most people (and I say "most people" because there is tremendous individual variation in brain architecture) is dedicated to several important functions. First and foremost, the frontal lobe is responsible for speaking ability, including expressive language and speech production activities. When my daughter says "I love you, sweet baby" to my granddaughter, her frontal lobe is controlling the action of speaking. Broca discovered more than 150 years ago that damage to the frontal lobe resulted in a loss of speaking ability even though the patient could still understand what was being said; from that observation he inferred that understanding spoken language originates in a different part of the brain than speaking, which indeed it does.[13] The frontal lobe is also the "strategic command center" for directing movement.

The *parietal lobe* is responsible for detecting and interpreting information coming from the body, especially with regard to touch. Special areas of the parietal lobe are responsible for sensing input from the fingers and hands, from the tongue, and from the bottom of the feet. When my daughter holds up her baby and feels the baby's soft skin with her hands, the parietal lobe is responsible for the sensation. When my granddaughter touches her mother's face, the parietal lobe is taking that information from her tiny fingers and helping her learn to interpret it. When I play "piggies" with her cute little toes, she receives touch input from her feet in the parietal lobe.

The *temporal lobe* is in charge of understanding what people say, that is, receptive language. This was discovered by Karl Wernicke about fifteen years after Broca's discovery that the frontal lobe was the seat of expressive speech. Wernicke found that patients with damage to the temporal lobe had trouble understanding what was said to them and appeared to lose their ability to comprehend language.[14] This finding has held right to the present day: studies show that damage to the temporal region of the brain is associated with reductions in the ability to comprehend spoken language.[15] When my granddaughter cooed to trigger her mother's verbal responses, Nina's vocalizations were analyzed in her mother's temporal lobe. When Katie talks back to Nina, the baby's receptive language area (Wernicke's area) is activated in her developing temporal lobe.

Finally, the back part of the brain, the *occipital lobe*, is responsible for processing and interpreting input from the eyes. The occipital lobe is the strategic command center for vision. When my daughter is looking at my granddaughter, her occipital lobe registers all the visual information her eyes take in and transmits it to the brain. Similarly, my granddaughter's immature occipital circuitry is being activated while she is looking at her mother's face.

Below the cortex and its four lobes lay other, subcortical areas of the brain. Nerve impulses travel up the spinal cord to the cortex of the brain through a series of nerve centers called nuclei. These nerve centers respond quickly to input from other parts of the body, such as arms and legs (brain scientists call these nonbrain parts of the body the "periphery"), and quickly deliver responses that may be needed for survival. For example, if you accidently put your hand on a hot stove, you do not have to consciously realize that your hand should be withdrawn as rapidly as possible; lower brain centers make sure this happens so you don't get burned.

You can think of these as hardwired alarm circuits that can act quicker than the higher cortical centers can. In addition, some of the subcortical regions are also responsible for the more "primitive" brain responses such as anger and pleasure, respond to and control hunger, and recognize and sort basic visual patterns and control repetitive motor behaviors such as walking and running—things you can normally do without thinking. But these lower centers are not capable of more complex, organized behavior such as talking—or solving math problems.

Two subcortical regions associated with emotion are the hippocampus and the amygdala. These are the areas that are activated by pleasure. When my daughter and granddaughter are happily interacting with each other, the emotions that arise from their interaction are processed in the subcortical regions. Pattern generation and pattern recognition are associated with the cerebellum, which is located in the back of the brain below the occipital lobe. Another subcortical region of importance is the basal ganglia, which is responsible for executing motor movements. As my granddaughter learns to reach out and grasp a rattle and shake it, she will be using her basal ganglia centers to coordinate the action. The cortex—in this case, the frontal lobe—gives the orders, and the basal ganglion coordinates the commands to the nerves that will activate the muscles needed to grasp the rattle and shake it. As these motor movements become routine, the patterns for completing them will be stored in the cerebellum so they can be repeated quickly and accurately.

Of course, brain functions are much more complicated than indicated in this quick primer—each area of the brain has many more duties, and each region is developed into much smaller subparts. But to nurture your baby and raise your child, it will suffice just to have some familiarity with the major cortical regions: the frontal, temporal, parietal, and occipital lobes; the emotion centers in the amygdala and hippocampus; and the pattern detectors and generators in the cerebellum.

The brain is also divided into right and left sides. These cerebral hemispheres are connected by thick bundles of nerve axons (white matter) called the corpus callosum. The frontal lobe, temporal lobe, parietal lobe, and occipital lobe are duplicated on both sides of the brain but are not directly replicated, and the right and left sides perform slightly different activities within the same regions.

A note of caution here: Much has been made of "right brain" and "left brain" thinking and differences between "auditory" learners and "visual" learners. The belief seems to be that because the left brain is associated with language skills in most people, there must be a parallel function with auditory learning. The right brain is thought to be responsible for visual learning. Although there is some validity to the idea that some areas of the brain are better at tasks such as seeing and listening, it is grossly misleading to assert broad functions as the sole responsibility of one side or the other of the brain. Studies of thinking and other tasks show that both sides of our brains are engaged and activated all the time; and the entire purpose (and function) of the corpus callosum is for each side of the brain to share information with the other so as to coordinate their activities.[16]

Despite this, myths based on oversimplification persist and have inspired the development of educational programs and special products that supposedly target and train specific left- or right-brained skills. For example, Thomas Biesanz's *Right Brain Math* book, DVD, and videos are marketed as a teaching approach "based on pattern recognition (right brain)"[17] that "bypasses many of the misunderstandings caused by language,"[18] even though there is no evidence that the activities selectively activate the right side of the brain—nor that there is even a right brain–left brain difference in learning math! Biesanz's strategies may help some kids, but the label is a marketing gimmick. Dianne Craft is a certified special-education teacher and learning consultant who also markets a number of products that distinguish "right brain kids" from "left brain kids" and offer "right brain methods" for struggling learners. "Fifty percent of the population is right-brain dominant," she claims,[19] and "80% of the struggling learners I see are right-brain dominant."[20] Marketing copy for her right brain flash cards says that "right brain kids learn best with picture, color, emotion, and humor." Do "left brain kids" learn best without any of those things? Whether or not her teaching strategies are helpful to some kids, her emphasis on left- or right-brained "dominance" is profoundly oversimplistic.

Parents should never fall victim to the mythology that certain activities or computer games are necessary for right brain or left brain development. Rather, it is important to focus on the activity *itself* and let the child's brain wire itself in the most efficient way for that individual child *in the real world*. Provide an opportunity to learn, respond appropriately (as in dialogic reading), and let nature take its course. This will allocate the neural resources to the locations and hemispheres that are best for your child's brain. Moreover, there is tremendous individuality (and individual difference) in the way brains are wired. As an example, a study of the location of Wernicke's area in individual patients indicated that everybody who could understand spoken language has a Wernicke's area, but while some were located in the upper temporal lobe, others were found in the posterior part of the temporal lobe, and still others were found in the parietal lobe.[21] The key point here is that everyone who understands spoken language has a functioning Wernicke's area, but its location will be tailored to fit an individual's unique brain map. It is foolhardy to try to force this function into a specific brain region, or to assume that everyone should have Wernicke's area in exactly the same location in their brain.

Similarly, there can be very significant differences as to which side of an individual's brain is used for processing tasks. For some people, a creative endeavor may activate primarily the right brain, whereas in others it is the left brain that becomes more activated. Creativity is an important ability that parents should continually nurture in their children. Studies of creativity show that this can be a left brain activity when telling stories or listening to stories, or a right brain activity when filling in pieces to a missing puzzle or having a flash of insight. A parent's job is to facilitate the development of creativity by reading stories and encouraging their children to make up and tell stories of their own.

Parents should also provide children with blocks, artist's materials, clay, Play-Doh, and other toys and materials that allow them to create. Who cares whether a child's brain does this on the right side or the left side, just as long as they learn to be creative? In reality, as brain studies show, creativity uses both sides of the brain, and there is no specific "creativity center" where creativity occurs. Rather, multiple brain regions are recruited during creative activities and creative thinking.[22] Part of what makes humans capable of our extraordinary creativity in the first place may be the existence of considerable differences in neural wiring between one person and the next when we engage in creative thought and action.

There are several regions that are responsible for problem solving and for decision making (e.g., the prefrontal cortex) that do appear to be consistently activated regardless of the nature of the creative activity. Other regions apparently activated are rather specific to the task. For example, the visual centers are activated when composing a photograph, the motor centers are activated when choreographing a dance, and so on.[23] Writing a play would involve thinking and planning centers (as in all creative activities) as well as visualization, language, and reading and writing centers.

The Truth about Brain Plasticity

The discovery of the nature and extent of brain plasticity has led to a tremendous advance in our understanding of what happens to the brain during the learning process[24]—and to an explosion of products claiming to trigger and enhance brain plasticity. Many products tout the harnessing of brain plasticity as a key benefit, and the notion that parents can build a designer brain smarter than anyone else's by using these products is certainly appealing. But what is "plasticity" and what should parents actually do to harness this aspect of brain development?

Plasticity is the brain's lifelong capacity to form new synapses, connections between nerve cells, and even new neural pathways, making and strengthening connections so that learning accelerates and the ability to access and apply learning becomes more and more efficient. This also includes the brain's capacity to deprioritize or prune "unused" wiring, or connections that don't continue to be useful.[25] For example, if you ever learned how to play a musical instrument, you may recall how, over time and with practice, you gained facility in all the elements involved in making music—learning the connection between actions and sounds, learning to read music, mastering fingering or breath control, etc.—and consequently gained the ability to play more and more complex pieces and to play more fluidly. And you may also recall that if you didn't continue playing and practicing in adulthood and then picked up your instrument twenty years later and tried to do what you'd done in younger years, you couldn't play quite as well as before.

That process of learning and "unlearning" music is a good meta-
phor for brain plasticity: laying down the brain wiring to begin
with and then losing a bit of that wiring if the skill—playing a
musical instrument, in this example—is not practiced. Also, as
with other aspects of plasticity, "pruning" is quite extensive during
the first three years of life, when the general architecture of a
child's brain is being sculpted by environmental input, including
input from an intuitive parent. Interestingly, there is another increase in pruning during adolescence, when brain architecture is
"finalized" for life as an adult.[26]

Animal studies have been quite informative in exploring brain
development, and much of what we know about plasticity comes
from research conducted on nonhuman primates, cats, and rodents. The research approach is deceptively simple: Expose the
animal to sound, sight, or another combination of stimuli and observe the changes in its brain.[27] Activity (exercise) stimulates and
strengthens development, in essence triggering brain plasticity. But
as with exercise, what you do, and how you do it, matters. Doing
pull-ups will strengthen the arms but will not directly improve
whole-body tasks such as running. To become a better runner,
you don't need to do pull-ups; you need to run! Similarly, watching
numbers flash on a screen will train the brain to watch numbers
flashing on a screen—but not how to do math. And more important, no one should fall prey to the myth that watching numbers
flash on a screen is *required* to learn math. After all, none of the
great mathematicians in history—even recent history—ever
watched numbers flash on a screen, but they did spend lots of time
working on math problems. I can assure you that neither Euclid of
Alexandria, who lived around 300 BC and is considered one of the
great mathematicians of all time, nor even Einstein in the twentieth century ever watched numbers flash on a computer screen
while learning math!

Developmental studies of plasticity trace the modification of brain architecture and brain wiring when it is exposed to novel situations. In this case, brain "wiring" means axon connections among brain regions and the activities those brain regions carry out. Rather like an architect drawing a wiring diagram for your home, indicating where the wires will go for the stove, refrigerator, air-conditioning, and so on, researchers have been drawing a wiring diagram for the brain. In the process they have established that in animals—and humans—the cortex of the brain is not a fixed entity but is, rather, being continuously modified by learning. It turns out that the "wires" in the brain are constantly reconnecting and will continue to do so based on input from the outside world.

One of the pioneers of this research is Michael Merzenich, now a professor emeritus at the University of California, San Francisco, and member of the National Academy of Sciences. In one of Dr. Merzenich's original studies, published in 1984, he conducted an elegant experiment demonstrating that in the sensory region of the brain (the parietal lobe) of owl monkeys, an area "coded" to interpret sense data from one of a monkey's fingers could, if the monkey lost that finger, convert to processing input from a different finger. In other words, the experiment showed that the function of this area of the brain is "plastic." As simple as that might sound, it was a revolutionary finding. Prior to these types of experiments, neuroscientists believed that after a region of the brain had been wired for one function, it could not then be rewired to do something else.[28]

Vanderbilt University neuroscientist Jon Kaas demonstrated similar results in experiments with human amputees. Writing in the prestigious scientific journal *Nature*, he reported: "The brain often reorganizes itself after damage to some of its sensory inputs, so that neurons that were responsive to the missing inputs come to respond to remaining inputs." He showed that, in the months of recovery after amputation of a hand, for example, the parts of the brain that previously registered hand sensation became responsive to sensations coming from the face or arm.[29]

Both of these studies reveal that the brain is plastic in the sense that you can "teach an old neuron new tricks." If a neuron became "unemployed" because the hand or finger initially activating it was no longer available to provide input, the neuron got a new job processing input from another region. It would be a waste of a perfectly usable neuron, or brain region, if the brain did not allow for conversion to some other use when the original function was lost due to accident or injury. The discovery of this kind of cortical plasticity makes perfect sense from the perspective both of healing and of efficient allocation of brain resources.

But what about learning and brain plasticity? Later studies by Merzenich and his colleagues demonstrated that plasticity extends not only to repair and healing but also to knowledge and skill acquisition. In order to test the neural responses to learning, they completed high-resolution mapping of brain activation while a monkey was performing a task such as tapping its finger. Merzenich then trained a monkey to tap its fingers in complex sequences and made new brain maps during the finger tapping. He found that as the monkey got faster and made fewer errors in the tapping sequence, new areas of the brain began "helping" and additional brain cells had been recruited to complete the tasks the monkey had learned. Moreover, as the monkeys used in the tests became more proficient at finger tapping, more and more of their brain power was used to support this task. Their "plastic" brain allocated more brain cells and nerve circuits to finger tapping as the monkeys learned[30] and became more adept at performing the activity. Because these studies used signals recorded directly from the surface of the brain, they cannot be directly replicated in humans. However, noninvasive human studies suggest that the plasticity seen in monkeys and other primates is probably quite similar to what happens in humans.

As an example, this kind of plasticity appears to be analogous to what happens when a child first learns to read. Initially, no part of the brain is wired specifically for reading. As the child learns to read, more and more brain cells and nerve circuits are recruited to the task as the child becomes a more proficient reader. The brain uses plasticity when a child begins to recognize words and comprehend what he is reading.[31] To be sure, *existing* language centers are expanded to now include reading, but new circuits for mapping written words onto preexisting meaning are also developed. The spoken word "ball," which the child already comprehends, now becomes associated with the letters B-A-L-L. In this way, learning to read is actually a form of neural plasticity. Computer-based letter recognition drills activate and train symbol recognition centers in the visual cortex using brain plasticity. But so does dialogic reading. And dialogic reading—intuitive and transactional—not only "wires" letter recognition centers, it also naturally harnesses neural plasticity to make axon connections to the language and thinking centers in the brain. Letter recognition drills do not.

These and other amazing discoveries about neural plasticity are often translated into commercial products touting enhanced "brain fitness" as a benefit. But just because an experiment shows that a particular activity triggers brain plasticity to enhance learning doesn't mean that the activity is *required* to achieve the effect, nor does it mean that the activity is the *only* means of generating plasticity.

In fact, all learning—of *any* kind—is a form of neural plasticity. An intuitive parent who teaches his or her child new words using language transactions while playing with real toys is harnessing neural plasticity every bit as much as—if not more than—the latest Baby Genius DVD or "brain fitness" computer game. Input of any kind—whether it is a mother talking to her baby, playing with blocks, sliding on the playground with daddy, learning math, listening to music (regardless of whether it is classical music or

disco or country-western or jazz), and playing special "brain training" computer games—activates neural plasticity.[32] There is nothing uniquely magical about computer-based brain plasticity
training—as least as far as the brain is concerned.

This is true even for the computer games developed by the
brain scientists themselves, who sometimes attempt to translate
their research findings into "brain-based" learning products. Michael Merzenich has developed and marketed computer games for
companies called Scientific Learning[33] and BrainSpark[34] that
claim to improve speaking and listening skills, and reading performance, in children.[35] As we will see, even companies and products developed by neuroscientists do not necessarily deliver better
speaking, listening, reading, or learning skills when compared to
teaching these skills in real-life activities such as language transactions or dialogic reading.

Professor Paul Yoder at Vanderbilt University and I made the
point in a paper published in the *International Journal of Developmental Neuroscience* that typically developing children learn to discriminate speech sounds quite efficiently with or *without* the
benefit of exposure to speech discrimination exercises or computer games.[36] In fact, their brains end up with a perfectly organized auditory cortex based on natural, transactional input from
their parents and others. This natural input is well suited to teaching the developing brain the importance of speech discrimination
as a means of understanding spoken language, not merely as an
overlearned "splinter skill" disconnected from language. We also
argued that *unnatural* auditory input—in this case, isolated auditory signals—would not result in the proper wiring or integration
of that input such that other brain regions were necessary to distinguish speech in the real world.

Let's take a closer look at studies comparing intuitive learning
to computer-based drill to gain a better understanding of the way
neural plasticity works in real-life situations. In addition to

discovering how plasticity works in the sense of touch, Dr. Merzenich and his colleagues have been the lead scientists in understanding how the brain becomes wired for speech perception. Some of this work has been done in animals and has shown that the *kind* of input that is heard—and the timing of that input—has profound effects on the auditory centers in the brain. For example, if rats regularly hear high-pitched noise, more neurons and a larger area of the auditory centers in their brains become dedicated to processing high-pitched noise. If rats are trained to expect food when a specific type of sound occurs (for example, a pulsing sound like a siren), more and more of their brain gets "recruited" to the task of detecting and locating this kind of sound. On the other hand, rats deprived of these types of auditory signals when they are young are much less proficient at detecting and processing these sounds when they are introduced to the rats in adulthood. But with training on sounds like sirens and other complex noises, those auditory-impoverished rats can still learn to seek food and become much better at detecting and processing complex tones.

This research led Dr. Merzenich and his colleagues to theorize that children who had problems learning to speak and to understand what was said to them were experiencing the same kind of problem as the auditory-impoverished rats. He proposed that the solution to this problem was, as with the rats, to conduct specialized, computer-based auditory training designed to engage neural plasticity to overcome the listening deficits.

On the human side, Professor Paula Tallal and her colleagues have shown that children with language-learning difficulties do indeed have trouble processing speech sounds. Auditory information in speech is both rapid and transient, and it is not surprising that some children have problems keeping up with the rapid flow of information. Putting the two research lines together, Dr. Merzenich and Dr. Tallal created—and marketed—special computer software to train discrimination of individual speech sounds and of nonspeech sounds such as rising and falling tones. That is, the phonetic difference in the English words "hat" and "bat" is the first sound in each word: an "h" for hat and a "b" for bat. Some children have difficulty hearing this fine difference, so the software was designed to target and develop that skill, harnessing the brain's plasticity and teaching it to discriminate these kinds of phonetic sound differences. In the hopes of improving language comprehension.[37] Alas, several large studies showed that their program didn't quite work out as the scientists had hoped. But the lack of independent scientific support has not stopped Scientific Learning and Brain-Spark from continuing to sell these products.

Although children did learn to discriminate between these kinds of sounds, those new skills didn't lead to improvement in their ability to understand what was said to them over and above classroom instruction or even inexpensive educational software.[38] What went wrong? No one would argue that the groundbreaking research the brain scientists, such as Merzenich and Tallal, did was accurate and illuminated essential principles of neural plasticity. But key to understanding why the auditory brain plasticity computer games didn't work is understanding how brain plasticity functions naturally and intuitively. Even typically developing children are born with relatively poor auditory processing skills, and their brains become wired properly *without* specialized computer training. In fact, intuitive, transactional learning is very well suited to ensuring that these skills develop. So even when there is a delay in developing auditory processing, the solution is not to isolate a "special" skill, such as speech processing, but rather to deliver additional transactional exposure to ensure that the child—and his or her brain—learns what he or she really needs to know, such as listening and speaking, rather than simply recognizing that "ba" and "da" are different sounds in English.

Of course, long before Drs. Merzenich and Tallal came on the scene and isolated the neural processes, and long before computers were invented, neural plasticity existed. Brain wiring occurred and continues to occur—extensively—without specialized, targeted, skill-focused intervention. Baby rats get their little auditory cortices wired via neural plasticity even when they are not being studied in a neuroscience lab, as do human children. In fact, studies of auditory plasticity in rats have to be completed in sound-proofed, isolated labs, otherwise the ambient noise triggers brain development in the auditory centers of their baby brains and interferes with the experiments! The point here is that naturally occurring environmental input is what ultimately activates neural plasticity and "wires" the auditory centers in the brain to function properly in the real world.

Similarly, before special software was available, children successfully learned how to discriminate between the words "hat" and "bat" because parental responses triggered brain plasticity and learning in the brain. Baby Adalyn, my third granddaughter, is eight months old and is babbling away while sitting in her high chair. Her father, my oldest son, Andy, and her mother, Molly, put some toys on the high chair tray. One of these is a duck, and Adalyn says "da" when she sees the duck. Andy and Molly are excited by this vocalization and say "duck" right after Addy says "da." They continue saying "duck" over and over, more than ten times in just a few minutes. Addy keeps saying "da," but after a while she starts saying "duck" too. While this is going on, everyone is having a jolly time, Molly and Andy smiling and moving the duck on the tray in front of Addy, who just loves the attention. Do you think this intuitive parenting episode is teaching Addy's developing auditory cortex to discriminate the difference between "da" and "duck"? I can assure you that brain plasticity is indeed occurring!

For scientists to use bits of sound, such as those that occur in "hat" and "cat" and "that," to study the way the brain processes sounds and ultimately gain insight into how brain plasticity works is a worthwhile and important goal. But to observe brain plasticity under these conditions may then mislead parents into thinking that it can only be triggered under scientifically controlled conditions or that the laboratory methods are the optimal way to harness plasticity.

Never forget that the brain will learn what it is taught. If computer software trains the brain to discriminate between little bits of sound, *that*—recognizing bits of sound—is what it will learn and become wired to do. But this will not generalize to the brain's ability to understand what someone else is saying, or to learn to read, because discriminating sounds is only a small fragment of what the brain has to do to comprehend spoken language and to read. If you want the brain to become wired for spoken language and for reading, then the input has to be real, functional, spoken language and dialogic reading. Breaking the speech signal into its component parts simply will not do the trick. And if you want the spoken language to serve as a tool for relational communication with other human beings, the input may also need to occur in the context of human social interaction, which involves even more areas of the brain.

When a child reaches for a hat lying on the floor, and her dad says "hat," this interaction triggers neural plasticity in the baby's brain. The child's brain is not only processing the phonic components of the word "hat," it is processing the visual image of the hat, the social context (playing with her dad), and the actual meaning of the word—a real hat. When dad intuitively (as is likely) puts the hat first on his head and then on her head, the speech sounds in the word "hat" are then associated with the perceptual properties of the hat as well as its function (covering the head). Later on, the child and her dad may read a book together and see a photograph of a bat (in this case, the flying mammal). Now the child hears her dad say "bat," which of course is phonetically different than "hat." But she is perceiving not only a difference in the speech sounds "h" and "b" but also the perceptual features of a bat and a hat, the social context in which the objects are encountered, and the functions of the objects. It is not surprising that simply teaching discrimination between "h" and "b" cannot possibly convey the information the child will need to comprehend the difference between "hat" and "bat" in the real world. Intuitive parenting *automatically* teaches all these elements simultaneously; it is automatically a *multisensory* approach. Touching, seeing, speaking, and listening are all providing context—in a safe, nurturing environment.

- Your child's brain comes ready to learn. An intuitive parent is confident in responding naturally and positively to his or her baby so that *brain plasticity* is triggered, ensuring that the whole brain is wired properly for a lifetime of learning.
- An intuitive parent knows that the brain *learns what it is taught*, so that it's better to expose his or her child to real-world experiences rather than computer games or drills and flash cards. For example, intuitive parents will engage in dialogic reading—sitting with their toddler and reading books—rather than drilling letter flash cards or computer-based letter games.
- Wiring the brain and neural plasticity *always* occur whenever learning occurs. Computers and flash cards are *not* required to wire the brain and may confuse a child or actually hinder his or her development.
- An intuitive parent knows that playing and responding to his or her child's *initiations* are the very best way to ensure that the various areas of the brain—vision, smell, touch, language, listening, etc.—learn to work together. Multisensory experiences are best. A child's initiations are the signal to an intuitive parent that his or her developing brain is ready to learn.
- Intuitive parents know that they are helping to lay the foundation for an integrated and optimal adult brain and will be naturally skeptical of get-rich-quick schemes that shortchange

them—and their child. Their child's brain becomes wired to *reason* and *problem-solve*, skills that can be adapted and applied to whatever knowledge and challenges the future holds far better than teaching his or her brain to parrot. Computer games and flash cards are no match for Mother Nature—and intuitive parenting—for brain development.

As we go forward, we will see over and over again that attempts to take shortcuts with regard to learning and wiring the brain in the name of harnessing neural plasticity cannot hold a candle to intuitive parenting when it comes to ensuring that your child's mind is built for learning and thinking well into the twenty-first century while actually maximizing neural plasticity along the way.

chapter 3
"The Critical Period": Truth and Lies

The purpose of this chapter is to prepare intuitive parents for the indirect—and direct—pressure they will face to push their children faster than their developing brains are ready to go. One of the more insidious rationales behind efforts to "raise the bar" on what very young children should learn—which parents will hear from well-meaning educators and product marketers alike—is the notion that there is a fixed, "critical period" for learning that a child must hit to achieve his or her full potential in life. After all (so the thinking goes), everyone *knows* that there is a developmental clock ticking when a child's brain is developing, and that it is therefore absolutely *crucial* that parents seize this precious and fleeting opportunity to ensure their baby's future success. Talk about parental stress!

This misunderstood notion of the "critical period" is, as we will see, a recurring theme in current parenting—and marketing—lore. It has certainly informed social and educational policies and programs that push children to learn at ever younger ages, but another of its tragic consequences is the sheer panic it can induce in parents that their baby will somehow miss *the* crucial critical period for brain development and always thereafter be unable to "keep up" with academic or social expectations as a result. In my work with children who begin talking late, parents routinely ask whether a child will be doomed to poor lifelong outcomes if "key" skills are not learned by the age of three—or within some other "critical period" they have heard about. These parents report reading or being told that unless their child is enrolled in a particular preschool enrichment program, or unless they purchase the latest "brain wiring" software and plug their child in, the opportunity for learning will be forever lost. Many parents—and professionals—seem to be preoccupied with the notion that a child's brain *must* be wired completely by the age of three—or else! This kind of stress can needlessly derail patient and positive intuitive parenting.

The origins of this panic stretch back nearly twenty years. In 1996, an article on brain development in babies and young children by Susan Begley proclaimed to *Newsweek*'s three-million-plus readers[1]: "[O]nce wired, there are limits to the brain's ability to create itself. Time limits. Called 'critical periods,' they are windows of opportunity that nature flings open, starting before birth, *and then slams shut, one by one*, with every additional candle on the child's birthday cake" (emphasis added).[2] Even more ominously, the article went on to imply that Head Start, a popular government-funded prekindergarten education program for low-income children, wasn't working as well as hoped because the critical learning window had closed by the time many of the children entered the program.

In the decade immediately after the *Newsweek* article was published, education policy makers and entrepreneurs continued to seize upon the notion of a "critical period" that "slams shut" to push for more and more "learning" in infancy and preschool years.

Parents—and children—are still suffering the consequences of this misleading view of how the brain develops and how children learn.

Parents have been bombarded by articles such as "To Shape a Life, We Must Begin before a Child Is 3"[3] and "Building a Better Brain: A Child's First Three Years Provide Parents Once-in-Lifetime Opportunity to Dramatically Increase Intelligence." One book even claims that performing the "right" kind of learning alchemy in the first three years can boost a child's IQ by up to thirty points![4] As we will see later in this chapter, the onslaught is, if anything, picking up steam, even in the face of serious doubts raised by brain scientists and developmental specialists.

But what does "critical period" really mean? Where does this notion come from and what is the scientific evidence on so-called critical periods? And, more important, what are the implications for intuitive parenting?

In brain development and in developmental psychology, a critical period is a time window thought to be crucial for acquiring a mental ability. Language development is a well-known example of an accomplishment that research has shown begins during a critical period, meaning that if a child's brain gets no language input from parents and others by a certain time, the child will fail to develop language skills properly.[5] Have you ever noticed that some people who learn a second language speak with an accent, even when their overall knowledge of its words and grammar is excellent? It turns out that if someone learns a second language *before* the teen years, he or she will probably *not* have an accent, whereas those learning as teenagers, or later, probably will. There seems to be a critical period for learning a second language, at least in terms of *pronouncing* that second language like a native speaker, that ends at around age twelve.[6]

But it turns out that even broad critical periods like this one for second language learning are actually quite rare in development and that they are not nearly so fixed as once thought. The notion of a window slamming shut on brain development, or that opportunities for learning have an "expiration date" is highly misleading at best.[7] Indeed, it now appears that attempts to artificially accelerate development in the name of hitting a critical period could actually disrupt the proper timing and developmental ordering of learning.

The great developmental psychologist Jean Piaget, who first described a general comprehensive path of intellectual development in children based on developmental stages, was often asked about how those stages could be accelerated.[8] Professor Piaget was deeply concerned about this question. His view was that children would learn when they were ready, and that seeking to accelerate normal developmental processes could inadvertently derail their cognitive growth. Piaget called this desire to speed up development "the American question," presumably because some American educators and parents were preoccupied with trying to hurry children along. Their assumption was (and is) that pushing development earlier and earlier will make the children "smarter" in the long run. But Piaget didn't believe that acceleration in childhood would necessarily translate into smarter adults.

Nearly forty years ago, education professor Lois Nelson argued that although attempts to accelerate cognitive development could produce short-term gains, the gains were not maintained long term.[9] She also noted that these short-term gains came at a high cost. Children who had been prematurely pushed to learn concepts for which their minds were not ready displayed increased passivity toward learning. Most children are naturally curious and want to learn, but those pushed too early seemed to lose interest in learning new things. Nelson also reported that the "thrust for attainment in the intellectual area may impede growth in other areas of personal and social development." In short, she argued, any benefits of acceleration were short lived and produced negative side effects in the form of reduced motivation for learning (passivity) and lags in social development.

Despite Dr. Piaget's and Professor Nelson's prescient warnings, the intervening forty years have only substantiated their findings: Schemes to accelerate learning do not produce long-lasting improvements in intelligence but do have long-lasting negative consequences, especially in the form of reducing a child's motivation to learn independently, and reducing self-confidence. Nevertheless, despite the research evidence, modern parents are under increasing pressure to push their children even harder and to introduce concepts earlier and earlier.

Is earlier really better?[10] Have forty years of introducing concepts earlier and earlier and subjecting even infants and toddlers to regimented drill and rote learning resulted in smarter children and produced a new generation of geniuses? Interestingly, innovators who society recognizes as geniuses, such as Steve Jobs and Bill Gates, are renowned for rebelling against any educational system that emphasized rote learning and failed to capture their insatiable curiosity. Indeed, any descriptive study of geniuses throughout history shows that they are uniformly rebellious toward rote learning and often are insistent on (and persistent in) following their own interests according to their own developmental schedule. And what makes a genius a genius if not the possession of high-level problem-solving skills and superior reasoning ability?

If earlier is always better in child development, why isn't ensuring that all children learn to walk and talk by the time they reach six months of age a national priority? Mother Nature and the usual course of development are remarkably consistent: The overwhelming majority of toddlers will learn to walk and start using first words somewhere between their first and second birthdays. This is true whether a child is raised in a crowded urban environment, on a farm, or in the suburbs and in fact seems to be true no matter where in the world a child is born or what language her parents speak. The ongoing national educational focus on pushing development earlier and earlier would suggest that these highly salient developmental milestones—walking and talking—would be natural targets for enhancement.

So why haven't we seen programs designed to ensure that all children walk and talk by six months of age? Because it is absurd to try to teach a six-month-old to walk or talk. They are physically and mentally incapable of doing so. And people generally seem to recognize that teaching a six-month-old to walk and talk is not a worthwhile goal. After all, the overwhelming majority of children will learn to walk quite well before they reach two years of age without any special intervention. Further, there is no evidence that walking or talking earlier would convey any long-term benefits in terms of a child's motor coordination, intellectual development, or speech and language skills.

Perhaps scientists could develop a training program to reduce the mean age a child walks by a few months. But what would be the point? And might there be potential unintended detrimental side effects to forcing children to try to walk before they would normally if left to their own devices? It is easy to speculate that pushing a child to walk before his or her joints and bones are ready could end up causing long-term harm. Perhaps the stress of standing up would prevent the knees and hips from aligning properly; perhaps the bones would become misshapen. Perhaps a toddler's proportional body configuration would induce an unusual gait that would adversely affect stride and balance in the long run.

It is fairly self-evident to everyone that working to accelerate walking and talking is a fool's errand. Everybody knows a newborn can't talk, and no one sees the point (or possibility) of a walking six-month-old. But when it comes to accelerating other kinds of learning, advocates haven't stopped to consider whether the ends really justify the means, or just seem to do so on a written test; nor have they factored in the documented and potential negative side effects on children—and on society as a whole. Perhaps these kinds of attempts to artificially accelerate development may be every bit as foolhardy as trying to teach a child to walk and talk by the time she is six months old.

Artificially Slicing Development into "Stages"

Child development specialists, and the test makers who adapt the information from child development studies to incorporate into standardized assessments, often employ the notion of "stages" as a way of classifying progress from infancy to adulthood. Milestones or developmental markers for each stage are often used in checklists or become items on tests. For example, most children begin walking by the age of twelve months, and developmental checklists will ask parents when their child started to walk. If a child doesn't begin walking by the age of eighteen months or so, it may be an indicator that the child's gross motor development is slower than average.

Stages of gross motor development include rolling over, sitting up, crawling, pulling up to a standing position, walking, and running. But in reality, these aren't really discrete, sequential stages. When a baby first starts walking, she is also still crawling most of the time; she didn't suddenly stop crawling when she started to walk. So there is no distinct dividing line between one stage and another; there is instead a transitional phase during which walking increases and crawling decreases. But because the age when a child starts walking can be an indication of overall development, parents are often asked to report the age at which their child first walked. No one, however, asks them when the child stopped crawling!

Why does this matter? Many developmental checklists and books on child development lay out stages a child passes through, often aligned with age levels when children typically reach these stages. Now, tying age to these stages can be useful in determining whether a child is developing differently than others—earlier or later. However, parents reading or hearing about the stages can misunderstand these checklists as specific timelines and become worried, or even worse, start to panic, if their child doesn't hit a particular stage "on time." These stages can also be misused as targets for acceleration; for example, a parent noticing that the "stage" for first words is around twelve months thinks: Wouldn't it be great if my child was talking by the time she is eleven or even ten months old?

In truth, there is considerable variation in the *range* of ages at which even normally developing children reach each stage. There are not precise age cutoffs wherein a child who misses the so-called deadline is necessarily "slow" or "impaired." For example, it is indeed true that the average age when children start to say words is around twelve months. However, if we were to look at language acquisition in a slightly different way, and asked when *most* children say their first words, the answer would be an age range stretching from ten months to eighteen months. Although it is fine when a child starts talking a bit early, this doesn't mean that the onset of first words was unusually precocious. Conversely, there is nothing grossly abnormal about a child starting to use words at eighteen months, so parents shouldn't push the panic button if their child doesn't achieve that "stage" by twelve months. The point here is that using first words is normal somewhere in the range of ten to eighteen months because this is the range in which children start saying their first real words.[11] Whether they start at nine months or eighteen months tells us very little about how smart they will be in kindergarten or later in life.

There is also considerable variation in how quickly a skill develops. For some children, first words come in and they add a few words here and there and make steady progress. My granddaughter

Adalyn's first word, "duck," came in at ten months of age, and baby Addy has been steadily saying a few new words every few weeks. Other children don't begin until a bit later but within a few months have added dozens or even hundreds of words and are beginning to speak in sentences. They may even have surpassed children who started using words months earlier than they did. Developmental stages are simply a set of guidelines and landmarks. They should not be viewed as strict rules for what baby should be able to do at a specific age, nor as targets for instruction or educational acceleration in hopes of "wiring the brain" more quickly and beating a mythical average cutoff age level.

In my clinical work with children with developmental disabilities such as autism, Down syndrome, and speech and language disorders, parents occasionally contact me, worried that their child passed his or her first birthday without saying their first words. On the one hand, I compliment them for checking in to be sure everything is OK with their toddler. On the other hand, if everything else is going well in terms of the child's play skills and social skills, I tell the parents it is perfectly fine if their child doesn't begin using first words until fourteen, sixteen, or even eighteen months of age so long as they start somewhere within the normal range and everything else, such as walking and play skills, is coming along in typical fashion. This is normal variation in development and is in no way a sign of bad parenting or a failure to properly stimulate their child's brain.

Slow onset of words *can* be a sign of developmental disabilities such as cognitive impairment, autism, or other speech or language disorders.[12] Parents of these children sometimes feel guilty and remorseful and believe that they should have pushed their child to speak when he or she was younger. Some parents say that they wish they had forced their child to watch Baby Genius educational videos to increase his or her vocabulary. But as we've seen, these techniques do not accelerate first words; in fact, their use potentially could have slowed things down even more. In our competitive society, these parents sometimes are subjected to well-meant but misguided advice or even criticism from neighbors, co-workers, and even other adult family members. When a child is slow to develop—except in those cases, mercifully rare in politically stable countries with adequate food supplies, when the child has suffered severe malnutrition or neglect—decades of studies have shown that it is not due to poor parenting. (We'll discuss intuitive parenting for children who are truly developmentally delayed or disabled in more depth in another chapter.)

The truth is that virtually no typically developing child is above average or below average *in all phases of development*. One may learn to talk early but struggle with number concepts later on. Another advances physically, and walks early, but then talks a bit later. In my own research, I have found that when preschool-age children talk in longer sentences, their pronunciation of the sounds in the words they are saying gets worse. That is, they may say the word "ball" with correct pronunciation in short sentences such as "I have a ball." But when they say something like "Mommy, please throw the bright red beach ball to me," they may leave off the "l" sound in the longer and more complex sentence. Trade-offs like this are extremely common in development.[13]

When a child makes an advance in one area, another area may not advance or may even regress.[14] This is important to bear in mind because curious children who like to learn things on their own may not necessarily sit still and listen very well. They may be highly intelligent in most ways but may not be able to retell a story or otherwise regurgitate what the preschool teacher talked about that day. Many other children are very adept at listening to and retelling stories—which is great! On the other hand, those same children may not be math whizzes, or may not excel at sports. There is considerable variation in human development, even among children in the same family.

In my own home sample of seven children, some talked a bit early and some talked a bit late relative to the usual developmental stage guidelines discussed above. One talked extremely late. Some were good at math; others had to work harder to grasp numerical concepts. Some were good athletes; others did not like to play sports. All were avid readers, but some liked to read nonfiction whereas others preferred literature. Their college-major concentrations have been all over the place! One was a physics major, another a history major, one created her own major as a science writer, another majored in human development, the next one in chemistry, and my youngest son graduated with a degree in political science. My youngest daughter is currently a senior in high school so I have no idea what she will choose to study in college. Given the complexity of the human brain and the diversity of the human species, it is hardly surprising that their minds and interests, as well as their development, have been so individual.

Given these circumstances, did it make sense for me to set out to wire their brains when they were babies in order to produce a physician, a teacher, an air traffic controller, a health-care product manager, or whatever they grew up to be? Of course not! What was important in raising them was to ensure that they had many opportunities to develop their reasoning abilities so that they were well equipped to follow their own interests as they grew up and became adults. As parents, our job was to ensure that all of them were exposed to multiple learning opportunities so their developing brains could gather the information they needed. We consciously made sure that their natural curiosity was always rewarded with parental attention and encouragement. And, as previously discussed, we also ran interference with teachers who insisted on rote learning or adhered to "canned" answers. I recall a sixth-grade science experiment for one of my daughters that did not come out as the textbook suggested it should. When the teacher instructed her to go ahead and change her data to conform to the textbook expectations for the experiment, you will by now not be surprised to hear that I firmly told my daughter *not* to do this but to report accurately what happened in the experiment. Afterward, I talked with the teacher at length about why she should not penalize my daughter for being a good scientist and turning in the results of the experiment even though they were unexpected.

In keeping with their different interests, my children have chosen diverse careers. The physics major went on to medical school and is studying to become a radiation oncologist—a physician who treats cancer using radiation—so he is putting his long-standing interest in physics to practical use. The history major is an elementary school teacher who works part time at a community college while raising her three small children, and the science writer works as a communication specialist for Johns Hopkins University. The human development major works as a product manager for a health informatics company, and the former chemistry major is working as an apprentice chef in a New Orleans restaurant. (No doubt he is putting his expertise in chemistry to good use creating wonderful sauces!) The political science major is an air traffic controller in the U.S. Air Force. My point here is this: There is no way I could have preordained or prewired my children's brains for the careers and education that their talents and their interests led them to. Rather, "child development" at our house was focused on nurturing curiosity, responding to each child's interests, and helping each one develop fluid reasoning and problem-solving skills. In this way they became prepared to take on educational challenges and career choices that they themselves chose.

Indeed, my children sometimes noticed our efforts to foster reasoning. One of the children once remarked (when she was in grade school): "Dad, when I ask you a question, I want you to tell me the answer . . . I don't want to think!" My wife and I were notorious for responding to their questions with "What do you think the answer is?" or "I'll tell you the answer after you guess." When they were babies, to be sure, much of our time was spent on caring for them: feeding them, bathing them, and generally nurturing them. After all, we were outnumbered seven to two! But in the process, we looked for and found ways to facilitate their mental development in a natural way, with fun and laughter and imagination being a big part of the mix. Even though the educational software industry was only in its infancy at that time, there was still plenty of pressure to purchase the latest educational toys and learning products. But then, as now, these things could not match what the children could learn from us, from one another, and from the simple process of growing up in an environment that nurtured their natural curiosity and reasoning abilities.

What does a baby really need to know? That his parents love him, will take care of him, and will encourage him and empower him to learn. This does not require special videos, special toys, or special DVDs or computer programs. There's no particular skill he *must* master by some predetermined date, especially by an arbitrary "critical age" of three—or any other specific age. Indeed, despite attempts to accelerate learning, there is no evidence that get-rich-quick learning schemes are translating to learning that is any earlier or any faster than children five years ago, ten years ago, or even twenty years ago.

Critical Periods: Myths and Realities

Tragedy struck early in young Julia's life. She was born in St. Louis to a reasonably well-off family, but her mother died when she was only two years old. Her father evidently became depressed and lost interest in working, so he sent Julia and her older sister to a foster home in Arizona. One year later, her father remarried and moved to Arizona to reclaim his daughters, but the family continued to move around and young Julia did not have any schooling or consistent academic instruction. Finally, when she was five years old, the family moved to San Diego so she could start school. She began catching up with the other students, but then when she was nine she came down with scarlet fever and missed another whole year of school.

Surely, this difficult start in life meant that many "critical periods" for brain development had been lost and young Julia was doomed to a life of academic underachievement. . . . Well, actually not. Despite a very difficult beginning to her educational career, Julia Robinson (1919–1985) grew up to become the first female president of the American Mathematical Society and the first female mathematician elected to the National Academy of Sciences.

How did she do it? After missing a year of school due to illness, she worked with a private tutor and began to blossom academically, especially in math and science.[15] In fact, she completed the fifth-through eighth-grade state mathematical requirements in a single year. By the time she entered public high school in San Diego, she was the only girl in the math and physics classes and received the Bausch & Lomb Honorary Science Award for her outstanding work. Julia entered college at San Diego State College and transferred to Berkeley for accelerated mathematics training. She received her PhD in mathematics from Berkeley in 1948, went on to a stellar career as a mathematician, and was elected to the National Academy of Sciences in 1976. It's clear from her life story that the "critical period" for wiring her brain extended far beyond early childhood and even early school age. Dr. Robinson's intellectual ability in general, and in math specifically, was slow to emerge but accelerated dramatically starting in middle school.

An unfortunate myth in active circulation these days has it that parents have a relatively fixed time window or "critical period" for wiring a child's brain properly to learn things like math. This misconception regarding brain development is all too common in child-rearing lore and parenting product marketing, and can dramatically raise parents' stress levels. "Oh my goodness, modern neuroscience tells me that I must wire my child's brain by the time she is three! Otherwise, I will miss the *critical period* to make my baby intelligent and doom her to lifelong neurological and intellectual mediocrity." This notion is sheer nonsense and reflects a complete misunderstanding of neurological critical periods. But it nevertheless crops up constantly in American popular culture today, even in serious scientific publications, and vulnerable parents who don't understand how to decode the scientific jargon and separate fact from myth may fall victim to pointless anxiety, wrongheaded guidance, and useless product purchases.

Here, for example, is a quote that appeared in a popular, respected science journal, *Nature*, in 2012:

> Language acquisition is just one of many processes that go through a "sensitive" or "critical" period—an interval during development when the neural circuits responsible for that process can be sculpted, and radically changed, by experience. . . . During critical periods, children can make rapid progress at discerning facial features that look like their own, recognizing spoken language and locating objects in space. *But within a few months or years, each window of opportunity slams shut, and learning anything new in that realm becomes difficult, if not impossible* [emphasis added].[16]

Wow, talk about scary. Miss that magic moment and it "becomes difficult, if not impossible" for your child to learn? And because this journal is respected, its dire message might inspire hundreds of tweets, parenting publication articles, blog posts, etc.

In another example, an article entitled "Q&A: What Are the Critical Periods in My Baby's Development?" on Disney's Babble Web site stated: "There are critical development periods that are time frames in your child's development during which she is ready to learn, master, or develop a new skill. . . . Some behavioral scientists believe that if a child is not assisted to learn a new skill in certain critical periods, she will not learn it on her own and may never learn it as well as if she had learned it in this 'critical' period."[17] A 2013 story appearing in *Business Insider* focused on the critical period for language learning and how feral children, who are raised with minimal human contact, can miss out. The article included a description of a hypothesized critical period for language by the well-known neurologist and linguist Eric Lenneberg: "His research suggests that a specific window exists for learning language, either spoken or tactile. Outside of it, grasping the basics of communication becomes extremely difficult."[18] It should be noted that feral children usually have intellectual disabilities in addition to poor language ability, so that these tragic cases may not be the best scientific evidence of a language-specific critical period. And an article on Brainy-Child.com distinguishes between "critical periods" and "sensitive periods," and says of the latter: "During this period, if there is a lack of opportunity for a certain type of learning, it is not gone forever (as it is for critical periods). Skills can still be acquired at a later stage in the individual's lifespan. However, skills acquired during the sensitive period makes [*sic*] the individual better than another who did not acquire those skills then."[19] This makes it seem that the brain-wiring deadlines of critical periods are more flexible in the form of a sensitive period, but still implies that brain wiring is highly dependent on ensuring that the right input is delivered at exactly the right moment, or at least within a fairly narrow sensitive period.

The truth is that child-rearing should be focused on building an adult brain by the time a child graduates from high school at around eighteen years of age. Of course, learning continues far beyond the age of eighteen, but the neural circuitry and networks for communicating across brain regions to sustain lifelong thinking and learning are largely up and running by that age. More important, because brain development continues throughout adolescence, parents have plenty of time to build an adult brain and should not try to cram everything in before a child's third birthday, sixth birthday, or even their twelfth birthday. There is absolutely no reason to panic if a child's development is not complete by the age of three. Neuroscience tells us that there will be ample brain development for the next *decade* and beyond.[20]

In an effort to ensure that a child hits all "critical period" marks defined by the so-called experts, parents may end up attempting to teach concepts before their child's brain is ready to process the information properly. Some mothers have said to me: "All these brain studies show that exposing my baby to the proper information at the proper time is crucial. What if I miss the right time or use the wrong kind of stimulation?" There is no need to micromanage learning through a series of critical periods with narrow time windows that have a specific expiration date, because brain development doesn't work like that.

Intuitive parents are far better off taking the long view, attending to what the child is and is not ready for, and thinking strategically: What is it that a child should know by the time he is eighteen? It is perfectly fine for a child to spend more time than the norm mastering an important skill such as reading—and certainly more effective in the long run than forcing him to read before he is ready. By forcing, one could inadvertently induce a learning disability or, worse, a lifelong hatred of reading. It is absolutely *not* essential that a child learn his letter sounds by the age of three. All that really matters is that a child becomes a fluent reader by the time he is an adult; or even better, has a very positive relationship with the written word and develops a lifelong love of reading.

A review of critical periods—what they are and what they are *not*—will no doubt prove useful.

Critical Periods and Neurological Development: More Myths and Realities

There are indeed a number of critical periods for very specific and limited aspects of development. Knowing when a particular critical period usually occurs, however, does not necessarily mean that missing the critical window will derail broader neurological development and retard intellectual potential.

Although these critical periods are an important aspect of how the brain ultimately gets wired, what is striking is that a more general *integration* of the various brain regions continues to develop through adolescence, which means the critical period for this integration is at least eighteen years! Indeed, one of the most important aspects of brain development, executive function, which is the ability to sort and prioritize input from different brain centers, does not fully come on line until early adolescence and is not complete until a child reaches adulthood. A teenager's thinking is quite different from an adult's at least in part because executive function has not yet been fully developed. Indeed, recent research indicates that executive function undergoes considerable refinement in the brain during the teenage years.[21] (Every adult with a teenager at home knows this!)

Thus, although it is true that to trigger brain development a child needs certain early learning experiences, including being exposed to stimuli that activate all five senses, unless a child is born blind or deaf, the input available from an everyday environment—both in terms of passive experience with light, touch, smell, taste, and sound and in terms of active, naturally occurring interactions with parents—is all that is needed to ensure that the brain develops properly during this critical period. Further, although there are critical periods for experiencing these senses, higher-level thinking ability does not rely upon a narrow "critical period" in infancy or early childhood. More complex neurological skills, such as integrating information from the various brain centers and reasoning with that information, are built upon years of experience and learning and are quite flexible in terms of brain architecture. This must be so, since even people who are born blind or deaf can think and reason, despite the fact that a critical period for wiring the brain to see or hear was missed completely.

While critical periods are real, they are also very limited in scope, and the scientific evidence revealing that they should *never* become a source of needless parental panic can be found by revisiting the discovery of true critical periods in brain development more than fifty years ago and by examining several mythological "critical periods" that have not held up under scientific scrutiny.

Critical Periods for Vision and Hearing: A Scientific Breakthrough

In trying to determine whether the timing of input from the senses makes a difference in how the brain develops, scientists have relied on experiments with animals so that they could control precisely when the brain receives input. For example, in a now-classic study published in 1963, David Hubel and Torsten Wiesel tested the importance of early visual stimulation by surgically closing one eye of kittens immediately after they were born and then reopening it three months later.[22] The kittens could see out of only one eye from the time they were born, and then out of both eyes after three months. The results of their study showed that the neural pathways for the eye that was open from birth were quite different from those for the eye that had been sewn shut for three months. Based on this study and countless others, scientists have determined that the timing of visual stimulation to the eyes is very important for the efficient development of the visual pathways and centers in the brain.

Thus, there is a critical period for vision. From a functional perspective, this means that failing to receive visual stimulation results in worse vision if sight is not "turned on" at the proper time in development. The ability to coordinate information between the eyes, such as developing depth perception in binocular vision, is also significantly impaired when both eyes do not receive proper stimulation at the proper time. Scientists report that, in humans, visual stimulation in both eyes is needed at a young age in order for binocular vision to develop properly.[23]

But does this mean that a well-established and credible critical period for developing vision justifies the need to expose a baby to all kinds of flashing lights, numbers, or letters to ensure that she will grow up to be smart? Or that failing to provide just the "right" visual stimulation during this critical period is needed to facilitate brain development? Actually, no. It turns out that babies should experience sensory input in both eyes before around eight months of age and that this input should be three-dimensional (solid objects) rather than two-dimensional (flash cards or video screens), but that there is no long-term advantage to specifically tailoring the input. In the natural environment, babies encounter their parents, blocks, rattles, cups, bowls, spoons, sticks, rocks, grass, pets, and so on. Think about all the different objects that babies encounter in the wonderfully diverse human cultures around the world! Any and all of these work to harness the power of this critical period, ensuring the proper development of visual pathways and binocular, or stereoscopic, vision. There is no scientific evidence that presenting special input—numbers or letters, or certain kinds of blocks—better wires the brain during this critical period for developing vision, and it is clear that babies who do not see letters or numbers until long after this critical period has passed often turn out to be outstanding readers and capable mathematicians.

This convincing evidence of a critical period for developing vision also has some important limits. Dr. Pawan Sinha, a professor of brain and cognitive sciences at the Massachusetts Institute of Technology (MIT), received the prestigious Troland Research Award from the National Academy of Sciences for his studies of blind children in India whose sight was restored long past the "critical period" for wiring the visual centers in the brain. Dr. Sinha found that these children could learn to see even when the surgery was completed after the age of five, six, or even twelve, causing a radical shift in determining who should be eligible for surgery to restore sight and, more basically, a corresponding shift in our understanding of the parameters of the critical period for wiring the brain for vision.

In a now-classic case study, Professor Sinha and his colleagues studied a woman from India who, before receiving eye surgery when she was twelve, could barely distinguish light and dark.[24] Despite this very limited early input, she developed high-level visual processing and three-dimensional binocular vision after surgery. The key here seems to be that since she wasn't completely blind, the neural pathways from the eyes to the vision centers in the brain were sufficiently developed to be further enhanced and refined when more robust visual input was available following the cataract surgery.

Dr. Sinha has been following up on this research, and it is clear that a critical period for vision means that the brain must have *some* visual stimulation from the eyes during the first years of life, but that this stimulation need not be high-quality visual input and, in fact, can be a relatively poor, degraded visual signal. In short, there is much more time for developing vision beyond the initial critical period. Applying the lesson of Dr. Sinha's studies more broadly, these findings fly in the face of the claims that parents need to provide specific brain stimulation at a particular moment during a critical period in infancy or early childhood. There is no need to panic or worry about trying to cram every conceivable form of "brain stimulation" into the first three years of life so that a so-called critical period will not be missed.

Studies on hearing using mice and rats have indicated that, as with vision, there are indeed critical periods for developing auditory pathways in the brain. One of the pioneers of this research, previously mentioned brain scientist Michael Merzenich, discovered that sensitivity to particular sounds could be enhanced if baby rats were exposed to particular sounds at the proper time in development. The rats that heard complex tones right after they were born were more sensitive to these kinds of tones and had more fully developed auditory circuitry in their brains as adults than did a group of adult comparison rats that had not heard these same kinds of tones early in life. He also reported that rats raised in soundproof cages whose brains received no input from the ears had very different auditory circuitry in the pathways and listening processing centers in the brain than rats that were not raised in soundproof conditions. These differences in circuitry remained even if the rats raised in the sound-isolation cages were later exposed to sound. As with visual development in animals and humans, there appears to be a critical period for auditory development as well. But studies have also shown that, as was the case for vision, neural wiring will occur in auditory pathways even if these critical periods are missed if the animal is exposed to at least some sound.

It is clear that for certain sense systems such as seeing and hearing, there is a specific, *optimal* time in early development for neural pathways to be established from the peripheral sense organs (such as the eyes and the ears) to the visual cortex and auditory cortex in the brain. This has been fairly well established through numerous studies and variations on those studies recorded in the scientific literature on brain development. However, these systems have to be only *minimally* stimulated during the critical period in order to be ready to receive more advanced input later in life. Brain development does *not* have to be *finished* during the critical period. Instead, there is considerable flexibility to receive more complex and sophisticated input long after the critical period has elapsed,[25] as long as a baby or young child has encountered learning opportunities such as those that intuitive parents naturally provide.

Lessons from Auditory Processing and Speech Discrimination

The process by which children develop auditory processing and speech discrimination skills provides an excellent example of the importance of critical periods in terms of both what is learned during a critical period and, more important, how missing that critical period does not necessarily end up having any negative long-term consequences.

The development of speech discrimination is fascinating. Professor Patricia Kuhl at the University of Washington completed some of the pioneering work on this topic and continues to make new discoveries.[26] She discovered that babies are born with the ability to discriminate sounds in any language. After all, there is no telling if a baby will be born into a family from Thailand, China, Spain, or the United States. Each of these countries has very different languages and very different sound systems. Individual speech sounds, called phonemes, can be radically different across languages. And in many countries, such as India, children are likely to learn more than one language, so the brain has to be prepared to process and interpret quite a variety of phonemes if, say, a baby in India is learning English and Hindi as well as a local language such as Malayalam or Gujarati. Some speech sounds are common across multiple languages, but others are quite rare and appear in only one or two languages.

Not only are there individual speech sound differences that must be distinguished in a particular language (such as "b" in "boy" and "t" in "toy" for English), but some languages, such as Chinese and Thai, also use different tones in the sound system. The syllable sound "ma" can have several different meanings in Chinese: If it is spoken in a high tone (high pitch) it means "mother";

but if "ma" is spoken with a rising tone it means "horse," and in a falling tone it means "scold." Babies learning Chinese must not only discriminate between phonemes and syllable sounds such as "pa" and "ma," but must also learn whether these syllables are pronounced with a steady high pitch or with a rising or falling tone. Because of this variation in the speech sound systems in human languages, babies must be prepared to learn whatever system they are born into, and their brains have to become wired to efficiently detect the speech sounds that are important in the language (or languages) they will ultimately learn.

Studies of infants' abilities to distinguish different speech sounds are intriguing. Because babies cannot tell us whether they are hearing an "m" or an "n" or some other speech sound, scientists have developed clever ways of mapping out what kinds of speech sound differences they actually can detect. One way of doing this is to record the baby's heart rate while playing repeated syllables through speakers in their crib. It turns out that if a repeated series of syllables such as "ba" "ba" "ba" "ba" is played, a baseline heart rate can be established. Then, if a different syllable is inserted in the string, for example, "ba" "ba" "pa" "ba," the heart rate will change if the baby detects the new syllable (in this case, the difference between "pa" and "ba"). Newborns and young babies up to about six months of age can detect a wide range of differences, even those that are not present in their parents' language. These babies can discriminate phonemes that are important for learning not only English but also Spanish and Hindi and even the tone differences in languages such as Chinese. But by the time a baby reaches her first birthday, the ability to detect phoneme differences that are not in the parents' language (or languages) has been substantially reduced.

These studies of phoneme discrimination in infants and toddlers are an excellent example of a critical period. When a baby is born, her brain is maximally sensitive to detecting differences in speech sounds from many different languages. Within approximately one year, this ability is dramatically reduced. One could say that there is a critical period in the first year of life for processing diverse phonemes, including those that are not in the language(s) her parents speak. Follow-up hearing perception studies with children and adults indicate that hearing a wider variety of speech sounds in infancy has an influence on the ability to discriminate phonemes later on in life.

If the speech sounds are present in their native language, listeners will be quite adept at detecting differences. However, if the sounds are not in their native language, listeners will have much more difficulty detecting differences. In the example of tone differences in Chinese, listeners who speak Chinese can readily identify the different tones that are meaningful in their native language. But English speakers who do not know Chinese and did not hear Chinese as babies will often report that syllables such as "ma" spoken in a high tone and "ma" spoken in a rising tone are the same, because saying "ma" with the high tone or with a rising tone still means "mother" in English. So, babies are better than their parents at detecting phonemic differences in syllables that are not present in their parents' native language(s), but become less able to detect these differences after passing through the critical period for phoneme discrimination.

Does this mean that someone who has "missed" the critical period for phoneme discrimination can never again learn to detect differences in speech sounds that are not in the language they learned growing up? Fortunately, the answer to this question is a definite *no*. Even though the critical period in infancy has passed, children and adults can readily be taught to discriminate phoneme differences that are not important in their native language. For example, as part of my work as a researcher on speech and language development, I've been trained in phonology, the study of speech sounds. I am a native speaker of English who also has some familiarity with Spanish, and I had no exposure to tone languages such as Chinese when I was a baby. When I first started listening to Chinese speech as an adult, I did not notice the tone differences in syllables such as "ma" (high tone = mother) and "ma" (rising tone = horse). But it took less than three months of intermittent practice for me to reliably discriminate these forms and phonetically transcribe the tone differences in Chinese and in many other languages I had never heard before.

The point here is that while there is indeed a critical period for sensitivity to speech sound differences in multiple languages, missing the critical period does not prevent the brain from being able to acquire this information long after the early-childhood critical period has passed.

As a professor, one of the courses I teach includes ways to transcribe speech sounds. Some of the students in this course have come to the United States from countries including China, India, South Korea, and Iran. Most are from the United States and have had limited experience with the speech sounds of languages other than English. In order to evaluate the effectiveness of my teaching, I keep close track of each student's ability to transcribe speech, including non-English phonology. The results of these efforts parallel my own experience: Students are relatively efficient at learning to transcribe the speech sounds in the languages that they have learned, but not very good at transcribing speech sounds in unfamiliar languages. But with practice they can readily learn to transcribe speech sounds from languages they have never heard before. Perhaps even more important, those students who had experience with multiple languages as babies don't necessarily do better than students who did not. That is, some students had "better" input during the critical period for speech discrimination when they were babies. But this input did not wire the brain for a lifelong advantage—at least in terms of transcribing speech sounds in my phonetics class!

What is required for a baby to acquire speech discrimination skills directly parallels the findings for vision. Parents simply need to talk to their baby in their native language(s) in order to prepare the auditory system and auditory cortex to process speech; a baby's brain will automatically tune in to the speech sounds in the language(s) he or she hears. No Baby Linguist DVDs needed! This speech input from his or her parents can subsequently be augmented and made more sophisticated later on in life. Special products are not required to wire a baby's brain for speech processing in his or her native language. Intuitive parents start talking to their baby quite naturally, usually from the moment he or she is born, and with increasing frequency as the baby responds. That means that, by and large, they have the critical period for speech discrimination covered.

After the initial critical period for processing rudimentary speech discrimination, the timing of the more sophisticated input is much more flexible than the early critical period. I have successfully taught adults in their twenties, thirties, forties, and fifties to reliably discriminate and transcribe speech sounds that are not present in their native language(s). After the stage has been set with naturally occurring auditory stimulation during the early critical period in infancy, the ears, auditory pathways, and auditory cortex are perfectly capable of more complex and efficient auditory processing that is *not* locked into a "critical period."

Another widely held, semimythic belief is that there is a critical period in the brain for language acquisition. This belief is based upon the observation that children can learn new languages and often speak them without an accent whereas adults generally have an accent when they learn a new language. Although there is much debate about the duration and age limit of this critical period for learning languages, many believe it to be approximately twelve years of age. A related notion is that if one acquires more than one language as a child, it is much easier to acquire new languages. Although it is true that children can more readily acquire a language without an accent, adults can actually be much more efficient at learning the words and grammar of a new language than most children.

The production of the speech sounds of a new language is often more difficult for an adult because the phonemes in their native language may conflict with the pronunciation of the speech sounds in the new language; therefore, adults will tend to have an accent in the new language. For example, a native speaker of Japanese may confuse "l" and "r" when learning English because these sounds are used differently in Japanese than in English. A Japanese speaker may say the word "rice" so that it sounds like "lice." Similarly, a native Spanish speaker will often say the English word "hit" so that it sounds like "heat" because while the long "e" occurs in Spanish, the short "i" does not. Pronunciation naturally tends toward the sounds that occur in the speaker's native language.

But these adult native speakers of Japanese and Spanish can readily learn the meaning of the English words "rice" and "hit." And they can learn to understand, speak, and read English, so the notion that there is an absolute "critical period" for learning a new language is false. Further, these adult English learners can be taught to substantially reduce the accent conveyed by their native language by practicing the pronunciation of English speech sounds that are absent in their native language.

This is also true for accents or dialects within a language: actors and actresses can learn new accents for use in their dramatic roles; and some of them, along with newscasters, politicians, and others seeking to advance their careers, try to reduce or eliminate their original regional accents, whether Southern, Boston, or Brooklyn born. This most certainly can be done many years after the critical period for language has passed.

In Defense of Patience: Lessons from Critical Period Research

The discovery of critical periods for brain development in the latter half of the twentieth century has yielded important insights into how neurological systems develop. But it is all too easy to overinterpret—and overhype—these discoveries in the mistaken belief that child development is a well-ordered, time-sensitive process and that parents who want the best for their children *must* systematically hit each critical period at exactly the right moment to maximize their child's intellectual potential. As we saw earlier, the research shows that this view is simply not true. Sense organs such as the eyes and ears do need to receive stimulation from the outside world in order to develop proper neural pathways and processing centers in the brain. But brain development is not a linear, time-ordered process, and raising a child to learn and succeed is not a matter of following a precise, minute-by-minute schedule or a precise wiring diagram. Brain development is triggered by naturally occurring input within an amazingly broad and plastic developmental window. Intuitive parents provide a good deal of that necessary input quite naturally, simply by caring for and interacting with their baby from day to day. After this basic wiring has been laid down, more complex development does not have a narrow critical period at all. Rather, the initial critical period apparently prepares the brain to process information at some point in the future, rather than only within a specific, limited time frame.

So, parents can take a deep breath, relax, and enjoy their baby while playing and interacting with them in naturally occurring ways. They are building an adult brain and will have nearly two decades of caring for their child in which to nurture her development. Savoring the day-to-day joys—and fun—of being a parent and spending time with their baby are precisely what is needed to properly wire an infant's brain. Hold your child in your arms, look into his or her face, and sing a lullaby! Not only will this be a

precious moment in itself, but you'll be providing all the visual
and auditory input your baby needs during this critical period in
his or her life.

- Intuitive parents are prepared to resist clever marketing, educational fads, and peer pressures that are based on the misguided notion that there is a so-called critical period during
  which they must pack everything into their child's brain.
- The scientific evidence is overwhelming—and convincing—
  that the brain is capable of learning throughout childhood and
  that some skills, such as executive function, continue to develop into the teen years. So there is no need to feel stress or
  to panic because you feel you are somehow shortchanging
  your child or dooming them to less than optimal achievement
  if your intuition tells you to be patient rather than trying to
  artificially accelerate learning in the name of hitting a mythical critical period.
- Hard-and-fast critical periods are rare. Most brain development periods are flexible, and there are ample opportunities
  for learning throughout childhood.
- Be skeptical of educational programs—and products—that tout
  the latest neuroscience on "brain plasticity" and "critical periods"
  as a means of pressuring you to enroll in a program or buy a
  product.
- Take the long view. You have plenty of time to foster learning
  in your child. Indeed, pushing things too far and too fast may
  actually undermine your child's development.

chapter 4

Enhancing Intelligence Using Intuitive Parenting

What makes a person "intelligent"? We can all agree that Albert Einstein was highly intelligent; the very name "Einstein" has become synonymous with "genius" in modern society. But what was it about Albert Einstein that is so recognizable as intelligence, and from the viewpoint of raising an intelligent child, is there something we can do, as parents, to help our children become "little Einsteins?"

We have a number of different images of intelligent people. There are those who readily recall a plethora of facts and obscure knowledge on demand—the kind who win lots of money on game shows like *Jeopardy* and who are in high demand for places on teams in trivia contests. Or we may conjure up an image of a scientist, such as Marie Curie, tinkering in her lab, making a brilliant discovery and winning not one but two Nobel prizes. Yet another image of intelligence is a chess master, poring over the chessboard before making the unexpected move that wins the match. This chess master may play several games at the same time against multiple challengers and make moves rapidly and decisively. Then there are the artists, writers, and philosophers who seem inconceivably intelligent in the way they express truths about the human condition through their powers of reasoning, imagination, creativity, and dexterity with language or artistic media—people like Plato and Leonardo da Vinci, Shakespeare and Jane Austen, Mozart and John Coltrane.

All these images represent one or more aspects of what we call intelligence. In layman's terms, intelligence includes knowledge and long-term memory (Plato and the *Jeopardy* champion), the ability to apply this knowledge to unique situations and solve problems (Curie and da Vinci), and to do these things rapidly and accurately (Mozart composing a new piece of music in his mind while transcribing a different piece; the chess master playing multiple games), and to be a creative artist (Shakespeare and Coltrane). But how does a baby become a world-class scientist, a walking encyclopedia, a philosopher, or a chess master? To answer this question, it is useful to understand something about the nature of intelligence, how it is measured, and how these skills can be learned.

Scientists have long been interested in the nature of human intelligence, how to measure it, and how to foster increased intelligence in children. The term "intelligence quotient" (IQ) was coined by the German psychologist William Stern at the end of the nineteenth century. Basically, Stern argued that intelligence could be quantified by calculating the ratio of a person's "mental" age and their actual or chronological age. This measure of intelligence is simply the ratio of the child's mental age divided by his or her chronological age and multiplied by 100. Thus, a six-year-old who knows pretty much the same things as other six-year-olds would have a normal IQ of 100. A six-year-old who knows as much as most eight-year-olds would be advanced and have a high IQ ($8/6 \times 100 = 133$), but a six-year-old who knows about as much as a four-year-old would have a low IQ ($4/6 \times 100 = 67$) using this scheme.

With advances in statistics and intelligence test development, IQ has been scaled so that a so-called average IQ is *always* 100 and meaningful variants occur at 15-point intervals. An IQ of 85 is thought to be slightly less than average, and an IQ of 115 is thought to be slightly higher than average. An IQ of 145 is considered highly intelligent, and an IQ of less than 55 often indicates that the person will, on average, learn more slowly than other children. Differences of only a few points are not meaningful; there is no real difference between an IQ of 101 and 106.

Stern and many of his successors in the intelligence testing community believed that IQ was an individual trait that remained static throughout life. Someone with an IQ of 100 at age eight was believed to maintain that IQ no matter how much older he or she became. In 2012, Professor Ian Deary at the University of Edinburgh in Scotland, writing in the scientific journal *Nature*, asserted: "So far, we know that intelligence differences show high stability from childhood to old age."[1] But Professor Deary also noted that what he meant by "childhood" began at the age of *eleven*.[2] The situation for babies, toddlers, and preschoolers is far different.[3]

The "destiny model" of IQ, wherein intelligence quotients are conceptualized as being pretty much set at birth and fixed for one's entire life, is problematic when applied to preschoolers—and an even worse problem when applied to babies. In practice, measuring IQ in a baby and then testing that same child at ages eight and twelve and again as an adult revealed that intelligence is not a stable trait in young children. Indeed, although there is a relative stability after a person becomes an adult, there is large variation in the scores of babies, toddlers, preschoolers, and even in early-school-age children.

As an example, consider how a verbal IQ, reasonably based on vocabulary levels in adults, can be wildly misleading and unstable when applied to babies. As we saw in an earlier chapter, the average age of onset of first words is approximately twelve months. However, it is not unusual for first words to appear at eighteen months or even later; nor is it unusual for some babies to begin talking at the age of nine months or so. Waiting until eighteen months old does not necessarily mean a child is unintelligent. Using the "quotient" method of measuring verbal IQ, a child who begins talking at nine months of age would be identified as having a "mental" age of twelve months because that is the average age when most children begin talking. (The child's chronological age would be nine months in the calculation.) To determine the quotient, then, you'd divide 12 months by 9 months and multiply by 100 for a quotient score—and this precocious nine-month-old would have a "verbal IQ" of 133, which is in the gifted range. Better start that college fund for an Ivy League tuition!

However, the luckless child who has the temerity to begin talking at sixteen months is in an altogether different verbal IQ category. His quotient would be 12 months (mental age) divided by 16 months (chronological age) times 100, which would result in a verbal IQ of only 75. Of course, it is absolutely absurd to believe that a verbal IQ score based on when a child begins speaking will dictate his intelligence in this domain as adults. There are a number of examples of real geniuses who did not begin speaking until age two or even older,[4] the most famous being none other than Albert Einstein,[5] who reportedly did not start speaking until at least the age of three. Other highly intelligent and otherwise gifted individuals who also began speaking late include Nobel Prize–winning economist Gary Beckman, renowned mathematician Julia Robinson, and physicist Edward Teller, who, among his other accomplishments, was on the scientific team that developed the atomic bomb and led the effort to subsequently develop a hydrogen bomb. According to a biography of Dr. Teller, published in the July/August 1998 *Science and Technology Review*, "little Ede Teller did not utter a word until he was three years old. His grandfather was afraid he might be retarded."[6] If Dr. Teller did not speak at all until he was more than three years old, his verbal IQ as a toddler would have been no better than 33, which is a very low IQ! Obviously, this was not an indication of his overall intelligence and future success.

These examples should make it abundantly obvious that IQ in a baby or toddler or even a preschooler is not a determinant of subsequent intellectual ability and is definitely not a stable measure of intelligence. Unfortunately, all too many modern parents and teachers continue to persist in believing in the myth that early intelligence levels dictate intellectual ability for life. Perhaps this is why there is such a misguided push in modern society to try to boost babies' and young children's IQ.

There is no need to feel stress or pressure to somehow set your baby or preschool child's IQ "switch" at *high* by their third or fourth birthday. Dr. John Bruer, head of the James S. McDonnell Foundation, an organization that supports research in cognitive neuroscience, describes this fallacy in his excellent book *The Myth of the First Three Years: A New Understanding of Early Brain Development and Lifelong Learning.* He argues persuasively that although a love of learning—and intellectual curiosity—should be nurtured in the first years of life, the next decade is at least as important for refining these aptitudes.[7]

The striking lack of stability in measures of intellectual ability in the first decade of life is likely to reflect individual variation in development from the time a child is a baby through adolescence, when overall brain architecture finally becomes relatively complete. This lack of stability may also arise from variations in the nature of the test items used to assess intelligence at different age levels. Intelligence testing originally was designed to be conducted with school-age children, adolescents, and adults, and the techniques used to test these groups may not be valid—or stable—in

preschoolers, toddlers, and infants. While specialists have continued refining the tests and the testing process in the century since
intelligence testing was first introduced, they have not yet succeeded in developing an instrument that can reliably measure intellectual ability in early childhood and then accurately predict
adult intelligence levels.

Nevertheless, intelligence testing continues, at ever earlier
ages and with profound implications. Parents who want to enhance their child's intellectual development end up focusing their
energies on helping their child artificially achieve high scores on
unreliable tests or entrance exams instead of nurturing real-world
reasoning ability. Educational programs and materials are marketed to teach young children to memorize and regurgitate test
answers, and education policies may inadvertently increase the
pressure on children and parents. Some states, such as New York,[8]
permit eligibility testing for gifted programs in kindergarten. It is
understandable that parents are anxious to prepare their preschoolers for these kinds of tests. But in doing so, they are buying
into fundamental misunderstandings about the nature of intelligence and its measurability. By spending more and more of their
baby's precious learning time on these "test prep" efforts, they
may actually be undermining the ultimate goal of increasing the
baby's real knowledge, reasoning ability, and overall intelligence.
A look at the development of intelligence testing will shed light
on this paradox, and illuminate why products and educational
programs designed to help parents "teach to the test" constitute
misguided attempts to artificially boost a baby's "mental" age.

One of the pioneers in the science of intelligence and test development, French psychologist Alfred Binet, began developing
what became one of the first widely used intelligence tests in the
nineteenth century after France adopted a law requiring all children ages six to fourteen to attend school. (School attendance had
not previously been compulsory.) His primary interest was in

developing a screening tool to identify students who would not be able to learn in the regular classroom without additional help.[9] By 1903, he and his colleague Theodore Simon had developed a series of test items designed to measure the intelligence of these school-children for that purpose. The test items included having a child repeat number sequences, demonstrate an understanding of vocabulary words (by, for example, pointing to body parts the examiner named), construct sentences from a series of words, and draw pictures from memory.

Looking back at the original Binet-Simon test through the lens of modern concepts of intelligence makes the test seem a bit primitive in some ways. For example, the intelligence score on the original test was highly dependent on a student's ability in French, so someone who didn't speak French would be scored as very unintelligent, even if they could score as highly intelligent when tested in their native language.[10] Although this would seem to be obvious, to this day intelligence testing still weights verbal skills very highly. That means that in North America the tests that include the kinds of items developed by Binet, wherein language proficiency is an inherent part of administrating and scoring, can be biased in favor of native speakers of English. Tests that weigh language abilities too heavily could misclassify children who are highly intelligent in math and other kinds of reasoning but not facile in English even if it is their native language.[11]

Also, drawing pictures from memory is not a good predictor of intelligence. There are many highly intelligent people who are not talented artists. Anyone with a progressive neurological condition, such as renowned physicist Stephen Hawking, would score very low on a test that required him to draw pictures from memory. And there are individuals who are quite proficient at drawing pictures from memory but who otherwise may have average or even below average intelligence. For example, the well-known neurologist Oliver Sacks described a young man with autism who was an amazing artist and could draw realistic pictures but also had significant gaps in his knowledge of the world.[12]

In the more than one hundred years since Binet's original intelligence test, there has been considerable refinement of theories of intelligence and how intelligence should be measured, and considerable evolution in measurement techniques. A more modern version of Binet's test—the Stanford-Binet Intelligence Scales, now in its fifth edition—was published in 2003. But while intelligence tests have evolved substantially to reflect developments in our understanding, and are useful tools when used properly, they still reflect certain assumptions about what intelligence means. It is instructive to examine those assumptions and the message they send to parents, whose access to educational opportunities and gifted programs for their child often directly depends on how well the child performs on such tests.

In the mid-twentieth century, American psychologist David Wechsler challenged the notion that intelligence was a single factor and revolutionized intelligence testing accordingly. Partially in response to the language bias in the original Binet-Simon intelligence test, Wechsler proposed that intelligence included not only verbal abilities but also nonverbal, "performance" abilities such as solving puzzles.[13] Another psychologist, Russell Leiter, constructed a completely nonverbal intelligence test in the 1930s for use with children who did not speak English.[14] This was an important breakthrough in the conceptualization of intelligence because it rectified the mistaken idea that people who could not speak and people who could not understand spoken language were automatically unintelligent. For example, deaf people were all too often thought to be intellectually disabled or otherwise unintelligent as young children, when in fact, aside from not being able to hear, nothing was wrong with their thinking ability.[15]

After Wechsler, Leiter, and others developed methods for assessing low verbal or nonverbal aspects of intelligence, theories of intelligence were expanded to include even more factors.[16] Today the definition of intelligence broadly includes "crystallized knowledge," which is the ability to retrieve facts (again, rather like a *Jeopardy* champion), and "fluid reasoning," the ability to apply these facts and one's experiences to new situations where problem solving is a factor of intelligence too.[17] Intelligence is thought to depend not only on "stores" of acquired knowledge—the facts that have been learned and stored in long-term memory—but on problem solving, which is the ability to use these stores of acquired knowledge flexibly and innovatively to reason and to solve novel problems.

The discovery that intelligence comprises multiple abilities rather than being a single uniform skill led to the further development of cognitive models and tests to assess these diverse abilities. One goal was to find a way to minimize the impact on scores of subjective judgments and interpretations made by the individuals administering the tests—biases that had already been found to diminish scores' reliability. In his now-classic 1904 paper entitled "General Intelligence, Objectively Determined and Measured," British psychologist Charles Spearman argued that newly developed statistical and mathematical analysis could be applied to the problem of measuring human intelligence; and in 1949, another British psychologist, Raymond Cattell, who, along with his wife, Karen, founded the Institute for Personality and Ability Testing at the University of Illinois, began to expand upon Spearman's approach, applying mathematical analysis to the multiple factors, or "domains," of intelligence Spearman had identified. Cattell used mathematical factor analysis to identify and measure the abilities that actually reflected intelligence, while also weeding out those that did not, such as drawing ability.

Despite Cattell's work, however, drawing tasks remained a part of intelligence testing for decades. I was trained to administer and score a test that included a drawing task in the late 1970s, when I was a college student working at the United Cerebral Palsy

Center in San Diego, and was skeptical about its accuracy even then. The drawing task asked a child to draw a person; the drawing was then scored on criteria such as whether it included fingers, facial features, and other details. The more details, the higher the IQ score.[18] My skepticism deepened (along with my awareness of how a test administrator's subjective judgments could impact a child's score) when I was assigned to work with a particular patient to teach him how to communicate.

The official reports on this patient described him as profoundly intellectually disabled, meaning he was a very slow learner with limited mental ability. But while I was teaching him to use a picture board to communicate—his cerebral palsy rendered him barely able to speak—I learned that he could read! I modified a typewriter so that he could operate the keys, and it turned out he could type out short sentences accurately describing what he had done earlier in the day, what he had eaten, and so on. Because he could do so much more than other patients also labeled profoundly intellectually disabled, I wondered how his intelligence had originally been tested. It turned out that he had been given a test called "Goodenough Draw a Man"[19] and was only able to draw stick figures.

I would hope anyone reading this would realize that assessing the intelligence of a person with cerebral palsy using a drawing test is downright foolish. I have always wondered whether this young man would have learned so much more if the people teaching him had realized how much more intelligent he was than this test purported to show. And while this is an extreme case of misinformation embodied in a test result, it was also the case for children generally: Subjective judgments about the quality of their drawings were taken as estimates of intelligence that could have broad impact on how others, such as teachers, viewed a child's potential, even though the estimates were generated using questionable items. A more scientific method of defining intelligence was needed because despite Cattell's excellent work, there were glaring—and persistent—errors in how IQ tests were being administered and interpreted.

John Horn and John Carroll later expanded upon Cattell's work. They conducted a comprehensive review of all the research on intelligence and intelligence testing and developed a new model asserting that nine "broad abilities" capture the breadth and depth of intellectual ability. This model, which has been substantially validated, is called the CHC theory of intelligence after its authors: Cattell, Horn, and Carroll. Today many psychologists, educators, and child development experts base their views on this theory, and consider intelligence to consist of multiple broad factors rather than a single monolithic "intelligence quotient." These multiple broad factors, in turn, are made up of a number of "narrow abilities," all of which contribute to overall intelligence.[20]

In order to facilitate intellectual development in babies, preschoolers, and older children, parents should understand which skills and abilities are included in each of these broad categories and understand how to ensure that their child receives opportunities to learn in *all* these areas. It is even more important for parents to ensure that a baby doesn't just master rote learning but develops problem-solving abilities in each of these domains. Intuitive parenting is the key to doing so.

Let's look at a description of each domain, explore examples of "narrow abilities" that contribute to mastering each of these domains, and examine what intuitive parents can do to help their children achieve mastery.

The Nine Essential Broad Intellectual Abilities

At the beginning of this chapter, we looked at some of the markers of highly intelligent people, including brilliant scientist Marie Curie, a walking encyclopedia with a large store of knowledge, and a chess master who could play several matches at once against multiple opponents and make brilliant moves rapidly. Each of these examples represents an important aspect of what scientists conceptualize as comprising intelligence: a) **problem-solving ability**, b) **stores of acquired knowledge**, and c) **cognitive efficiency**. Problem solving is defined as the ability to conceptualize—and think through—novel questions and situations. Stores of acquired knowledge are the library of memorized information that is readily accessible in long-term memory—the "facts" a person knows. Cognitive efficiency is how quickly the brain operates.

The nine broad intellectual abilities can be subclassified within these three fundamental aspects of intelligence.

- *Problem solving* requires 1) fluid reasoning, 2) visual spatial thinking, and 3) auditory processing.
- *Stores of acquired knowledge* include the general ability to reliably access information stored in memory, which requires 4) long-term retrieval and the actual memory content domains, which consist of 5) comprehension knowledge (language recognition, including vocabulary), 6) reading and writing, and 7) mathematics.
- *Cognitive efficiency* includes 8) short-term memory and 9) processing speed.

There is overlap among the domains—after all, intelligence includes an ability to integrate these discrete skills. For example, skill in mathematics relies not only on the store of acquired knowledge (long-term memory) an individual has developed but also on an ability to use this knowledge to solve problems (fluid reasoning). Indeed, intelligence requires these broad abilities to be integrated efficiently. For parents who want to facilitate mental development in their baby and young child, it is most useful to consider intelligence as the confluence of problem solving, accessing an ample store of acquired knowledge, and doing so rapidly and efficiently.

Parents who understand these domains and skills will be able to assess whether their baby is laying the groundwork for developing each ability, and they'll be able to review educational materials and enrichment toys to determine what aspects of intelligence the materials target. To that end, parents first need to add to their own "store of acquired knowledge" an understanding of each ability and of the ways in which psychologists assess it in children (and adults). The following descriptions are intended to provide parents with a practical working knowledge of those abilities so that you can help your baby and child develop them during daily caregiving routines. By considering each skill in the light of how babies learn, you can successfully provide your child enrichment opportunities for *all* aspects of intelligence.

Again, I don't mean for you to view these descriptions of individual abilities as an invitation to drill your baby on isolated skills. Rest assured, I am *not* recommending that parents run out and purchase "baby learns calculus" CDs to accelerate development of mathematical abilities. Rather, I want to encourage parents to ensure that *integrated* learning opportunities are available within the baby's normal, everyday environment and through intuitive interactions with you that naturally enhance all these intellectual abilities. More important, parents should not focus exclusively on one aspect of intelligence, such as long-term memory (rote learning) to the detriment of other skills, such as fluid reasoning. I also hope that intuitive parents will recognize the terrific job they are doing when they build their child's intelligence.

Problem Solving (Thinking Abilities)

These broad abilities include fluid reasoning, visual spatial reasoning, and auditory processing. Although other abilities, such as mathematics, are actually a combination of stored knowledge and problem-solving (reasoning) abilities, these three are clearly primarily concerned with the ability to reason and think through novel problems. Because so much of human information processing is done through visual and auditory channels, each of these senses has its own problem-solving domain.

FLUID REASONING

Stated simply, fluid reasoning *is* the ability to solve problems. Thinking through number series, making predictions, playing chess, and designing experiments are all examples of fluid reasoning. Solving the Sudoku puzzle in the daily newspaper is an application of fluid reasoning. When Einstein developed the theory of relativity, he was using fluid reasoning to understand and model the relationship between matter and energy, and to explain that relationship in the succinct equation $E = mc^2$.

Can fluid reasoning be measured? Psychologists have employed many different strategies and types of problems in their efforts to do so. Some tests measure fluid reasoning using pattern recognition. At the simplest level, used with young children, this includes demonstrating a series using geometric shapes such as circles, squares, and triangles. The examiner shows the child a pattern such as circle-triangle-circle-triangle and gives the child an opportunity to demonstrate what shape should come next (in this case, circle). In order to complete this item successfully, the child must mentally recognize the pattern and provide the next item in the series based on the established pattern. Increasingly complex series are utilized to assess older children and adults on this task.

On other measures of fluid reasoning, the test taker must mentally recognize the rules or logic of an unfamiliar pattern in order to provide a correct answer. For example, a child could be shown three large squares and then be presented with a small square and asked how the small square is different from the others. The required response here would be "It's smaller." Other measures of fluid reasoning include predicting the next items in a mathematical series, such as "Provide the next two numbers in the following sequence: 2-4-6-8." (The answer would be 10-12.) A more complex testing of fluid reasoning would be to provide the next numbers in the famous Fibonacci series: 1, 1, 2, 3, 5, 8, 13, 21, 34, 55, and 89. To solve this puzzle, one must recognize that the next number in the series is the sum of the two preceding numbers. So the next number in the sequence would be 55 + 89 = 144. The common theme in all these activities is the ability to generate solutions to puzzles and series when only part of the information is available.

It is important to bear in mind that innovative thinking requires on-line fluid reasoning. That is, an unknown solution must be generated quickly and without previous practice on that item. Drilling babies on vocabulary items, flash cards, and such could teach by rote memorization but would not actually induce the problem-solving abilities needed for fluid reasoning. Problem solving is an *active* mental process that cannot be learned in a passive way. The baby must learn to think and generate solutions, even if they are initially incorrect. In essence, simply telling a child the answers to a number series such as "2-4-6-8" or showing a child the answer to a particular problem on a flash card or a computer program will not provide experience in problem solving. Children should be encouraged to think and solve problems rather than memorizing answers.

Children must learn by trial and error and be given proper feedback and multiple flexible examples. Also, it is vitally important that parents encourage innovation in problem solving. Your child should frequently be hearing phrases like "Try another way," "Why do you think that happened?" and "What comes next?" Play games that explicitly require a child to think and anticipate the next step. With toddlers, this can be as simple as alternating big blocks and small blocks, or alternating red blocks and yellow blocks and giving them the opportunity to add the next one in the pattern. After they become adept at two items, add three (big, medium, little) and different features (red, yellow, blue) and so on. In older children, this can be done with numbers (even/odd, multiples, etc.) and by asking them what they think will happen next in a story before you read the next passage or page to them. If an answer is not plausible, do not immediately tell the child the correct answer; instead, be sure to ask, "Can you think of something else that might happen?" Be sure to nurture the ability to reason and to guess as a part of your intuitive parenting.

VISUAL SPATIAL THINKING

Fluid reasoning and problem solving in the visual domain is called visual spatial thinking. The ability to hold a geometric shape in mind and rotate it mentally is a form of visual spatial reasoning. So is being able to figure out the identity of an object when shown an incomplete drawing of that object, and so is being able to look at a drawing of a maze and mentally deduce the path out of the maze. Everyday examples of this include using a map and compass to plan a hike or trip, looking at an abstract painting or drawing and deducing meaning from the image, and even using a car GPS system to navigate through an unfamiliar city. Artists, architects, and engineers all use visual spatial thinking constantly. Artists must conceptualize images and visualize what they hope to communicate in the finished product. Architects must visualize the buildings they are creating, and engineers of all sorts visually imagine the bridge, mechanical device, electrical system, or even the software they are writing.

Because a baby's visual system comes on line relatively early in its development, there are ample opportunities to facilitate visual spatial thinking in infants and toddlers. In its simplest form, intuitive parenting for visual special development could include moving an object multiple times across the baby's visual field and stopping and shaking the object at the same point before continuing the movement. This will teach the baby to anticipate when the object will stop and shake. This can be enhanced by using a brightly colored rattle so that in addition to the visual cue, an auditory event is paired with the novel visual event (stopping and shaking).

Practically speaking, puzzles, Legos, train sets, mazes, connect-the-dots games, *Where's Waldo?* books and other types of "hidden picture" games, and "creative" materials such as clay, Play-Doh, and plaster of Paris are all materials that can facilitate development of visual spatial reasoning. In the computer realm, role-playing games wherein the characters must navigate mazes and mental rotation games such as Tetris require visual spatial reasoning. Note here that intuitive parents facilitate this aspect of intelligence by interacting with their child while playing and inquiring about their thinking. It is fine if the child follows a pattern to build something with Legos, for example, so long as the parent does not lead them through all the steps. The goal should be to allow the child to discover the solutions by thinking them through on her own. If the Lego structure collapses, that is an excellent bit of data for her developing brain! Do not start using video or computer games until a child is three or four years old, and ask her to explain her thinking to you as she solves the maze. A good question to ask while a child is playing is, "What will happen if you go this way?"

AUDITORY PROCESSING

Thinking through number series, identifying sequences, and using visual mental imagery to solve problems are relatively straightforward examples of problem solving. But how would one use the auditory sense to solve problems? And why would psychologists classify auditory processing as a thinking ability rather than an automatic, passive process?

The ability to utilize and organize auditory information is indeed a thinking ability. The auditory system, like the visual system, is complex and organized to give humans a competitive advantage in the environment. A visual spatial thinking task could involve identifying an animal when shown a drawing or photograph of the animal cut into puzzle pieces. An analogous auditory processing task would be identifying a word when only the individual parts of the word are spoken. For example, if the following phonemes are presented—"P" "I" "K" "L"—auditory processing can be utilized to deduce that the word made when the sounds are assembled is "pickle."

In languages with phonetic alphabets, where letters represent the spoken sounds of the language (including Spanish, Italian, Arabic, and English, with a partially phonetic alphabet), reading aloud requires visual identification of the letters, but actually pronouncing what is written requires auditory processing to translate letters into verbalized words. People who are trained in phonetics can read aloud texts from languages they do not understand as long as the phonetic alphabet fairly represents the way that the words are spoken in that language. For example, as a trained phonetician, I can read the Italian sentence "Come ti senti oggi?" (How do you feel today?) with proper Italian pronunciation even though I do not speak or comprehend Italian. Auditory processing can be employed to identify and assemble the phonetic sounds on the printed page into verbalized words, so that one can deduce that "ti" in Italian is pronounced the same way as the English word "tea."

Measures of auditory processing include identifying words when only a few of the letter sounds have been provided, identifying tone sequences, assembling speech sound sequences (phonemes) into whole words, and discriminating the differences between speech sounds such as "b" and "g." As with visual thinking, rudimentary auditory processing ability begins to develop very early in infancy.[21] There is even some indirect evidence that some aspects of it begin to develop even before a baby is born. Because of this, parents should provide a variety of auditory stimuli to their baby and toddler, including different environmental noises such as animal sounds, rattling, ringing, clicking, rain pattering, gravel crunching, thunder rumbling, the sound of bath water running or popcorn popping. Of course your baby's most important source of auditory information is your voice. Hold your baby within one foot of your face (facing you) and speak (and sing!) using a variety of pitches and intonation patterns. Although the baby will not necessarily comprehend the words, the speech input is vitally important for developing auditory processing.

For older children, music, singing, and repeating nursery rhymes; imitation games such as clapping patterns and "mockingbird" games wherein a parent and child take turns repeating longer and longer sentences (such as with "This is the house that Jack built"); and playing word-rhyming games are all excellent activities that develop auditory processing. Listening and repeating, as well as retelling stories, is also excellent. And as your child develops, so can the sophistication of the auditory input. Your child may enjoy listening to ball games on the radio with you, or music of various styles from various eras and cultures.

These three abilities—fluid reasoning, visual spatial thinking, and auditory processing—are foundational elements of problem solving. Problem-solving ability also requires the ability to remember and recall to mind as needed basic information that is stored in long-term memory. Problem solving can only be effective when there is a sufficient knowledge base or store of information to apply to the conundrum at hand. For example, solving a Sudoku puzzle requires automatic knowledge of the numbers and number symbols 1 through 9. Solving crossword puzzles requires a fairly extensive vocabulary—and often some knowledge of history, literature, and popular culture—in addition to the reasoning ability necessary to solve clues. These stores of acquired knowledge include not only long-term storage ability (rather like the hard drive of a computer), but also the information content contained in the memory. The next section will describe the various knowledge "pools" that scientists such as Cattell, Horn, and Carroll believe contribute to overall intellectual ability.

Stores of Acquired Knowledge

How the brain makes memory traces and stores information has been the topic of considerable scientific study and experimentation over the past twenty years. Important discoveries have been made about how the brain stores knowledge and retrieves this knowledge for real-world applications.

Memory itself is partially a problem-solving activity. That is, the brain is not like a recording device in which everything is stored verbatim. Rather, pieces of information are stored, then reassembled to recall events. As with the visual spatial thinking task wherein a child can identify an animal from only parts of a photograph of the whole, people "fill in the gaps" using logic and reason when accessing long-term memory. However, "crystallized" knowledge must be available for analysis in order to remember people, places, and things as well as facts. Some of the people we think of as smart often have prodigious memories and can rapidly and accurately recall information. This aspect of intelligence—stores of acquired knowledge—involves long-term retrieval skills, comprehension knowledge, and those aspects of reading and writing and mathematical knowledge that have been learned and stored in people's minds so that they can be readily retrieved when needed.

LONG-TERM RETRIEVAL

Long-term retrieval refers to the ability to memorize and then recall information on demand. On intelligence tests, long-term retrieval is often measured by having the examiner read an unfamiliar story and then come back after several hours to test how much of the story, and the facts in the story, the subject can remember. Another variation on this is to introduce abstract symbols and then, after completing other kinds of tests for three or more hours, to return and retest the child's memory of the symbols. In practical terms, long-term retrieval is used every day and consists of being able to remember information that was learned previously, and to use it in a new context or endeavor. Preparing a complicated recipe from memory, retelling a favorite story, remembering client details in a sales meeting, recalling times tables from memory, and successfully remembering the directions to a restaurant in an unfamiliar city that was last visited several years ago all involve long-term retrieval.

The actual extent to which babies can store information in long-term memory is currently an interesting area of study. Because babies are incapable of saying "Oh yes, I remember seeing that same stuffed animal last week," researchers have to make inferences about what babies remember by studying their facial expressions, monitoring their autonomic functions such as heart rate, and using noninvasive brain imaging techniques. It is fair to say that there is plenty left to learn regarding just how much babies remember day to day, week to week, and month to month. But until a child reaches an age when she can talk about her previous experiences, it can be difficult to know just how much she remembers.

However, it is clear that even babies can remember events and objects. If you continuously record a baby's heart rate, you'll see that it increases when she sees something new (in essence, she is registering surprise). The rate will not increase if she has seen the object before. From that, scientists can infer that babies do have some form of long-term memory.

Many parents also report that their older children can recall events that happened when they were toddlers. I know this first-hand. One of my sons injured himself when he was almost two years old. I was the only one who saw what happened, and I took care of his injury. But I never talked to him or anyone else about it, and no one else could have told him what happened because there were no other witnesses. Yet when he was eight years old, he gave me many details of his injury and talked about how I had cared for him—information that *must* have been recalled from his long-term memory.

On the other hand, memory is an active process that includes assembling cognitive narratives from stored information. It is *not* simply like playing back a video or audio recording or streaming a video. Jean Piaget talked about his childhood memories of nearly being kidnapped while being cared for by his nanny. This was an important event in young Piaget's life: He vividly recalled sitting in his carriage, watching his nanny tussle with a stranger attempting the kidnap, and recalled seeing a policeman chase the kidnapper away while waving his police baton. He even recalled seeing the scratches his nanny received on her face when she fought off the kidnapper. But when he was fifteen years old, more than thirteen years after the alleged kidnapping episode, the nanny wrote a letter to Piaget's parents admitting that the whole episode was a hoax—she had made it up. Because the memories were real to him and seemed to come from his own long-term memory, Piaget hypothesized that these realistic mental images of the incident were created, stored, and retrieved based on hearing stories about the attempted kid-napping. Nonetheless, these memories were just as "real" to him (before he learned the truth) as events that actually happened. Piaget argued that imagination can impact memory and that recall-ing events is not necessarily a photographic (or phonographic) pro-cess. More recent studies have supported Piaget's views on memory development: It is not photographic, and memories are influenced by a number of factors, including thinking ability, maturity, and previous experience with the information being recalled.[22]

Parents who understand that development of long-term memory includes more than remembering dry details and uninteresting facts can facilitate their child's long-term memory development by tying information to interesting stories and engaging learning opportunities. One of the reasons that Piaget's memory of the attempted kidnapping episode was so salient in his memory was that he himself was the central character in the story. This is an important lesson for parents: Storing information in long-term memory should not be a passive experience, which is what happens when the baby or toddler sits quietly viewing DVDs or educational software. Memory can be much more efficiently facilitated if the baby, toddler, or young child is directly involved in the learning process as an active participant—an actor in the story and not just a member of the audience. Establishing routines, such as taking walks, telling stories, and having a child recall their experiences, will also help to build memory.

COMPREHENSION KNOWLEDGE

Since the earliest days of intelligence testing, language ability—and specifically vocabulary knowledge—has been recognized as important aspects of intelligence. We tend to think that someone with an enormous vocabulary who can use language to communicate precisely is very clearly intelligent. Conversely, individuals with smaller vocabularies who communicate awkwardly at best may be (sometimes mistakenly) thought of as being less intelligent. Naturally, the situation is a bit more complicated than just measuring who has the largest vocabulary. However, nearly every intelligence test includes numerous vocabulary items, and in widely used intelligence tests for children and toddlers, more than half the test items involve vocabulary. But it is noteworthy that scientists identify the intellectual ability the tests are assessing as "comprehension" knowledge rather than "vocabulary." This means that this aspect of intelligence involves in-depth knowledge of the words and their meanings, not just rote word memorization skill.

Scientists test comprehension knowledge using antonyms (opposites) and synonyms (words with a similar meaning) in addition to word definitions. Intelligence tests will often include questions such as "What is the opposite of ____?" Easy items include things such as the opposite of "in" (out) and the opposite of "up" (down). More complicated items in tests for middle- and high-school-age children could include asking for the opposite of "demure" (brazen) or the opposite of "ubiquitous" (rare, or uncommon). Similarly, tests of comprehension knowledge could include synonyms such as "What means the same as ___?" Easy items could include "big" (large) and "car" (auto), whereas more difficult items could include "ridiculous" (absurd) or "Machiavellian" (scheming). The point here is that simply identifying or naming pictures does not demonstrate comprehension knowledge. Rather, the relationships among words, including superordinate classes ("animal" is a superordinate class for pig, cow, dog, cat, horse, sheep, elephant, etc.), words with similar meanings, and words with opposite meanings, are needed for a high degree of comprehension knowledge. Of course, toddlers and young children will simply be learning words and their meanings, and intuitive parenting is especially supportive of language learning and new vocabulary acquisition. By teaching your child words in a real-world context, you will be setting the stage for more complete comprehension knowledge as he or she matures.

There can be no doubt that making sure babies, toddlers, and preschoolers have numerous daily opportunities to learn new words is an important activity for fostering the development of intelligence. Indeed, learning new words and playing word games with children should be a part of the daily routine.

This doesn't mean, as the makers of Baby Einstein products seem to assume, that you could show a baby pictures of objects, say the names of those objects, and thereby increase the baby's functional vocabulary. As is the case with long-term memory, children's word knowledge is integrally related to how they *experience* the objects, actions, and adjectives these vocabulary words represent. Playing with the objects and moving the objects around while the parents talk about the objects and their actions is essential to comprehension. A child's early vocabulary learning should be based upon his or her own experiences. Because of this, trips to the zoo are more likely to trigger vocabulary acquisition than sitting in a high chair watching photographs of various zoo animals flash by on a computer screen.

A young child can and should also learn vocabulary from reading books with his or her parents. Reading stories about animals, especially when the book has engaging photographs or illustrations, is also a very salient method of expanding vocabulary. And after a child begins to read on his or her own, reading is an excellent way to learn new vocabulary. Researchers have long known that putting a word in context enhances memory for that word. The brain stores narrative scripts that support recalling that word. For example, showing a picture of a scorpion and labeling it will trigger memory, but if the scorpion is introduced in a story that talks about what it looks like, what it eats, and, of course, the dramatic claws and stinger while showing a picture, recall is much better.[23]

Comprehension knowledge should not, of course, be limited to naming photographs or showing pictures.[24] When a child is three years old, or even in some cases as young as two years old, parents can begin expanding vocabulary knowledge by talking directly to the child about word classes. For example, animal toy sets can be grouped into zoo animals, farm animals, and pets; shapes can be classified according to color and size; and vehicles can be classified into cars, trucks, trains, and airplanes. Grouping the toys—and thus the words—is important in giving the child an opportunity to mentally classify vocabulary into what scientists call "semantic maps," which is a crucial aspect of comprehension knowledge. Grouping also provides an excellent opportunity to talk about simple adjectives: An elephant is "big," and a mouse is "small." This tiger is "in" the cage, but this one is "out." These shapes are "blue," but these others are "red."

Parents should be aware of the difference between vocabulary (words) and grammar (syntax and morphology). Comprehension knowledge focuses primarily on words and word knowledge, whereas formal knowledge of grammar is considered a reading and writing skill.[25] This distinction is important because vocabulary and grammar develop and are acquired in very different ways,[26] even though both are very important as a child learns to talk.[27]

Grammar includes the rules for combining words into phrases and sentences (syntax) and for modifying word tense (morphology). For example, a grammatical rule for changing a statement to a question is to start the sentence with a "wh" word (e.g., "where") and move the helping verb (in this case, "is") so that it switches places in the sentence with the subject (Mary). Using this rule, the sentence "Mary is going" can be made into the question "Where is Mary going?" Grammar also includes the little bits of sound that distinguish different forms of a word, such as singular forms ("book") from plural ("books") and present-tense forms ("walk") from past tense ("walked").

This distinction is important from a learning standpoint because Noam Chomsky, Steven Pinker, James Morgan, Jean Berko-Gleason, and many other cognitive scientists and linguists have argued convincingly that learning the rules for combining words into sentences, and the rules for generating the various tenses that transform singular into plural and present tense into past tense is an inductive process, *not* a form of memorization. Thus, comprehension knowledge includes vocabulary learning and general word knowledge, but not the grammatical aspects of learning to speak and understand language. At the risk of oversimplifying the distinction, children develop grammar by listening to their parents speak. Words, on the other hand, must be learned more explicitly, by listening to their parents speak *and* by being shown the objects (nouns), movements (verbs), and attributes (adjectives) to which these words refer. Professor Pinker provides detailed analysis of this topic in his book *Words and Rules*. An intuitive parent always delights in presenting new words to his or her child while they are naturally interacting.

READING AND WRITING

Although it is certainly possible to be highly intelligent without knowing how to read and write, there are sound reasons for including reading and writing ability as one aspect of "stores of acquired knowledge." The ability to read permits accessing the knowledge of others to add to one's own current knowledge (crystallized intelligence). In addition, reading is often the source of additional vocabulary knowledge as one reads unfamiliar words, determines their meaning, and adds this knowledge to their comprehension knowledge vocabulary.

Unlike grammar, which is not explicitly taught yet is acquired by practically everybody, reading and writing are learned skills. Children must be explicitly *taught* how to read and write, and most children are unable to pick this up on their own (although there are certainly cases of children teaching themselves how to read). Regardless of whether one is learning a phonetic spelling system (letters representing spoken sounds) such as Spanish or English or a nonphonetic writing system where symbols or icons are used to represent words, as in Chinese, or a combination of the two systems, the visual representations for the spoken words are memorized to the point of automatic recall in those who become fluent readers.

This latter point is extremely important when considering the nature of reading and writing ability and its contribution to intelligence. Writing systems are devised in order to represent spoken words. This means that the written symbols have a correspondence to oral vocabulary so that, at least in the initial stages of learning, it is important that the visual (written) symbols for words be mapped onto vocabulary the child *already knows*. Otherwise, they may be able to pronounce the words and in some sense "read" by sounding out the words, but they will not *understand* what the written words mean.

Over the last decade, there has been a push for introducing reading earlier and earlier in a child's life. Learning programs are being heavily marketed to parents trying to teach babies to read. Because writing is a visual representation for words, one wonders what aspects of reading a baby can actually learn when he or she has not yet developed word knowledge upon which to map the visual symbols.

There is a condition called hyperlexia that occurs when a child can read words but has no idea what they mean. I've seen cases like this in my clinical work. One four-year-old boy could read virtually any word, but could not select objects from an array that included the words he had just read. For example, if he saw a card with the printed word "elephant," he would look at it and say the word "elephant." And if you said the word "elephant" and gave him a blank piece of paper and a pencil, he would write the word "elephant" correctly. His printing looked exactly like typewritten text using a courier font; like some children with autism, he was very meticulous in his printing. But if you showed him a card with the word "elephant" spelled out and showed him a picture set that included an elephant, a car, a cow, and a dog and asked him to point to the animal whose name was written on the card, he could not do it. He could recognize and "read" words but did not comprehend what the written words meant. Fluent readers are generally able to sound out unfamiliar words they encounter when their meaning is unknown, and so in that sense are hyperlexic for unfamiliar words that can be sounded out. But unlike the hyperlexic boy who understood very little of what he read, these fluent readers comprehend *most* of what they read. They often sound out a word as part of an effort to understand what it means, to begin to become familiar with it and guess at its meaning in the context of the sentence, not just as an end in itself. And they do not sound out every word while reading.

This is an important distinction. Studies in the United States indicate that many children in elementary and even middle school have a working knowledge of phonics but have difficulty comprehending what they read.[28] This may be due, in part, to efforts to teach phonics to younger and younger children, when their vocabulary and grammar systems are still very immature and incomplete. Perhaps this practice is resulting in a form of hyperlexia in these young children because they do not understand the words that are being drilled. While I don't want to oversimplify a complicated situation, I do think it's fair to say that teaching reading to children should involve more than teaching speech sounds or phonics that the letters represent. We should also be making sure children *comprehend* the words they read.

It is also noteworthy that countries that do not formally teach reading or phonics until a child reaches age seven or even eight have very high literacy rates—in some countries, even higher than in the United States.[29] Finland, for example is the world's top country for student achievement, but teaches reading at a later time than in the United States—and has higher literacy rates.[30] A possible reason for this is that the language system (and vocabulary knowledge) is much higher in a seven- or eight-year-old than in a three- or four-year-old. At this older age, many more of the written words can be stored in long-term memory along with vocabulary knowledge that was previously learned.

An intuitive parent understands that reading and writing are forms of *language*. Even more important, these parents intuitively know that didactic, direct instruction on skills such as phonics should wait until a child's oral language is well established and grammatical skills are nearing adult levels—which means around six, seven, or even eight years of age. This is not to say that reading should be avoided until a child enters school. The stage is set for enjoying reading during early childhood, using intuitive parenting activities such as dialogic reading. Intuitive parents read to their children every day—or nearly so. They pick stories that are imaginative and that are interesting to toddlers and preschoolers, and books with big, attractive pictures and few words. Vocabulary books with photographs are also fun.

In addition to reading the words, intuitive parenting includes encouraging a child to make up her own stories while reading the books and interacting. A way of introducing technology—and reading—is to take a series of photographs of your child while she is playing or completing a routine such as going to the store with mom or dad. The idea is to capture each event—and then have her retell the story. This then becomes the written "text" for the story.

For example, the story of "going to the store with dad" could include a picture of dad putting his coat on and a photo of him getting the keys; a photo of the child putting her coat and shoes on; a photo of getting into the car; then arriving at the store; and so on. These photos then become the theme of the story. Show the pictures to your child and ask her to tell the story in her own words. Write down what she says and use word processing software to write down *her version* of the story. Import the pictures to complete the book. This is a highly effective way of introducing reading because the child herself experienced the elements in the story (it is about her) and you also know that she has the language (vocabulary and grammar) that the text represents because you wrote down what she said. Even if you add a few words—or new grammatical forms—here and there in the story, this too is in accord with intuitive parenting because these become language transactions within the story. Children love these kinds of stories because in them they are a "coauthor."

As your child gets a bit older, say, in grade school, this same approach can be used to teach story writing and journaling. Again, using a camera to photograph key elements in the story is helpful. Many children enjoy writing a story about what they did with one parent and then read what they wrote to the other parent, or to an older sibling, cousin, or grandparent. Again, because they "lived" the story, writing—and reading—it is far easier than it is for stories involving unfamiliar people or situations. Some children, like my youngest son and my youngest daughter, enjoy illustrating the stories rather than using photos, drawing pictures for each element or scene as they create their book. An intuitive parent encourages this form of reading—and writing.

MATHEMATICS

The final category in stores of acquired knowledge includes rote information on mathematics. The ability to problem-solve is *not* what is being considered under mathematic-quantitative knowledge. Rather, this domain involves knowing basic quantitative information such as numerals, times tables, math facts, such as addition and subtraction, and the other kinds of established principles needed to engage in math problem solving. Stated differently, stores of mathematical and quantitative intelligence include knowing that 5 × 6 equals 30, 10 − 2 equals 8, and 5 + 9 equals 14 without having to consciously think about it or count on our fingers.

As with reading, this kind of math knowledge is a type of crystallized intelligence that has been learned and stored in long-term memory for ready and fluent access so that it can be drawn upon to solve new problems. Helping a child develop math ability includes ensuring that he or she understands that numbers—and mathematical symbols—represent real-world concepts (such as adding up the number of cookies on a plate), and that these symbols are to be practiced sufficiently to be recognized rapidly and automatically as well as intuitively. This is similar to recognizing that letters represent sounds and that these in turn form words and phrases that have meaning. Math comprehension and reading comprehension both involve *understanding* the ideas or concepts depicted by the symbols (numbers and letters) rather than simply *recognizing* or *memorizing* the symbols and parroting their names. The goal should always be to ensure that children develop an intuitive sense of quantity, so that numbers seem to naturally "make sense" and that the numbers and symbols of mathematical operations (e.g., "+" and "−") have meaning in the same way that the symbols "b" "a" "l" "l" refer to a small spherical object that can roll and bounce. This kind of knowledge is different than being able to solve complex equations that one has never seen before and that require not only stores of quantitative knowledge but also require fluid reasoning, or the ability to take known information and apply it to new situations or new problems.

It is clear that the visual systems of babies are fairly adept at noticing and registering quantitative differences in visual fields. This can be measured using electrical brain waves that show differences in neural activation when different quantities of the same toy are placed in the baby's visual fields. But noticing a difference in quantity isn't the same as learning and storing this knowledge in long-term memory for fluent recovery. Some parents show their infants and toddlers number symbols such as "1," "2," "3," and so on while naming these with the words "one," "two," "three," etc. Later on, when the baby is a bit older and begins to talk, parents are proud that they can hold up a card with the numeric symbol "2" and their toddler knows the name of this number. But children who are taught in this way often do not actually know how many items "2" refers to. As with reading, it is very important that *comprehension* of the visual symbols (letters and words for reading; numbers and equations for math) is the learning goal. That is, when a child is ready, it is fine to teach him the names of letters and number symbols as a form of comprehension knowledge (vocabulary). However, it is vitally important to make sure that he actually *understands* the words that the letters spell and the quantities the number symbols refer to.

For babies, this can include giving them items one at a time and counting as each one is delivered to the baby. For example, when one of my sons (who ended up with a physics degree and went on to medical school) was a baby, he loved frozen peas. When he was sitting in his baby seat, we would give him the peas one at a time while saying: "One pea" and "You have one"; then "Another pea—two peas," then "Another pea—three peas," and so on up to ten. As a variation on this baby game, we would sometimes put five peas in a bowl in front of him and count them down as he ate them. "Five peas," "One is gone," "Now there are four, four peas—oh, you ate it," then "Now there are three peas left," and so on until "You ate them all up—five, four, three, two, one, zero. All gone."

As a child gets older, concepts such as fractions can be illustrated by breaking up cookies when he or she is eating them. "A whole one," then "Break it in two, now you ate half," then "Here's another whole one," "Break it in four pieces—now you ate a quarter," and so on. This kind of rudimentary quantitative information should be a part of the child's store of acquired knowledge so that the symbols "1," "2," "3," and so on that they learn to name are well understood. And unlike language and subsequent reading, wherein the language base is naturally acquired in everyday verbal interactions with parents and others, both the knowledge base and the symbol system for mathematics must be taught.

It is also important for children to develop a general number and quantity sense. Piaget conducted some experiments where he poured exactly the same amount of milk into both a short wide glass and a tall skinny glass and asked preschoolers which glass had more milk in it. Even though Piaget made clear that he had poured exactly the same amount of milk into each glass, most of the children responded that the tall skinny glass had more milk than the short wide one. With experience and repeated exposure and brain development, the child eventually learns that even though the glasses look different in terms of dimensions, they actually hold the same amount of liquid.

The point here is that parents may intuitively know about mass and quantity and differences in these dimensions, but their babies do not. As with vocabulary, reading, and writing, mathematical knowledge should be an everyday part of the parents' interactions with their children so that these stores of acquired knowledge are developed and reinforced in their children's everyday activities.

Cognitive Efficiency

The third primary area contributing to overall intelligence is cognitive efficiency. In the example of a chess master who plays multiple games at once, the ability to quickly make decisive moves is a factor in our impression that this person is highly intelligent. Efficiency, then, is the ability to problem-solve accurately and to retrieve the stores of acquired knowledge rapidly and efficiently. Psychologists have described this as "the cognitive clock," "cognitive timing," and "processing ability." In CHC theory, the two abilities that are considered measures of cognitive efficiency include short-term memory and processing speed.

We know that the brain's cognitive "clock" increases in speed as a child grows. A toddler's cognitive efficiency is fairly low whereas a teenager's is much higher, meaning that children can solve problems faster and faster as they grow up. This is due in part to changes in the structure of neurons in the brain. As explained in Chapter 2, as a child grows, nerve axons are surrounded by a fatty sheath called myelin[31] that speeds up neurotransmission. As you may recall, myelinated nerve cells are what make up the "white matter" in the brain. Nerve axons in babies are relatively low in myelin, and so their nerve impulses are relatively slower than what is seen in older children, who have myelin in a much larger proportion of their neurons (more white matter in their brains). Yet increased cognitive efficiency is more than just a matter of developing more myelin; it is also improved through changes in the cerebral cortex that occur as a result of learning. Stated simply, practice and advances in the other aspects of intelligence contribute to more efficient thinking.[32] As we make more and more nerve connections between one "data point" of information and another, the various areas of the brain become more integrated and cognitive efficiency improves.

Although scientists are confident that myelinization and cortical organization improve cognitive efficiency, there is an ongoing scientific debate over whether (and how) this development can be accelerated, and if an individual's "clock" can be altered through specific practice or learning. One might argue that it is obvious that the cognitive efficiency of recalling and reciting rote information like the multiplication tables or a memorized poem increases dramatically with practice. However, this could be the result of improved storage of these items in long-term memory rather than any speeding up of the cognitive clock. The question would be whether learning one's times tables would then speed up the cognitive clock when one encounters a new memorization task. At this time, there's certainly some evidence to suggest that cognitive efficiency does improve with practice, but it's not clear that intellectual abilities other than cognitive clock speed aren't responsible for the improvements. In other words, rote memorization and drilling children on one body of knowledge doesn't, so far as we know, have any ancillary benefits in terms of overall processing efficiency when it comes to learning a different body of knowledge.

The broad area of cognitive efficiency is subdivided into short-term memory and processing speed. Let's take a closer look at each of these—and at how intuitive parents *can* naturally facilitate the development of cognitive efficiency.

SHORT-TERM MEMORY

Short-term memory is the ability to hold in mind small amounts of recently presented information, and to utilize it. This is distinct from what I call the "mockingbird circuit," or the ability to simply repeat or parrot information. To be sure, a primitive form of short-term memory is required to enable someone (or some animal) to imitate, but what psychologists mean by short-term memory is the ability to hold information in mind for access and modification. People with echolalia, a communication disorder, repeat what they hear verbatim. If I were to say, "I went to the store," someone with echolalia would always say: "I went to the store." But in a test of short-term memory, "I went to the store" can be repeated with alterations such as "store I to went." The key here is that in order to produce "store I to went," the individual words have to be held in mind and their places in the sentence moved, which requires short-term memory. In echolalia, the child cannot "break into" the sentence and change the word order.

Although this seems like a rather trivial skill, it is also clear that short-term memory is crucial to acquiring new information rapidly and effectively. Consider a classroom situation in which the teacher is providing a lecture on geography. If the student is unable to hold the information the teacher just provided in the lecture in short-term memory, he or she would very quickly become lost and unable to keep up with what the teacher is saying. If a student can't hold the word "Constantinople" in short-term memory, then a teacher explaining that Constantinople is a city in Turkey that is now called Istanbul will be completely incomprehensible, regardless of whether the student knows the meaning of the words "Constantinople," "Turkey," and "Istanbul."

Unlike long-term memory, which is used to store information to be retrieved over and over again, short-term memory is the ability to hold recent information in mind and operate on it rapidly and accurately. Some items in short-term memory may be transferred to long-term memory, but most items will not. Studies of the neurological basis of short-term memory indicate that short-term memory traces are lost fairly quickly. From an intellectual perspective, short-term memory is needed so that information recently presented can be inspected and, if needed, operated on.

Because the assessment of short-term memory requires active responses, including naming objects and numbers that have been recently presented, it is not surprising that the nature and extent of short-term memory in babies is unknown. From a theoretical perspective, psychologists tend to think of short-term memory as being "innate" or instinctive, and some have theorized that nearly all of a baby's memories are relatively short term. While it is clear that babies will recognize changes in the visual field relatively quickly and efficiently and that their auditory systems are relatively adept at noticing the different sounds in the environment, including speech sounds, it is not clear to what extent short-term memory is developed and utilized in these kinds of activities.

One can see short-term memory coming on line in toddlers

who have begun speaking. Many will begin imitating syllable sequences but will change the order or add new elements, indicating that these elements are being stored and accessed from short-term memory. Preschoolers will repeat short sentences and phrases while changing the word order or the tense of some of the words. For example, if a child saw the classic children's television show *Mister Rogers' Neighborhood* for the first time and then attempted to sing its theme song, he might transform the line "It's a beautiful day in the neighborhood" into "A neighborhood day beautiful." These kinds of errors are natural and no cause for concern. Indeed, when children imitate phrases and change them up a bit, it is a good sign that they are mentally "breaking into" the verbal string and processing it in their own way instead of simply echoing it.

As is the case with cognitive efficiency, short-term memory does develop with age. Young children have difficulty reversing even two elements; for example, they may have trouble saying the words "dog" and "hat" in reverse order when asked to do so. By the age of six, many children can do this with a sequence of three words; most nine-year-olds can do four or more items; and most adults can hold five or more words in short-term memory and operate on them in this way.[33]

PROCESSING SPEED

The second cognitive efficiency broad intellectual ability is called processing speed. Within the context of the CHC theory, processing speed is defined as the ability to automatically perform cognitive tasks when under pressure to maintain attention and concentration. Note that the decisions made in such tasks are relatively simple and are not designed to tax higher reasoning.

Processing speed is defined as the ability to complete mental tasks of moderate difficulty rapidly and accurately. In practice, processing speed is measured using a series of timed tasks of short duration (two or three minutes) that require little in the way of complex thinking or mental analysis. The notion here is not to stretch problem-solving ability but to assess the speed with which the mind operates when completing simple tasks that are not automatic. To sample processing speed, a test might present a picture on the left side of a row and five or six pictures on the right, with one of this array a match for the "target" picture on the left. The goal is to rapidly scan the row to find the match for the picture on the left. The number of items completed is then scored to estimate a person's processing speed.

Note that processing speed is distinct from another type of cognitive speed measure called reaction time. Reaction time is defined as an individual's quickness in reacting (e.g., pressing a button when they see a flash on a computer screen), rather than the processing speed needed for scanning and detecting salient features to make decisions. Reaction time also depends directly on hand-eye coordination, whereas processing speed does not.

As with short-term memory, practicing tasks that utilize processing speed will improve efficiency for those particular tasks, but there is considerable debate about whether the broad cognitive clock can be sped up. And, as with short-term memory, the clock does speed up as a child develops.[34] In a two-minute time period, a three-year-old can scan and make a simple decision on an average of five items, and a four-year-old can accurately complete an average of fifteen items. By age five, most children complete twenty-five or more items correctly within two minutes, and an eleven-year-old can usually complete more than forty items. Adults can often complete more than fifty-five items in two minutes. But if one practices scanning pictures as described above and becomes more efficient, this does not then transfer to more items correct on another measure of processing speed. For example, if the number of items correct on one kind of task is increased from twenty to forty by practicing, shifting to a different kind of processing speed task will often yield a score of about twenty in that person. Like short-term memory, processing speed shows fairly substantial development from preschool through elementary school and into adulthood.

The development of executive function—the ability to coordinate and route information to the proper brain centers for processing—also continues into adolescence. The brain region primarily charged with managing executive function for the whole brain is located in the prefrontal cortex, which, as mentioned in Chapter 2, is a region in the front of the brain just beneath the brain areas utilized for speech and language. Neural imaging studies indicate that information input from multiple brain regions into this executive function center is important in developing the ability to actually coordinate and process the information. The development of that coordination and processing ability is associated in turn with improvements in processing speed. The key here is that the nerve pathways carrying the impulses are sped up through myelinization and that the child's experiences with different but simultaneous input streams from visual, auditory, and/or tactile data cause the brain to learn how to handle these different input strands more efficiently. Because of this, cognitive efficiency and executive function develop and improve through multisensory, "whole-brain" learning—the kind you can provide through intuitive parenting.

An intuitive parent need not get bogged down in the nuances of the debate over whether the cognitive clock can be sped up (and if so, whether there's any benefit in doing so). What matters is that you foster and inspire your child's thinking, within the real world, in response to your child's initiations and through play. Young children do the same things over and over again, with slight alterations. An intuitive parent builds on these routines and encourages a child to think—and talk—about what they doing. Fun games that encourage these qualities are I Spy and games in which the child names five words that start with a "b" sound (or if a child knows his or her letters, names five words that start with the letter "b"). You can also play a game in which you and your child take turns thinking up different word classes: "I wonder how many farm animals you can name?" "How many friend's names?" "How many kinds of fish?"—and so on. Take turns so that your child gets to ask you to develop some categories. Throw in some mistakes from time to time and let him or her correct you—for example, by saying "snake" when the category is farm animals. Give your child some time to notice the mistake, and if he or she doesn't, say something like "A snake? Oops, that isn't a farm animal! It's a reptile." Including an occasional mistake will hold a child's attention and gives him or her some control over the game as well.

In older children, an intuitive parent can set up time targets—and rewards—for routine tasks such as household chores. This can also be done for homework. Some children enjoy trying to say as many multiples of numbers as they can within a specified time, which can be a good way of combining processing speed and mathematical knowledge. The key here is to encourage cognitive efficiency and build knowledge simultaneously. After all, an intuitive parent doesn't break intelligence "training" into small pieces using drill; he or she facilitates thinking within the powerful context of everyday play and caregiving activities. Let's take a closer look at how this can be done.

Reasoning Trumps Rote Memorization

It is clear that intelligence is more than just recalling facts on demand or having particular acumen with flash cards. Indeed, real intelligence and real genius are founded on the ability not only to accurately recall information from long-term memory, but also on the ability to solve problems rapidly, efficiently, and innovatively. Because of this, facilitating intellectual development in babies, toddlers, and preschoolers should *not* rely exclusively on drilling rote information or on having a child passively view learning DVDs or computer applications. Also, attempting to "teach to the test" using individual, isolated tasks or exercise such as work sheets will not increase a child's intelligence. Forcing a child to memorize and recite their times tables by age two may be impressive, but this will not ensure that she becomes a mathematical genius, and in fact may actually end up hindering her ability to solve mathematical problems using reasoning.

An intellectually enriching environment for babies and toddlers as well as preschoolers includes developmentally reasonable opportunities to learn *all* nine broad abilities in functional, day-to-day contexts. Problem solving is perhaps the most important of these abilities for developing future intellectual ability, and providing opportunities for your child to practice it is vitally important. From the earliest stages, when babies first learn to move and coordinate their sense systems, an intuitive parent provides opportunities for exploration and learning, remembering that trial and error is key to the learning process. Intuitive parents don't try to do everything for their child; nor do they keep a child from trying—and making—mistakes. The foundations of reasoning can be seen in a baby figuring out how to reach and grasp a cup, a block, or other object. For a toddler, having opportunities for stacking blocks, building things, playing with imaginatively designed toys, and telling simple stories (in which you can also change up the circumstances and the ending) are all ways an intuitive parent can encourage reasoning.

After a child begins to talk and to understand what others say, an intuitive parent directly encourages thinking by asking questions such as "What comes next?" or "Will it fall when you put another block on top?" When her child answers, an intuitive parent says "OK, let's try it out!" rather than simply providing the right answer or even confirming that the child's answer was right.

Intuitive parents naturally provide opportunities for their

child to explore visual spatial and auditory information. They provide toys that make noise (not too loud or they will drive you crazy!) and toys for building in which pieces can fit together in various ways. When you purchase a toy, think about how your child will be playing with it. What are the various things a child can do with the pieces of a toy? What can they learn from it? After buying a new toy, watch your child play with it and see what they do. Also think about how long they play with it. Good toys have flexible uses; a child will not quickly discover them all but will keep coming back to them again and again. When Nina was a toddler, my wife gave her some foam blocks of various shapes that could fit together in different ways. At first Nina just stacked them, but over time she made more and more complicated structures. She played with them for months. They were a great toy for a toddler—and one that encouraged visual spatial reasoning.

Helping a child acquire a large vocabulary is also very important, but you won't achieve the goal by repetitively naming photographs or using flash cards—or simply throwing words at him or her. Your child should become familiar not just with the vocabulary words but with the actual items and concepts the words represent, and how these items, concepts, and words relate to other items, concepts, and words. In addition to naming objects (nouns), modifiers such as shape, size, color, and comparatives (big, bigger, biggest) and action words (verbs) should be an integral part of a child's everyday play-based experiences. This helps your child develop a large store of memories rooted in his or her own experiences. Finally, it is important to bear in mind that reading, writing, and mathematical abilities, as integral parts of intelligence, have to be taught to babies and toddlers through experience, with direct instruction reserved for when a child gets older and goes to school. A baby or a toddler or even a preschooler should *not* be taught as if they were already in school. They will build thinking ability—and natural curiosity—through play, and when they do so they will be all the more ready for more advanced and more structured learning when the time comes.

In the next chapter we'll take a deeper look at why drill and memorization are not sufficient techniques for helping young children—especially babies and toddlers—develop intelligent minds.

- Intelligence is not simply a matter of memorizing facts. There are other important skills, such as reasoning ability, that are crucial.
- Intelligence tests, especially in young children, are not highly accurate, and using the wrong test will yield an inaccurate estimate of intelligence.
- An intuitive parent cultivates his or her child's reasoning and thinking ability and balances the various domains rather than emphasizing only one or two exclusively to the detriment of other intellectual abilities.
- The development of intelligence is not "set" in infancy, preschool, or even elementary school. IQ remains relatively fluid until a child reaches the age of twelve, or even older. An intuitive parent does not rush to teach his or her child how to take an intelligence test or memorize test answers and knows that nurturing thinking and reasoning will pay lifelong dividends for the child.
- An intuitive parent knows that learning is enhanced when a child tries things on their own and that trying—and making mistakes—is an important part of building an intelligent brain.

chapter 5

Raising Lifelong Learners

The total amount of knowledge a child acquires between birth and adulthood is staggering. This knowledge includes how to speak and understand at least one language; a typical adult understands more than seventeen thousand words.[1] It includes how to read, how to write, and a sense of numbers as well as innumerable facts in a variety of subjects such as history, social studies, literature, biology, physics, and chemistry. It also includes the nuances of social interaction, cultural conventions, and how to "fit in" and succeed in a complex, dynamic society. And this is just a tiny fraction of the information your child's brain will accumulate over a lifetime. Just as important, there will be new ideas and new technologies that are not currently available or even on the horizon! And your child—and her brain—must be prepared to integrate these discoveries and technological advances into her daily life.

The sheer amount of information we learn in a life span is awe-inspiring. How in the world do we do it? The answer has profound implications for teaching infants and young children in ways that ensure optimal brain development. Our brains can be wired to readily acquire new information, but then we also have to acquire it. Curiosity inspires us to explore, to seek more information. And we can reason. The human mind is particularly adept at reasoning, so we can build upon what we already know to generate new insights and knowledge. Scientists who study these kinds of learning sets—those that build upon rules or principles—call this "generative learning."[2]

Because of our capacity for generative learning, turning a brain into a passive storage device that simply retrieves rote facts on demand dooms that brain to do far less than it is capable of doing. In essence, to teach a baby or child to learn through memorization is inadvertently to wire a baby's brain for passive, rote learning at the expense of reasoning and active problem solving. This is particularly tragic in light of the fact that it is *impossible* for even the smartest human beings to use rote learning to memorize all the knowledge they will acquire (and need) by the time they reach high school, much less what they will encounter during a lifetime. The key to maximizing a baby's brain potential is to encourage active generative reasoning that is not limited to passive rote learning. Intuitive parents naturally facilitate generative learning by encouraging their child from the outset to try new ways, learn from trial and error, and be an active partner in the learning process.

Generative Learning and Language Acquisition

Language acquisition provides a splendid model for illustrating the meaning of generative learning and of the way that reasoning generates infinite possibilities for knowledge acquisition. In a world of more than seven billion people,[3] more than 99.9 percent learn to speak and understand at least one language, and many will learn more than one. But virtually none of these seven-billion-plus people ever learn their native language through explicit language instruction or rote learning. It is a sure bet that most do not have access to special language-learning DVDs, videos, or computer games, or even vocabulary-building flash cards. Yet all become experts in both speaking and understanding their native language. So how is this done?

Professor Steven Pinker notes that children primarily learn language simply by hearing their parents talk. Parents do not explicitly teach their children how to talk, nor do they routinely provide lessons on grammatical rules for generating correct sentences.[4] Studies show that parents give children direct feedback on "politeness" forms such as "please" and "thank you," but give almost no feedback on the actual rules for assembling words into sentences. How much of the formal grammar learning in elementary school do you recall? Just what is a past participle, gerund, or infinitive anyway? Do you need this formal knowledge to carry on a conversation in your native language? Children learn to use these forms correctly long before they are taught in school. Further, parents cannot possibly teach a child everything he or she will ultimately hear and say even if they wanted to. It is *impossible* to memorize every word, phrase, and sentence that one will say or hear during a lifetime. This is because language is creative, an infinite and flexible code for conveying ideas with various words and grammatical structures, and can always be used in novel ways.

Textbooks on linguistics illustrate the infinite nature of language using examples such as the Mother Goose nursery rhyme "The House That Jack Built,"[5] which can be uniquely and infinitely varied. You probably have heard the sentence "This is the house that Jack built," and you may recall the next phrase in many versions of the rhyme: "This is the malt that lay in the house that Jack built."[6] But you've never heard "This is the brewmaster who stole the malt that lay in the house that Jack built," because I just invented that line. I was able to create this new version with proper

English grammar and meaning so that you are able to comprehend this sentence even though you have never read (or heard) it before.

Our brains are wired at a young age to generate and comprehend sentences in our native language even if we have never received explicit instructions on the nuances of grammar. We can also intuitively know whether a sentence we have never heard (or read) conforms to English rules of grammar. We know that "Where the woman is going?" is an incorrect question form even though we may not consciously know that the grammatical rules of English require that the helping verb ("is") be moved from its customary place in front of the verb it is helping ("going") to an earlier place in the sentence (preceding the subject "the woman") to make a proper question: "Where is the woman going?"

Indeed, it turns out that children learning through reasoning will intuitively pay attention to exactly those aspects of their parents' input that advances their current knowledge level. Parents do not need to be language experts and spoon-feed or drill pronunciation, words, phrases, and sentences; babies are born with the ability to deduce the rules for language based on relatively limited input from their parents. In fact, their brains will automatically focus on those aspects of the parent's talking that advance their current level of knowledge. Through this natural process, children learn the grammatical rules for generating an infinite number of sentences. The key to building a sophisticated, facile "language" brain is to expose a baby to a few examples of the grammar of the language they are learning and give them plenty of opportunities to learn new words in a meaningful context using intuitive parenting techniques. No special training or programs are needed for you to be your baby's language instructor par excellence!

Children can generate adult-level sentences by the time they are three or four years of age without any explicit instruction on sentence construction. Again, this is not because parents drilled them as infants or toddlers on how words are ordered in the language they're learning or because they explained the difference between the passive and active voice by saying: "Now, remember, when the topic of the conversation is the recipient of an action, our usual subject-verb-object word order is inverted to an object-verb-subject order."

Dr. Keith Nelson at Penn State University showed that three-year-old children could quickly learn to use passive constructions without any explicit instruction if their parents just modeled a few real-life examples.[7] While playing with a set of toys, the parent acted out scenarios designed to mimic how passive forms are used in everyday conversations. "Oh, look!" "The dog is barking at the cat." "Uh-oh, now he is being chased by that mad cat!" This sets up the dog as the topic of the conversation and then as the recipient of the action by the object of the previous sentence, which is the natural way that passive voice is used in everyday conversations. This is intuitive parenting at work, naturally enabling generative learning. Nelson's groundbreaking work showed that this form of intuitive language learning not only applies to grammar but also to vocabulary and verb markers, such as use of the past tense. In essence, all aspects of language can rapidly be acquired in this way.

Perhaps even more astounding is that children learning more than one language readily "code switch" between languages. For example, in English, an adjective usually precedes the noun, as in "red car." In Spanish, the adjective follows the noun, so that "red car" in English becomes *"coche rojo"* in Spanish. Children learning to speak both English and Spanish quickly learn to say "red car" when speaking English and *"coche rojo"* (car red) when speaking Spanish. They almost never say "car red" in English or *"rojo coche"* in Spanish. Parents do not have to explicitly tell their children: "When speaking English, you must say the adjective first and then the noun, but when you speak Spanish you must say the noun first and then the adjective" for their children to learn these rules.

When a child learns a new noun or a new adjective, or a new noun *and* a new adjective, she will instinctively use the proper word order when speaking English or Spanish. Similarly, even when the new words are learned first in English, the child will immediately translate the words using proper Spanish grammar: noun followed by adjective. So, if a child learns about a bear that lives in the Arctic and is called a "polar bear," she will generate "*oso polar*" without her mother or father ever having to present a flash card or DVD or special computer program to help her memorize the rule. This syntactic rule is generative in the sense that after the child learns the rule for adjectives and nouns, forms that she has never heard before will automatically be incorporated into the grammar. And in the case of a child learning English and Spanish, she will automatically include the new words into *both* grammars, even when they use different rules.

We could not possibly explicitly teach a child every word combination he or she will hear and say. Thankfully, the natural learning process allows the child to *discover* the rules for English or Spanish—or Mandarin Chinese or whatever language they are learning through verbal interactions with parents; interactions that signal to the child's brain key parameters of that language. Formal language instruction is not needed. The way to teach babies, toddlers, and children is to help them *discover* knowledge through a natural developmental process. Their immature brains come ready to learn in this manner. All that parents need to provide is the opportunity for the learning to occur by talking to their child.

The same is true for many other kinds of learning as well. Rather than aiming to have children memorize specific forms or pieces of information to be recalled on a rote basis, it is far more efficient to wire their brains to enable them to take a limited set of information and, through an inductive process, learn new things and generate new knowledge. If one knows a set of rules or principles—and some basic facts—unknown information can be deduced. So, the focus of teaching a baby or young child should be problem solving, reasoning, and other kinds of abilities that will allow them to become lifelong learners as well as creative and innovative thinkers.

Whole-Brain Learning

Among the reasons why drilling and rote memorization don't help a child develop the reasoning and problem-solving skills necessary for generative learning is that there are striking, fundamental differences in the regions and neural pathways of the brain that are activated by these very different tasks.

One way of studying what's happening in the brain during different learning activities is to look at patterns of neural activation. How many areas of the brain are working together during that kind of learning? What kinds of neural resources are recruited to solve a problem as compared to the neural resources engaged in memorization? Brain imaging studies provide an answer that may surprise you: The brain works much harder, and many more brain regions are working together, during tasks that require thinking, while memorization taps only those areas of the brain directly responsible for completing the task.

Literally hundreds of brain imaging studies have been conducted over the past half century that look at what a brain is doing when it is engaged in recalling memorized information. To summarize the results in a somewhat simplified manner: The primary regions dedicated to storing and recalling language information (words, for example) are located primarily in the front part of the brain, the frontal lobe. When research subjects are asked to say the names of objects in photos or drawings, most show increased activation in those brain regions, meaning that there is an increase in blood supply to the front of the brain and increased electrical activity. Scientists believe that increased activation in this brain region means that the frontal lobe, especially on the left side of the brain, is responsible for verbal naming.[8]

Interestingly, clever researchers can alter the region of activation in the brain for naming responses by showing subjects different kinds of pictures.[9] For example, Professor Elizabeth Kensinger at Harvard University and her colleague Daniel Schacter at the Athinoula A. Martinos Center for Biomedical Imaging showed that if adults are shown pictures with emotional content, the areas of the brain that regulate and process emotions, namely the amygdala and hippocampus, get activated along with the usual memory centers in the frontal lobe.

As an example, if a scientist shows a research subject a picture of a bird and asks the participant to name the picture, the frontal lobe of the brain "lights up" on scans of electrical activation and blood flow. But if the scientist shows a picture of an actor showing anger, the areas of the brain associated with processing emotions also light up. This can also be done with pictures of animals or people the participant has an emotional attachment to. If a picture of an unfamiliar dog is shown, the frontal lobe is activated, but if the picture is of a subject's beloved childhood dog, the frontal lobe *and* the emotional centers light up. This finding is noteworthy because it shows that brain activation can be enhanced beyond passive retrieval and naming. Certain parts of the brain are dedicated to storing and retrieving information acquired using rote learning, and when a person has a deeper knowledge of the words, that is, if they contain emotional content, additional neural resources in diverse brain regions will be allocated to processing the information.

In sum, what these brain imaging studies show is that passively viewing flash cards or images on a screen while a parent or narrator calls out the names of the objects depicted will result in much weaker, "shallower" brain activation than that which occurs when learning and storing more information about the words.

Let's consider as a general example the brain activation needed to learn the answer to the problem "What does 2 + 3 equal?" using a flash card. In terms of brain architecture, the flash card requires activation of the visual center that stores the image of the flash card and the symbols "2," "3," "+," and "=." When the parent or teacher reads aloud the equation depicted on the flash card, it activates the auditory center that encodes and stores the verbal information "2 + 3 = 5." With a relatively limited amount of practice, a child, even a young child, can be taught to reflexively say "five" when shown this flash card (using the visual center for recognizing the card and the language area to recall and recite the answer).

As a comparison, let's teach the child the same information using real objects, such as fruit snacks. Although superficially the question and answer are the same ("2 + 3 = 5"), consider the differences in the learning context and support for learning an intuitive parent provides. For the flash card, the parent or the computer program says, "2 + 3 = 5." There is no basis for *thinking* on the part of the child other than to passively process this information input using the brain's visual and auditory centers. Then, the next flash card is presented, and the child's neural engagement in the task is minimal. In contrast, when the intuitive parent takes out three fruit snacks she says, "Look, here's some fruit snacks! How many do we have here? Let's count: one, two, three! Here's two more, you can have them: one, two! How many do you have now?" At this point, the child is given a chance to answer. If he says "five," give him some more and count those too. If he doesn't answer or gives the wrong answer, praise him for trying and then say, "You had two and then three more! You have five! Let's count them: one, two, three, four, five." Then the child holds the fruit snacks and gets to eat them.

What is happening in the brain? As with the flash card, the visual center and the auditory centers are both activated. But what else is happening in the child's mind? Consider the other senses involved in processing the fruit snacks. These have an odor, so the olfactory system is activated, they have a texture, so the tactile centers are activated, and, perhaps more important, the brain is engaged in sorting out these different types of sensory information; therefore, the prefrontal cortex (executive function) is also activated. Even better, the verbal and language centers in the brain are now active. And the social interaction with the parent and the fruit snacks is activating the pleasure/reward centers in the brain.

As simple as these differences between flash cards and experiential "real world" learning seem, neuroscience studies confirm that solving problems—in this case, figuring out how many fruit snacks were presented—is much more powerful in terms of brain activity than sitting back and looking at flash cards. In general, reasoning of any kind is a whole-brain process.

The areas of the brain for reasoning also include the frontal lobe, and this makes sense because recall is a part of problem solving and the front of the brain is the "general" commanding the coordination of the "troops"—the rest of the cortex. When we are thinking about a problem, we recall the things we know about the task at hand. But researchers have found that multiple, astoundingly diverse areas of the brain are activated in problem solving than in rote memorization and recall, involving regions in the front, middle, and back of the brain as well as a key area of the cerebellum. The top of the frontal lobe is used in planning (including planning complex motor activities); the lower sides of the brain (in back of the frontal lobe) are used to locate or "find" objects; another region is used to understand the meanings of words and also to process speech sounds; a region located in the back of the brain is used to visually decipher complex shapes; and the left part of the cerebellum—a primary sensory and motor processing part of the brain located below the cortex, in the back of the head on top of the spinal cord—is also activated for executive function, verbal working memory, and spatial processing. And all these diverse cortical and subcortical centers are coordinated and brought to bear to solve problems. Talk about a "whole-brain" activity!

There is an elegant symmetry to all the different skills the brain recruits to solve problems: Planning, search skills, meaning, sound processing, spatial reasoning, and executive function are all coordinated to generate an answer. Intuitive parenting seeks to activate the child's whole brain by encouraging problem solving in an interactive context. Play activities, toys, and real-world learning materials automatically and simultaneously engage brain regions normally devoted to memory, listening, moving, and seeing. A baby's brain has the latent potential to integrate information coming from all these regions in a miraculous manner, but experience, in the form of problem solving, reasoning, and, importantly, making and learning from naturally occurring mistakes are all needed to ensure proper brain wiring.

Watch a three- or four-month-old as she learns to grab an object. At first, the hand and arm coordination is not good enough to let the baby reliably grasp the object. The coordination between the visual centers at the back of the brain and the motor centers at the front of the brain aren't communicating very well, so the baby can't make her hands go directly to where she is looking. And even if she manages to move her arm to the proper place, getting her fingers to grasp the object is another problem. A baby will look at her hands and the object over and over again, and her failure to grasp the object will give her brain just a bit more information on how to successfully solve this problem. By the time she is about five or six months old, instead of clumsily batting the object, she can smoothly reach out and grab a large object, such as a rattle or block, whenever she wants. My six-month-old grandchildren are adept at quickly snatching my eyeglasses off my face!

Note that, as with language, the parents don't have to explicitly teach a child to do this; all that's needed is to place objects within reach and let nature take its course. The process requires a baby to try—and to fail—in order to make progress. She learns from her naturally occurring mistakes, and her brain *needs* this feedback to solve the problem. A brain wired for rote learning and passively storing and retrieving "facts" on demand is far different than a brain that solves problems. Making mistakes and using data from failures to ultimately solve a problem are both key attributes of generative learning.

Naturally, the process is a lot more fun when mom and dad participate and laugh about misses and encourage trying as well as success while also moving the object back into reach when the baby knocks it away. Being an active part of the play and reacting to the baby will make this learning more efficient while also laying the emotional and neurological groundwork for the baby to enjoy solving problems.

- Raising a lifelong learner means getting the right start using intuitive parenting and transactional learning. Lay the foundation by following your child's lead—and by letting him try things on his own.
- Intuitive parents bear in mind that drilling a baby on "facts" will strengthen only those brain regions and neural pathways supporting rote learning and parroting, whereas engaging in interactive learning and problem solving will strengthen those abilities and the broader neural regions and pathways supporting fluid reasoning.
- It is foolhardy—no, *impossible*—to preplan or micromanage every aspect of what a child needs to learn. Early on, empower your child to acquire new knowledge in partnership with you and on his own.
- Encourage and praise attempts even when these result in failure or the wrong answer. As we will see in a later chapter, the brain needs accurate input, so do not tell a child that an

answer is right when it is wrong. But it is also important to recognize and encourage *trying*. Of course, success and right answers should also be praised.

- Learning from naturally occurring failure and mistakes is an essential part of the learning process and helps your child's brain to become properly wired. Always keep your child safe, but also be sure that he or she is allowed to try new things, even if you know that their way won't work. When failure or mistakes occur, offer encouragement to keep trying.

chapter 6

Confidence, Resilience, and Persistence: Natural Benefits of Intuitive Parenting

As we have seen in previous chapters, modern efforts to acceler-ate learning are directly intended to increase children's intelligence—and their test scores. But as important as intelligence is, it is becoming increasingly clear that other skills, such as faith in one's own abilities (confidence), the ability to overcome setbacks (resilience), and stick-to-itiveness (persistence) are also extremely important determinants of whether children will ultimately succeed in life. As a "veteran" parent, I would say that fostering these qualities in children should be very high on every family's list of priorities. Thankfully, intuitive parenting will help instill these traits in your child in a way that pushing achievement test scores or intelligence test performance could never do. Let's see how and why this works in real-life situations.

Parents Mary and William must have been worried about their son. Both were pillars of the community; Mary served on the board of a local bank, was active in Junior League, and helped raise funds for civic organizations. William Sr. was a prominent lawyer and community leader. Their son, William III, attended an exclusive prep school. But he was argumentative and headstrong, and could be, as he himself later put it, a "sarcastic, smart-ass" kid.[1] As a teenager, young William had trouble in school—sometimes skipping classes, sometimes failing to turn in schoolwork—and was even banned from the computer lab for stealing computer time from a local company.[2] And although he was smart enough to get into Harvard University, he dropped out before graduating. Naturally, his parents were troubled by this decision. "Mary [his mother] and I were both concerned about it—I think she a bit more than I," William Sr. said. "Her expectations and mine were very ordinary expectations of people who have kids in college—that they get a degree."[3] As a parent myself, whose own teenagers were sometimes rebellious and nonconformist, I can imagine how concerned William's parents were throughout these ups and downs during his upbringing—especially during his teen years and early adulthood.

William III is none other than Bill Gates, who went on to found Microsoft and become one of the world's richest people and one of its most dedicated philanthropists. There is no question that he was intelligent from his earliest years, but perhaps even more important were the confidence, persistence, and resilience he brought to bear while pursuing his ideas. Even when things weren't going his way, either at school or in business, he stuck with it and didn't give up. He always believed in his ideas and his abilities. His family enjoyed competing with one another in games and sports, and when he lost a competition, his parents didn't tell him that he had won; losing a game was not called "success" in order to bolster self-esteem. His mother insisted that Bill and his siblings study hard and participate in sports and music lessons, and she imparted discipline with regard to their manners, responsibilities, and social conduct. When Bill did well, he was praised; but he was also told when he was not putting in the effort or not doing what was expected of him.[4] His parents instinctively ensured that his

developing brain received authentic input—and nurtured persistence, resilience, and confidence in their son.

You may be thinking that because Mr. Gates is highly intelligent,
everything would have worked out fine in the end anyway, even if he
wasn't so resilient and persistent. But research tells us something else.
Professor Joan Freeman at Middlesex University in England completed a long-term follow-up study of 210 highly intelligent children
who were part of a special gifted program in which they received
more attention and opportunities to learn than did children in regular classes. One could speculate that many of these students would go
on to get advanced degrees and/or forge distinguished careers in
teaching, science, technology, medicine, law, politics, or creative arts
such as writing. Or that, like Bill Gates, they would become entrepreneurs and build successful companies. Dr. Freeman defined "success" very broadly in her research; essentially, she was exploring
whether "giftedness" in school translated into accomplishments later
in life. She sought to avoid stereotypes of success and misclassifying
as unsuccessful people who ended up working in rewarding careers
that weren't necessarily prestigious or especially high paying. But the
study indicated that many of the students Dr. Freeman followed did
not meet even her broad classifications for success. It is clear from this
research that simply being intelligent is not enough to ensure that a
child will actualize his or her full potential as an adult.

How many of us would have persisted in developing the theory
of relativity after not immediately getting into college and then
while working as a patent clerk, as Einstein did? There are many
potential reasons why gifted students, like Bill Gates, might choose
not to continue their education; and certainly many may find different ways to continue expanding their knowledge and abilities in
life and work. But Dr. Freeman's study points to several reasons
that have to do with the process of education itself, including burnout, the consequence of pushing students to excel in school to the
exclusion of engagement in other pursuits that engage them, and

through burdensome amounts of homework or boring, routine work that doesn't engage their minds.[5] It is also possible that many of these highly intelligent children were taught using rote memorization, with insufficient emphasis on problem solving, resilience, and perseverance, so that while they were able to score high on entrance exams, their skills did not translate into long-term academic success or success in life. The results of this study and others like it suggest that, in addition to intelligence, confidence, determination, and a positive self-image are important factors in a child's ability to actualize his or her potential in work and to forge a fulfilling adult life. And that for parents, the goal is not just to help wire a child's brain for effective learning and intellectual development but also for confidence, persistence, and resilience.

Confidence is a faith in one's ability *and* in the truth or accuracy of what one knows. A confident brain has a high degree of certitude for the truth of the information it knows. Confidence can be established using rote learning, at least for the information that has been drilled and as long as one does not encounter questions and problems one hasn't already been taught how to answer. But raising confident children includes not only helping them to have certitude in the accuracy of the information that's been stored in long-term memory but also helping them establish a belief in their abilities to overcome setbacks—an attribute that, as the previous chapter clarified, cannot be developed using rote memorization alone.

Intuitive parents know that children must discover that they have the ability to reason and solve problems on their own. Intuitive parenting naturally supports—and enhances—this process. It is noteworthy that parents can also undermine confidence by consciously or unconsciously teaching that even a child's best effort is "never good enough." To expect a toddler or preschooler to know as much as, or act like, an older child before they are sufficiently developed either mentally or emotionally is to set them up for failure. They are inadvertently being taught that no matter how successful they are, it is never good enough.

Resilience is the ability to deal with setbacks, obstacles, frustrations, mistakes, deficits, and disappointments and still maintain a positive outlook. If a child is always reliant on her parent to provide her with the answers she needs and to solve her problems or to "fix" her frustrations and disappointments ("You're right, honey, that test wasn't fair, so your low grade is the teacher's fault"), it will be very difficult for her brain to develop resiliency. Resiliency is achieved by failing, dealing with failure, and then succeeding.

Persistence is the willingness and the desire to continue working on a task even when one is not initially successful. For children, this involves continuing to put forth effort even when mom, dad, or a teacher is not standing over them providing the motivation. Some parents are persistent in pushing their children but may inadvertently neglect to help instill the internal or *intrinsic* motivation to master tasks that is prerequisite to developing persistence and perseverance. Children who have learned to solve problems and to follow their own natural, instinctive curiosity will be persistent; they don't need mom or dad to keep pushing because they've learned—and their brains have experience with—trying different approaches and trying different solutions until success has been achieved. The persistent child—and his or her brain— knows that effort will be rewarded with new knowledge and interesting discoveries, which is what intuitive parenting fosters.

Essential Mistakes and Necessary Failures

At a basic level, babies learn confidence by succeeding on their own. When they learn to coordinate the input from their eyes, arms, hands, and fingers to successfully grab a cup, for example, their success instills confidence. And the long process of learning involved in mastering the skill has also taught them the value of persistence and resilience. Parents can foster persistence by encouraging the baby to keep trying even when the baby fails, and then rewarding his or her successes with praise and approval. In the same way that this naturally occurring exercise sets the stage for whole-brain activation for problem solving in later life, parents' participation, encouragement, and demonstrated thrill at their child's successes augments and reinforces all the benefits and rewards of this natural process. As an added side effect, it naturally teaches the baby delayed gratification and the rewards of hard work as well as how to overcome the frustration of falling short of a goal.

What is delayed gratification, and why should intuitive parents try to instill this trait in their children starting when they are babies? In animal learning experiments, this simply means that the reward for a behavior doesn't get delivered instantly. After a rat has learned that a food pellet comes after pushing a lever, it will keep pushing the lever even though the pellet isn't delivered every time. Of course, if the reward *never* comes, the rat eventually stops pressing the lever, but it will be persistent with the behavior for quite a while. It is easy to overlook just how important this is in people, who can postpone gratification for much longer than a rat can! I work at my job for a whole month before I get paid, and the money I am saving for retirement won't come for at least another decade—longer if I am lucky and am able to keep working. But, it is also clear that a desire for instant gratification is very common as an inherent part of growing up—and as a powerful marketing ploy. It is the old fable of the grasshopper and the ant: One must endure labor and frustration to achieve long-term success.

The 1971 film *Willie Wonka and the Chocolate Factory* featured a character named Veruca Salt, who wanted everything right now. She even sang a song entitled "I Want It Now!" which poignantly illustrated a spoiled child who continually seeks instant gratification. One could argue that most children are predisposed to be a bit like Veruca—so as an intuitive parent, you should consciously foster development of delayed gratification. Failing to do so will have adverse consequences for your child—and for you!

There are two keys to achieving this: First, temper tantrums and other unwanted behaviors should not be rewarded by giving in. This will ensure that requests for instant gratification do not increase. Second, teach a child that having to wait for a reward is part of the family culture. As with so many aspects of development, these lessons are a natural part of intuitive parenting. When a child is young, a treat or dessert is delivered after he or she has eaten more nutritious food (and of course these "reward" foods should be limited and never given to appease a child). As a child gets older, he or she can be included in the family discussion of vacations, going to the movies, going out to dinner, and so on. "We are saving money so we can go to Universal Studios during spring break." "Your mom and I are taking sack lunches to work so that we can all go out to dinner on Saturday." "If you do your chores without being told this week, we can go see *Frozen* at the theater." These are all examples of letting a child explicitly know that there is virtue in delayed gratification and that desired outcomes do not occur without sacrifice and work.

Moreover, helping to cultivate confidence, resilience, and persistence remains key to your baby's ongoing development through toddlerhood, preschool, and on into adulthood. It is impossible to lead a life that is free from setbacks, and everyone fails at least some of the time. Naturally occurring successes and failures teach babies, and wire their brains, to have faith that their ongoing efforts will eventually pay off, even when things aren't going so well at the moment.

Suppose that, in an attempt to accelerate their baby's progress through the developmental stage of learning to grasp a cup, a parent didn't just react by putting a cup back into the baby's reach when baby knocks it onto the floor but, rather, put the cup directly into the baby's hands, molded baby's hands and fingers around it, and guided her on the movements involved in lifting it to her mouth. What learning opportunities were missed, and what did the parent actually teach the baby?

First, in this scenario the baby is not permitted to fail—or I should say, is not allowed to learn by failing and then trying again. More insidiously, the baby is learning to rely on her parent to guide her through what she needs to learn. The foundational elements of problem solving have been derailed, and the brain is deprived of the opportunity to become organized to deal with failure. In terms of confidence, the baby can follow the parent's lead and accomplish what she has been shown but will have no strategies for adapting or modifying her tactics when things go awry (say, when a cup is bigger and heavier) or when parents (or others) are not there to show her what to do. She will also learn to wait around until her parent gives her the solution to a problem. So, by setting out to show the baby how to grasp the cup, perhaps in a well-intentioned effort to accelerate her learning beyond what the developmental charts indicate or to keep her from experiencing the "pain" of failure in the false belief that this is emotionally harmful, the parent actually *prevents* the baby from developing confidence in her own abilities. The result is similar to what happens when parents lead children by the hand in teaching them how to score better on tests, and end up wiring the children's brains to become recording devices rather than reasoning devices.

In order to facilitate confidence, resilience, and persistence, parents must give their child opportunities to naturally develop these traits. Failure is not a catastrophe; it is a learning opportunity. Setbacks will not cause permanent emotional harm to your baby—in fact, they are necessary for healthy development! An intuitive parent reassures children that making mistakes is human and that no one is right all the time, and that it is fine to make a best guess or an attempt to accomplish a task, even when the guess is incorrect or the attempt is not successful. Parents can model this in everyday life by making guesses themselves, even when they don't yet know the answer. For example, you can pose a question such as "I wonder when Grandma will arrive?" and guess at an answer: "I think it will be two o'clock!" Or, you can make a guess about some fact you genuinely don't know, such as the date a particular movie was made, the name of a character in a book you read as a child but have forgotten, or some trivial factoid, such as how much a bushel of okra weighs (26 lbs.). Make a guess yourself and show your child it is nice to make a correct guess, but OK to be wrong too. Always provide positive and truthful feedback on your child's efforts: "You are right!" or "Hmm, not quite, why did you think that?" or "Good guess, try another answer!"

Confidence, resilience, and persistence and, ultimately, self-esteem are by-products of natural development. These qualities cannot be synthetically produced using contrived, artificial learning scenarios. Intuitive parenting—knowing what *not* to do, providing enthusiastic encouragement for your child's efforts, and rewarding the learning *process* and not just the *product*—is key in helping your child develop them.

Shallow Learning

How does an emphasis on rote memorization versus reasoning affect a child's development of confidence, resilience, and persistence? To answer, let me first explain the concept of shallow versus deep learning.

When a child learns using a flash-card-drill educational approach, with enough practice he or she will be able to recall and parrot the items drilled and provide correct answers for material that has been memorized. The child will have a lot of confidence recalling and reciting that information—so long as it is presented in a form they recognize. For example, it is becoming common for some parents to drill their preschooler on "math facts" for numbers from 1 to 10. They hold pictures of each number ("1," "2," "3," and so on) in front of their toddler, who is sitting in a high chair or strapped in a car seat. Or they may have their child watch a DVD or computer program that does essentially the same thing. Initially, the parent says "Look, Suzy: one" or "This is a number one." After several presentations, the child is prompted to answer a question: "Suzy, what number is this?" If the preschooler doesn't know the answer, she is then prompted: "It's a one, say 'one'!" Naming each of the numbers is established using this procedure so that in a relatively short time the toddler is saying the name for each of the numbers when prompted. That works out pretty well if the goal is to have her eventually identify a number symbol on a kindergarten readiness test or other rote recall task.

But although the child can name a picture of the number, unless quantity knowledge has also been learned and the whole brain has been engaged, she will not know much about the actual quantity this number represents. Many preschoolers I know demonstrate rote learning knowledge for numerals: When I show them a number symbol, they can correctly name that numeral. And they do this quickly as well as accurately, which is very impressive. If I hold up a printed numeral "6," they will say "six." However, when I ask them to give me six pennies after putting ten pennies on the floor in front of them, they are unable to do so. This is true even when they can name a numeral "6" symbol correctly every time when I show them a flash card or the written "6" in a book or on a computer screen. If I just went by what they could name, I would be misled into thinking that their developing brain was wired properly for math.

I call this ability to correctly identify number and letter symbols and to name pictures in the limited context of specific items when prompted "shallow" or "partial" knowledge. Teaching (and learning) beyond shallow knowledge and knowing more than just the rote answers to test items should be the goal of every parent. To get beyond shallow learning to deep, three-dimensional, whole-brain learning, *all* rote memorization should be supplemented with real-world knowledge. This is even more crucial when a child has initially been taught using rote memorization with two-dimensional cards or on screens such that their brain is already "prewired" for shallow learning. These children all too often have not touched or played with the items depicted on the cards or screens or otherwise explored them to augment the memorized information. And because they are sitting in a high chair or car seat, they have limited access to the objects they are learning about and are not given the freedom to explore the objects in their own way. In truth, rote memorization should occur only *after* a child has grasped the concept.

It is also important to bear in mind the actual learning context that rote memorization and "teaching to the test" entail. The parent or teacher is the primary or sole source of the information and also the source of the feedback on whether an item was correctly named. Also, the parent or teacher provides the nature of the reward and its delivery. The child's role is to sit back, watch the parent or teacher present the information, listen to the word or words the parent presents, and then repeat what the parent said in order to win the reward. By now it should be clear that this process does not involve any problem solving that is *initiated by the child*. No transactional learning is happening! The child learns that he is successful when he parrots the information provided by his parent or by the teacher. This approach will not foster persistence or resilience. After all, why should the child continue to exert effort when the reward (from the parent or teacher) is not present? He is being conditioned to try only when someone else is present to motivate him and gives the reward.

What happens when the child encounters information or questions that have not previously been presented in this context? In his book *NurtureShock*, Po Bronson reports on children who are identified as "gifted" at the time they enter kindergarten.[6] Naturally, the overwhelming majority of these children are very good at answering test questions that have been previewed and prompted by their parents in order for their children to qualify for gifted programs. I understand why parents are concerned with this, given how competitive our education system has become. Most parents are sincerely trying to do the best they can for their children. But children who have been trained to perform well on tests, though they might get into preferred programs, are not automatically being trained well in terms of lifelong confidence, resilience, and perseverance. If educators are uneducated enough to set up a system of rationing "gifted" classroom placement based on misguided testing, who can blame parents for figuring out how to get their children into one of these scarce places?

However, as Bronson points out, when children who have been trained this way are given problems they have not seen before or for which they have only partial information, they are far less willing to guess than are children not so trained, and will sit back and wait for the adult to provide the answer. And why should we expect them to do anything else? That is precisely the way they have been learning since they were babies, and they are very good at it. That is the way their brains have been wired from an early age, and they've been consistently rewarded for this behavior.

This kind of learning is fine for taking tests and getting good scores and gaining entrance into gifted programs in kindergarten, but what about confidence, persistence, and resilience—and a lifelong love of learning? These children have been provided with very few opportunities to learn by trial and error. They have had limited opportunities to succeed after failing. Because the correct answers are provided and their knowledge is founded upon two-dimensional shallow learning, they often have very little experience having to work through adversity and problem solving in the academic or even in the home environment. If they encounter new information that resembles what has been explicitly taught or has been drilled previously, everything goes great and they can answer questions rapidly and accurately. But when the new information doesn't resemble prior information or is presented in a way they don't recognize, their brains are not very flexible; what they've learned through rote learning and memorization is not useful to them when they attempt to divine the correct answer or find a solution to a problem. Broadly, they lack the internal motivation to use reasoning.

I administer psychological tests as part of my work at Vanderbilt University School of Medicine. In a widely used achievement test, math problems are presented both vertically and horizontally. By this I mean that the child is asked to solve problems that look like:

$$\begin{array}{r} 3 \\ +5 \\ \hline \end{array}$$

and $3 + 5 = ?$ Of course, the answer to both of these is eight. But it is not at all uncommon for children who have been drilled with flash cards to be able to answer the problem if it is presented in vertical form but not in its horizontal ($3 + 5 = ?$) version. These same children are also often unable to look at a picture with three cars on one line and five cars in the next row and correctly answer the question "How many cars are there in this picture?" I hypothesize that because many flash cards are written in the vertical form, the children are familiar with how this problem looks and "know" the answer. Indeed, one can speculate that their developing visual cortex was wired to process the vertical version of the problem. But they seem to have some trouble with the components of the actual math problem and don't seem to grasp the underlying concepts so that something as simple as changing the format from vertical to horizontal derails the ability to answer correctly.

Many kindergartners and first-graders can correctly count to three and correctly select three items, and they are also able to count to five and correctly select five items. But in order to go beyond simply recognizing a picture of the problem in vertical form, they also have to know that "plus" (+) means adding these things together and that the line underneath the vertical form and the "equal sign" (=) mean the same thing, and that whereas the answer goes under the line in vertical problems, it fits to the right of the equal sign in horizontal form. In other words, if the child understands the concepts behind the symbols, and what "plus" and "equals" mean, the format in which the problem is presented won't matter. They will recognize the actual *problem to be solved* and provide a solution.

Children who have experienced problem solving are noticeably more confident and more persistent on these kinds of tests. They may say things to themselves like "I haven't learned this kind yet, but it looks like this other one" or "I'll try adding these numbers, this looks like I should add." They also seem to have an intuition about the right answer and are remarkably transparent in their reasoning. Many seem to say things like "I think this is right, but I had to guess." In contrast, the rote memorization learners either skip the problems they don't recognize or will even say to me (as the examiner), "I don't know how to do this one" or "I can't do this one unless you show me."

To be sure, it is fine for children to indicate that they don't know how to solve a particular type of problem that they haven't encountered before. This particular achievement test for math incorporates material all the way up to trigonometric functions, and it would be highly unusual for any kindergartner or first-grader to recognize sines, cosines, and tangents. But what is striking to me is that the rote memorization or flash card learner will say "I can't do this one unless you show me" even when *exactly the same problem* that they can answer correctly in one form is presented (vertical) in a slightly different form (horizontal). They seem to make little or no effort to try to decipher the new form. If they haven't seen it on a flash card, all too often they do not have a strategy for figuring out the correct answer, even when they have at least a shallow knowledge of the information. Worse, they seem to lack confidence that they can solve the problem at all and don't make guesses or persist in trying different solutions. They either recognize the answer quickly or they don't try. They don't seem to believe they are capable of thinking their way to a solution.

Children Will Learn What You Teach Them

Human beings are naturally quite clever, and when given the opportunity, display reasoning abilities in diverse situations.[7] However, it is important to bear in mind that while reasoning means applying known information (and processes) to new information, *learning* is the by-product of *teaching*. If a child is taught to respond to flash cards or canned computer programs, that is what she will learn. If a child is taught to explore objects on her own and, by trial and error, learn how that object works and what it can do, she learns to problem-solve.

This discovery process is fundamental to learning and crucial for developing reasoning skills. A parent knows that a ball is a sphere that rolls, and can drill a child on these facts. And the child can memorize the words "a ball is round and it rolls." But a child who *discovers* these attributes and *then* maps the words onto these concepts has a deeper knowledge than the child who memorized the facts. She learned that the round shape means that a ball is more likely to stay in motion than an object of a different shape, such as a block. When a child discovers the attributes of these objects, a parent watching his or her child's play is in a position to provide the labels—ball, round, roll; block, cube, doesn't roll—at the precise time that these concepts have a real, three-dimensional meaning for the child.

You can "roll" a block, but it doesn't stay in motion very well, does it? You know this and you could tell it to your toddler, but it is far better for brain development to give the child a block and a ball and let nature take its course. Then you'll be in the perfect position to provide the input precisely at the right moment when it will have the optimal impact on learning and brain wiring. If you are spending time with your toddler and have learned to follow the child's interests and their initiations, he or she will roll the ball (a great opportunity to comment: "Roll, you rolled the ball") and push the block. The child may discover this in another way, by simply dropping the ball and the block, which will also show that the ball moves differently than the block. Because a parent already knows this about the ball and the block, it is easy to miss the fact that a toddler discovering this on his or her own is having a "eureka" moment in terms of brain development and problem solving.

The toddler's brain is learning, "Hmm, when I operate on two objects the same way, they don't act the same way!" and "Ah, this one has a different shape, and it tends to stay in motion much longer." If later handed an oblong, football-shaped object, this toddler will have a *knowledge base* for deducing how the football-shaped object will move when dropped (or rolled) and a *strategy* for testing this deduction. In contrast, a child who learns by rote may be able to parrot "a ball rolls" because he was drilled on this answer, but he will be unable to answer the question "What will this one do?" when given a football-shaped object. That child must be *told* the correct answer (which he will then remember).

Praise for Intuitive "Honest" Praise

For many years, the conventional wisdom has been that praising a child at every opportunity boosts confidence and self-esteem. In a 2015 cover article for *Southwest* magazine entitled "Enough Already! Praise Gets Heavy, Why Can't We Stop?"[8] Heidi Stevens writes: "[R]eckoning with failure is key to kids' growth, but they're buried in [sic] mountains of flattery." But if praise is so beneficial, why would parents want to cut back? In recent years, new research has shown that the wrong kind of praise—and too much praise—actually undermine confidence. Worse, unearned praise and nonspecific praise will derail natural development of resilience and perseverance. One of the leading researchers in this area is Professor Carol Dweck at Stanford University.[9] A study she completed on fifth-graders illustrates the point that the wrong kind of praise can actually backfire. In this study, children were given problems that required effort to solve but were relatively easy, so that most were able to get the correct answers. Afterward, half the students were told they were smart, and the other half were praised for their *effort* ("You worked hard!"). Then the students were given a choice of taking on more difficult problems or a test just like the first one, which they now knew they could do (that is, they were not going to learn anything new). Ninety percent of the children praised for effort were eager to take on the harder problems, but a majority of those who were simply told they were smart stuck with the easier problems they already knew they could do. Scientists argue that simply telling children they are smart—or awesome, or geniuses—actually sets them up to keep from making mistakes that will undermine the image of being "smart."

But moderating praise is easier said than done. In *NurtureShock*, Bronson[10] describes the great difficulty he had reducing and modifying this type of praise to his son—even after he became convinced that it was not good for the boy to hear it. All parents want their children to know how terrific they are, no matter what happens, but this must be balanced against the need to foster their development. In the case of praise, the old saying "You can't have too much of a good thing" is, in fact, false. Too much praise transforms a good thing into a bad thing.

It is important to know when to deliver praise and when not to, and to understand what form this praise should and should not take. If a child is praised for trivial, commonplace efforts and events ("Wow, way to go, you woke up this morning!"), your praise will lose its reward power and simply become part of the background noise. Why work for something you will get anyway, regardless of whether or not you try? Nonspecific praise like "You are awesome!" also undermines confidence, because a child has no way of knowing what this really means (awesome why? as opposed to what?) and what it takes to achieve "awesomeness."

Let's look at what makes praise a positive reward and at its role in increasing confidence, resilience, and perseverance. Remember that a reward *must* increase a target behavior or it is not a reward! In fact, if the target behavior decreases, what you think is a reward is actually a punishment. Studies on the "you are smart" and "you are awesome" forms of praise show that even though the words are positive, the desired outcome (more exercise of intelligence or continued good behavior) is reduced, so the praise actually functions as a punishment. Also bear in mind that any reward, when delivered too often, loses its power to shape behavior. The technical term for this is *satiation*. Praise delivered too often can do the same thing. It is not at all unusual for children as young as seven to "tune out" a doting parent's praise: They have become satiated with it. [11]

Also bear in mind that parental attention and response are an inherent part of intuitive parenting and can be powerful rewards in themselves. When a child brings you her latest finger painting, suppress the urge to say "You are the next Picasso!" and instead ask her what she drew (if you can't tell), why she picked the colors she did, what she was thinking about when she painted the picture, and so on. In short, show a genuine interest in her painting. This is a "praise transaction," intuitive parenting style. All people, especially children, enjoy having someone who is interested in and curious about us and what we are doing engage us in this way.

Remember, the goal of praise should be to increase desired behaviors, in this case having a child continue to express herself creatively in positive ways. In the long run, you want your child to gain confidence in expressing herself, to persist in creative endeavors, and to be resilient when encountering obstacles, challenges, and other people's differing perceptions ("Why do you think I could *not* tell that this is a picture of an elephant?"). Those behaviors and skills, not empty praise, are what will foster your child's self-esteem in the long run.

Remember, too, that your attention to and interest in what your child is doing can remain a form of praise even when he or she makes a mistake or fails to achieve a particular goal. In fact, these moments provide a valuable opportunity to reward persistence and resilience by praising *effort* and encouraging a child to try again or try another approach. Your continued engagement shows your child that mistakes are not the end of the world and don't make him or her any less intelligent or less "awesome" in your eyes.

Intuitive parents keep their focus on patiently nurturing their child into adulthood. Confidence, persistence, and resilience are important lifelong traits that will serve a child well in school, on the athletic field, and in building friendships. They will remain important for young adults in their first jobs, when they go to college, pursue a rewarding career, and form committed relationships. And these traits will be very useful indeed when these adults become parents! Let's look at some ways to nurture confidence, persistence, and resilience as a child grows.

Encourage toddlers and very young children to do simple things such as bring you their shoes, put away their toys, help you load the dishwasher, fold the laundry, weed the garden, and so on. They will learn, by watching and participating, that tasks such as these are a normal part of life. Years ago, when I built a large deck in my backyard, I had the children bring me nails and do other small chores to help out. I told them that we were making the deck together. I will admit that including them meant the job took a lot longer, but we made some good memories, and when my adult children come home, they sometimes talk about building the deck together. I also had them help when I painted, fixed pipes, and worked on the cars. These things weren't drudgery for them when they were young; they actually liked to help out. Of course, that changed over time! (With regard to working on cars, a word of caution: There is nothing more frustrating than dropping a bolt, barking your knuckles, or burning your finger on a hot exhaust pipe. Naturally, this can result in a stern one-way discussion with the car, using a rather direct vocabulary and vernacular not used in polite society, one that your kids will learn after only one presentation and, of course, repeat to their mother!)

As children get older, they can take on more responsibility. We had rotating responsibilities for washing dishes, sweeping, folding and putting away laundry, mowing the lawn, and other tasks needed to keep the household going. All the children, both boys and girls, were expected to "pull their weight" and perform these chores when it was their turn. There was sometimes wailing and gnashing of teeth, but they all learned that this did not get them out of the work. Indeed, a helpful rule was that I was always willing to listen to any complaints, but only *after* the work had been done. The children sometimes tried to complain before doing their chore, but I told them to come back when they were done. After they were done, of course, they rarely came back to complain!

Intuitive parents also model integrity and good sportsmanship—and nurture these qualities in their children. Play simple games with young children and show them that there are rules to follow. If they cheat (and it is not unusual at all for children to sometimes cheat), let them know that this is against the rules—and that there is no satisfaction in winning by cheating. When the game is over (or the race is run) make sure to congratulate the winner and request that your children do so too. It is fine to compete hard and push to excel—as Bill Gates did while growing up—but it is also important to manage temper and learn to lose with grace. And it is vitally important to cheer success in others. When a sibling, friend, or classmate accomplishes something, be it on the ball field or in the classroom, show your child by example how to be genuinely happy for that person—and not jealous or resentful.

We would sometimes set up absurd playacting to illustrate poor manners or poor sportsmanship. One night at the dinner table, several of the children were not using good manners. My wife and I were hard put to keep correcting each of them (after all, there were seven of them). So I hit on the idea of imitating their bad manners. This evolved into "pig night," when we ate outside on the deck (the one we had built together) and had to use bad manners. It was all in fun but also drove home the point that manners are important.

Teen years can be especially challenging because teens, by nature, will push the limits. Their developmental "task" at this age is to separate from you and become independent, but their early efforts to do so often mean simply rebelling against the parents they also remain dependent upon, and against any and all rules their parents have established. You may have worked hard to foster persistence in your child; now your teen may demonstrate how well they have learned that skill by persisting in testing your patience and your boundaries! It is better to have a few simple rules, and to enforce them, than to constantly nag or make threats that you have no intention of following through on. Taking away privileges is effective only if you actually take them away—and if they do have the privilege in the first place. But bear in mind that the goal is to help build your child's good character rather than to arbitrarily assert your authority for its own sake.

Of course, all of this is the result of starting off with intuitive parenting from birth. Children will naturally take on more and more discipline and responsibility and gain self-confidence if they are learning these traits from their earliest years. Because their intelligence is based on real knowledge rather than memorizing rote test items, and because they've been encouraged to keep trying when they make a mistake and have learned to successfully overcome challenges and setbacks from their earliest years, self-confidence, resilience, and persistence will be a lifelong part of their character.

- In addition to fostering intelligence, intuitive parents consciously nurture confidence, resilience, and persistence. By enlisting their children as partners in the learning process, and encouraging them to try things on their own, they teach their children that mistakes are a natural part of learning and that failure is not the end of the world.

- An intuitive parent models work as a regular part of daily life and encourages even toddlers to join in. Responsibility is fostered and developmentally appropriate tasks are expected to be completed with good effort. All children are held accountable in the sense that chores are assigned and parents positively enforce discipline.

- An intuitive parent models supporting others for their efforts and complimenting others for their accomplishments, and expects his or her child to do so as well.

- Competition is fine whenever it fits in with the family culture, but good sportsmanship, graceful winning, and especially graceful losing are *always* modeled by parents and should be expected in children.

- The goal of intuitive parenting is to build good character and lifelong "people skills" in your children. The wrong kind of praise can actually *punish* confidence, persistence, and resilience in the sense that it can inhibit the development of these traits. Genuine parental interest in their child—naturally arising from transactions and responding to a child's initiations—are a very powerful reward and a natural form of praise.

- Praise real effort rather than nonspecific attributes: "Nice try, can you do it another way this time?" rather than "You are a genius!" Mistakes are learning opportunities—so long as your child doesn't stop trying.

- Finally, it is important to nurture a sense of optimism by helping your child understand, when things are not going well,
  that they will get better. It is fine to be empathetic when they
  are sad, but to foster confidence, resilience, and persistence,
  your child will have to learn to overcome the negative feelings, doubts, and frustrations that are natural and inevitable
  parts of life.

chapter 7
Behavior–and Consequences

The brain is an amazing organ. It is the body's "command center" and ensures that a person is well equipped to survive and thrive in diverse environments. Through neural plasticity it can rewire itself to adapt to the kind of information it receives as new challenges arise. Scientists have long conceptualized the brain as a statistical computing machine:[1] It takes in an astounding amount of information and sorts and filters it in order to make the best decisions to enhance a person's odds for thriving in a particular environment and winning the competition for survival.

At the heart of this process is not only the quantity but also the *quality* of the information the brain receives. Intuitive parenting delivers high-quality input to the brain in addition to high quantity. By accompanying and interacting with their children as they encounter new situations and new problems, intuitive parents naturally wire their children's brains for adaptability—an attribute fundamental to maximizing the brain's potential. Stated simply, the brain needs accurate input, including the experience of real consequences—the by-product of explorations, mistakes, successes, failures, and results and the absence of results—in order to become properly wired.

"Real consequences" means that the results of a child's actions are natural and authentic. If a child attempts to solve a math problem or spell a word and the result is a wrong answer, the child needs this feedback. It is fine to praise effort if that is your intuition, but never tell a child that he is right when he is not. In grade school, my oldest son was on the basketball team. Once, they lost a game by a lopsided score. Many of the parents gathered around after the game and told the team that they played well. But one of my son's younger siblings said, "Wow, you guys really got creamed!" This was the plain, unvarnished truth. There is no need to berate a child when he is wrong, but it is very important to provide a developing brain with accurate feedback.

In the modern world, however, parents may be misled by popular myths, mistaken beliefs, and misinformation that inadvertently deprive their child's brain of accurate input and thereby derail proper brain development. A review of learning theory may help parents understand the importance and impact of reinforcement, rewards, and consequences.

Learning theory is the study of how humans, and human minds, acquire new information from the surrounding environment. There has been a scientific revolution in learning theory in the past century—akin to the revolution in the neurosciences—that offers a wealth of new knowledge useful to all parents. First, learning theory informs parents how to teach their children and how consequences affect development. Second, it helps parents understand why their children behave in undesirable ways and how to help *change* these behaviors. The first aspect is more straightforward than the second, which often requires some detective work on the part of the parent. But both can help you better understand how your child's brain works and how to alter its wiring in positive ways. It can also help intuitive parents understand why some learning, even when it is "by the book," goes awry.

The developing brain is predisposed to "bind" events from the different senses in time, and there is extensive neural circuitry devoted to this task.[2] And this is also true for unrelated events that inadvertently (or randomly) happen at the same time. For example, imagine that a baby is sensitive to loud noises and that her father starts vacuuming while her mother is feeding her peas. Her brain may mistakenly classify eating peas as a cause of the frightening noise of the vacuum, so that she may then refuse to eat peas in the future even if she really liked peas before this happened. The brain naturally binds events together and *learns* what is positive and negative in order to increase positive events and avoid negative events in the future. The baby then behaves in light of what she has learned—by refusing to eat her peas. Because of this, the timing of when events occur is very important, so that the brain properly and correctly associates the action with the consequence—or cause and effect. In this case, because of timing, the baby mistakenly (superstitiously) believes that the vacuum noise is a consequence of (caused by) the action of eating peas. The intuitive parent observes this kind of superstitious learning and, if eating peas is a desired outcome, makes sure to avoid vacuuming or making other loud noises in order to prevent a repetition of this mistaken association. On the other hand, when a superstition like this inadvertently occurs, which it will sometimes, an intuitive parent knows that he or she will now need to *dissociate* the events (vacuum noise and eating peas). This can be done by avoiding vacuuming while baby is eating *and* by pairing eating peas with a positive event, such as smiling and encouraging, reassuring talk.

To explore this aspect of learning and its impact on behavior in more depth, let's start by breaking learning into basic components and defining a "target behavior" as basically anything a child says or does that you can see or hear. If the child reaches for a block, that's a behavior. If she or he says "Mama," that's a behavior. If he cries, that's a behavior, and when she throws a temper tantrum, that is *really* a behavior that will get your attention. And let's acknowledge that we can infer feelings and emotions from observing behaviors. For example, when a baby cries, we infer that he is experiencing sadness, hunger, fatigue, or some other internal state that he finds aversive. Together, these ideas provide a framework for understanding how scientists studying development measure behaviors and how behaviors are learned.

Scientists recognize that any behavior can increase, decrease, or stay the same. Learning principles, which I will explain more thoroughly below, tell parents under what conditions their child's learning can increase, decrease, or stay the same, and what causes these increases or decreases (or stasis). This is very valuable knowledge, given that a goal of intuitive parenting is to increase desired good behaviors and to decrease unwanted behaviors in their children.

The Boy Who Feared White Fur Coats

In order to understand learning principles, the first step is to identify a target behavior. What is it that the parents want their children to learn? This must be done thoughtfully to understand the factors that are operating on that behavior to maintain it, increase it, or cause it to decrease. Learning science has provided the tools to do this with a high degree of accuracy and precision.

To illustrate, let's start with an animal example, since animal behavior is more straightforward and easier to control than human behavior. Assume that a scientist studying rat behavior wants to train a rat to press a lever. This skill has to be taught to the rat because rats don't normally press levers in nature (it is not an instinctive behavior). We could simply wait until the rat inadvertently pushes the lever—of course, we may have to wait a very long time, and the rat might never cooperate—but learning theory provides a training paradigm to efficiently teach a rat how to press a lever.

First, the scientist/trainer watches the rat as it wanders about the cage. Exploring its cage is instinctive behavior; the rat doesn't need to be trained to do it. Then when the rat spontaneously or even arbitrarily moves toward the lever located in the cage, the trainer delivers a food pellet to the rat in a slot located in close proximity to the lever. Notice that the trainer is responding to the rat's spontaneous initiation of the target behavior, not taking the rat in hand and moving it toward the lever, nor forcibly pressing its paw on the lever. Because the rat's diet has been under strict control to ensure that it is hungry, it quickly moves toward the pellet slot and eats the food pellet. Not surprisingly, the rat quickly repeats the behavior that produced the reward by moving toward the lever. It has learned that the consequence of moving in that direction is the appearance of a food pellet.

However, because the goal of the training is to teach lever pressing, not simply turning and moving in the direction of the lever, in the next trial, the rat has to move *closer* to the lever before the trainer provides a food pellet. Eventually, using a process called shaping, in which the rat gets the reward only when it performs a behavior ever closer to the target (lever pressing), the rat will eventually touch the lever. After another reward, it will touch the lever right away, but now the trainer gives the food pellet (the consequence) *only* after the rat actually presses the lever. From then on, the rat receives a food pellet only whenever it presses the lever.

This target behavior is easy for scientists to quantify. They can simply observe and count how many times a rat presses the lever during a specific time period, under specific conditions. Guess what happens to the number of lever presses when the rat is trained in this way and is *rewarded* for pressing the lever? Initially, before teaching started, the number of lever presses was zero. But after the rat has learned to press the lever, it will repeat this behavior dozens of times until it maxes out its physical ability to lever press. Of course, when the rat is no longer in a food-deprived state and its hunger becomes satiated by food pellets, the reward loses its power, and lever pressing declines.

The same thing is true for humans. When parents' rewards to their children reach the point of satiation, the rewards lose their power to increase behavior and instead spoil the child's motivation for those rewards and for completing the behaviors that earn the rewards. This is what was described in the last chapter: When too much praise is given, the parents' praise no longer acts as a reward for their child—especially if the child learns that they will get the praise whether they earn it or not. A rat will stop pressing the lever if it receives the food reward, even if it does not press the lever or if it is no longer hungry for a food pellet.

The key components in this learning example are the target behavior (lever press), the reward (food pellet), and the contingency of the reward. The trainer has to time the delivery of the food pellet so that the rat is engaging in the target behavior or initiating a prior behavior that can be shaped into the target behavior, or the learning process won't work and the rat will not learn to press the lever. If the timing is off, so that the rat gets rewarded for something other than the target behavior, the rat's progress toward learning to lever press gets derailed. The same thing can happen in humans.

Now let's look at how a reward system works when an intuitive parent responds to his eight-month-old child who is starting to talk. The baby's initial attempts at speech often consist of babbling, or making syllable sounds like "da-ba-da-du-ga." A parent hearing these syllables rewards his baby by looking at her and smiling. Parents will often talk back to their babies and act as if (pretend) the babbles are part of a meaningful conversation. In a process similar to how the rat was gradually taught to press a lever, these parents are intuitively teaching their babies to turn these babbles into real words. Say that the baby in this case says "da-ga." Her father looks at her, smiles, and says "Dada! You can say daddy." The baby enjoys attention from her dad, and says "da-da-da-da." Her father says "Yes, daddy!" This reward triggers even more attempts by the baby and more happy responses from her dad. My grandpa nickname is "Poppa." I picked this name in part because it is easy for babies to pronounce and learn. When I was watching baby Nina for a week when she was about a year old, I responded to her in this way and she started saying "Poppa" clearly and named me—and my picture—Poppa after only a few days.

While humans do share some of the behavioral and neural processes seen in animals, particularly in other primates, there are limitations to the lessons we can apply from the lab to your own parenting strategy. Take the infamous "Little Albert" experiments conducted nearly a century ago in 1920 by Professor John Watson and his graduate assistant Rosalie Raynor. They used loud, startling noises to teach a toddler to fear innocuous objects. The toddler, identified as "Albert B.," the son of a nurse in a local hospital,[3] was subjected to experiments that would be considered highly unethical by today's standards. Watson and Raynor used conditioning techniques previously developed by Russian psychologist Ivan Pavlov when he trained dogs to salivate when they heard a bell by ringing a bell when he fed them. After first showing Albert B. a white rat to ensure he had no instinctive fear of them, Watson and Raynor "paired" showing him the rat with clanging an iron rod. At first he showed no fear of the rat. But after they started clanging the iron rod, the little boy, frightened of the noise, began crying whenever he saw the white rat thereafter. After this training, he cried when shown the rat even after Watson and Raynor had stopped clanging the rod.

Little Albert's brain had become wired to associate the frightening sound with the white rat: The fear response he'd had to the loud clanging had been transferred, in his mind, to the presence of the rat. But even more important, Watson and Raynor found that Little Albert now also cried whenever a white rabbit, a white dog, or even a white fur coat was shown. Little Albert's brain connected the scary noise with *any* animal or object with white fur or hair. His brain learned that the noise and the white fur were associated events. (Although it was not recognized as such at the time, this is also an example of neural plasticity in action.)

The Little Albert study, and further queries into pairing—the process of creating firm (even if false) associations between actions and consequences, or causes and events—have shown that training of this nature can result in the activation of emotional control centers in the brain even when the emotional content is no longer present. It also shows that an emotional response can be transferred to objects and situations that did not originally produce those responses (as in transferring fear of a clanging rod to a rat and then to a fur coat). In short, Watson and Raynor discovered that emotional responses in the brain can be altered in humans using learning techniques. Parents see how these learned associations work all the time in modern life, for example, when harmless things such as vacuum cleaners produce terror in their toddler. Their child may have initially responded fearfully to the loud noise a vacuum makes, but subsequently she experiences fear and becomes inconsolable when she sees a vacuum or a picture of a vacuum, even when the appliance is not turned on and thus is not producing any noise.

But it is also clear that this learning technique can be used to manipulate emotions in ways that have adverse effects on normal human development. Unnatural cues can be used to distort brain function so as to condition a child to respond inappropriately or incorrectly to harmless events. Is it ethical or even reasonable to instill a hysterical fear of rabbits or fur coats in a toddler? What are the long-term negative consequences of doing this?

Such experiments showed that emotions such as fear—or happiness—can be transferred to innocuous objects in a developing child's brain. This discovery is still in wide use today—in advertising. Indeed, Professor Watson subsequently left his university career to become an advertising executive, and ultimately a pioneer in the use of "sex appeal" to sell products. He's the guy who first conceived of the idea of using ads showing attractive (if conservatively dressed, at least by today's standards) young women using a product to condition an emotional response in potential customers. As with Little Albert, the idea was to pair an emotional response, in this case attraction to a beautiful woman, with a product that might not itself be attractive in order to transfer the positive emotional response to the cigarettes, beer, shaving cream, or whatever else a company wished to sell. Inducing the brain to *transfer* the positive aspects of the attractive model to the product is a highly effective technique.

And it's a technique frequently used today to market the latest toy or game or breakfast cereal to your children, though the beautiful woman used in adult ads has been replaced, of course, with "kid-friendly" emotional appeals such as cute cartoon characters or happy children depicted using the product. One study of 147 commercials for high-calorie food products shown during children's television programs found advertisers using emotional appeals that associated their products with positives like happiness, fun, and play; peer acceptance and social enhancement; and "coolness/hipness."[4] A well-prepared, intuitive parent will anticipate advertisers' attempts to wire your child's brain in the hopes of getting them to pester you into buying the latest toy or game or snack food. After all, the Little Albert study showed how effective and long-lasting this kind of learning can be!

After a child learns to talk, intuitive parents can use verbal information to interpret and explain to children the context for behavior and consequences.[5] They can, for example, reassure a child that a vacuum cleaner is actually harmless. My oldest granddaughter, Nina, was terrified of vacuum cleaners as a baby and toddler, but when she was eighteen months old, her parents were able to patiently tell her that everything was OK and that the vacuum wouldn't hurt her. She still gets nervous when she is in the vicinity of a vacuum cleaner, but she no longer cries hysterically. In addition to using verbal information to provide reassurance, parents can also provide emotional support by hugging, smiling, and using other nonverbal communication.

Parents can also use words to inform their child about whether they will or won't purchase a desired toy. Be forewarned that young children, because their brains are convinced that the desired toy or game will make them happy, and with a time sense locked into the here and now, may be quite insistent. But intuitive parents understand that a) the insistence—which may include tantrums—is transient and based upon conditioning, not reality; b) giving in to the child after the child throws a tantrum or complains will *reward* (and thus *increase*) the tantrums and complaining; and c) they should be helping their child to develop a resistance to buying on impulse, a worthwhile goal with important, positive long-term implications for the child. It is useful to have a consistent, preplanned strategy ready when your child is exposed to advertising.

Parents' ability to interact verbally with and provide emotional support for their children is unique to humans and is a powerful influence on development. It is important to bear in mind that the strict conditioning scientists use to train and experiment on animals should *never* be used with children. Animal training and conditioning techniques were developed without reference to the complexities of human emotions and relational interconnectedness. Using such techniques to derail a brain circuitry primed to learn normal emotional responses as a child develops into a well-functioning, mentally healthy adult is definitely not a recommended parenting practice! Humans are both social and emotional, and to dispassionately separate the learning process from the supportive social and emotional context of parental nurturing can have devastating consequences—as happened in the Little Albert study. I certainly did not raise my own children as if they were animals in Pavlov's, Watson's, or Skinner's labs—even though, as a scientist, I knew how and could have done so if I wished.

But being aware of how conditioning works is vitally important for parents in recognizing when a child has learned something that is not helpful, and in being equipped to salvage the situation and get things back on track. Awareness can also help parents become intelligent consumers who can critically evaluate educational software, products, and teaching techniques to judge whether they aim to alter the normal learning and conditioning process in ways that they do not wish their baby to be subjected to, and to make informed decisions about what goes into their baby's brain.

Learning, as Pavlov's dogs and Watson's experiments with Little Albert and his advertising programs show, also alters the brain's response to a behavior. When lever pressing is paired with a reward such as a food pellet, the pleasure centers in the brain associated with food are now activated and transferred to when the rat presses the lever. And the rat will continue to lever press (or continue any other behavior that becomes associated with food) even when the food pellet is not delivered, at least for a while. The lever-pressing behavior now sends some of the same messages to the brain that the food pellet sent. Also, a rat once trained to lever press will quickly regain this behavior even when it has not had an opportunity to lever press for a long time, if it is hungry and the pellet reward is reintroduced—brain plasticity means that its brain has now been wired to lever press. The conditions that ended up wiring the brain for lever pressing have, at least to some extent, permanently altered the rat's brain. Luckily, when it comes to humans, parental mistakes—and we parents all make them—do not permanently disrupt a child's development. After all, if there were no way for a child's brain to overcome parenting mistakes, our species would have died out long ago!

But it is important to consider the long-term consequences on the child—and on her brain—when we implement new forms of learning—and rewards—such as using computer programs and rote memorization to wire a baby's brain. Just like lever pressing in rats, which is not a naturally occurring behavior and does not translate to how a rat behaves in its normal environment, parents should think through normal learning and conditioning responses, and how these are being altered, when teaching a child in a radically new way that humans have not previously experienced—ever. On the one hand, humans are amazingly adept at incorporating new technology into their daily lives. On the other hand, indiscriminate application of technologies at the wrong point in development may have unintended—and potentially adverse—consequences.

For example, indiscriminate video and computer program training in infants and toddlers (before natural conditioning has wired the brain properly) could result in unanticipated conditioning and emotional responses in their developing brains. Are normal social attachments to parents and naturally occurring rewards being altered in much the same ways as Watson and Raynor altered Little Albert's fear responses to white rats? What are the long-term consequences of displacing a child's normal trial-and-error learning and natural curiosity by pounding information into their brains from a computer screen or flash cards before normal emotional associations and pathways for learning have been laid down? Parents would be wise to think through their educational choices in terms of what their children are being conditioned to do.

One time, my wife and I were considering a fairly rigid academic environment for our youngest daughter. We liked the culture of the school as a whole, and the principal was terrific, but the class we visited was led by a drill-sergeant-style teacher. Children were not encouraged to ask questions, and the instruction was clearly based on rote recitation, no matter what lessons were being taught. Punishment for errors or classroom transgressions, in the form of negative comments and stern looks, was swift and sure. As I've mentioned elsewhere in this book, rote learning definitely has a place in teaching and in child development, for example, in helping children gain facility with math facts after they know the concepts behind those facts. But we worried that our daughter's natural curiosity and reasoning abilities would be permanently altered or displaced in that particular environment at that time in her development.

There is no way of knowing whether there would have been any harm, or benefit, for that matter, in enrolling her in that classroom because we ultimately decided on another school for her. I can say that she is now doing very well in an academically challenging college prep high school, has gotten accepted into the college she wanted to attend, and has not lost her curiosity at all. But the point here is that in the process of making our decision, my wife and I carefully considered the learning and *conditioning* context of the way in which she would be taught, and what this might do to the emotional response and reward centers in her brain.

To help parents better understand the relationship between learning, conditioning, emotional responses, and activation of reward centers, it may be helpful to describe how behavior increases and decreases during the learning process, once again first drawing on straightforward animal models as an illustration.

Reinforcement: Increasing Behavior

When a particular target behavior is being taught and learned, there are several possible outcomes. When the result of the process is that the target behavior increases, we call that process "reinforcement." It is important to understand that whenever a behavior increases, this is reinforcement regardless of whether the parent—or anyone else—*believes* it is a reward. The source of the reinforcement can be external (praise from a parent, a cookie, getting to play with a favorite toy, etc.) or internal (satisfying curiosity, a desire to learn, etc.). In addition, there are two kinds of reinforcement: positive and negative. In our rat's learning, the delivery of a food pellet as a consequence of its pressing a lever served to reinforce the target behavior of lever pressing, as is proved by the fact that the frequency of the behavior *increased*. When the stimulus (the food pellet) serves to increase the target behavior and the target behavior then increases the frequency of the stimulus, we call this "positive reinforcement."

But suppose we change up the learning paradigm. Let's start with a new rat, one that has not previously learned to press a lever for food. Now, a bright light is flashed in the cage every ten seconds, disturbing the rat, and every time the rat presses the lever, instead of receiving a food pellet, the flashing light is turned off. The consequence of the lever press is termination of the flashing light. Guess what happens to the target behavior (lever pressing)? As with a food reward, lever pressing increases, so this is a type of reinforcement; but this kind of learning is called "negative reinforcement" because the response stimulus (the consequence) of the rat's behavior is to decrease the *aversive* stimulus of the flashing light. When the stimulus is decreasing while the target behavior is increasing, we call it negative reinforcement. When people wear sunglasses to avoid glare from the sun, it's a form of negative reinforcement. If they wear sunglasses to look cool and elicit positive comments from peers rather than to avoid glare, it's positive reinforcement. When they wear sunscreen to avoid sunburn, this again is negative reinforcement.

To help you keep the distinction between positive and negative reinforcement in mind, remember that the first word ("positive" or "negative") refers to what is happening with the *stimulus* and the second word refers to what is happening to the *target behavior*. The consequence can either be increasing or decreasing, and that tells us whether the reinforcement is positive or negative.

So what do rat-learning paradigms have to do with teaching human babies, toddlers, and children? It turns out that many aspects of human learning follow these same principles. Positive reinforcement consequences for humans include attention from others; approval from others; access to desired food, toys and activities; and many other stimuli. Humans can also learn from watching others get rewarded for *their* behavior. So when a baby vocalizes and her mother talks to her and smiles in return, the mother is providing positive reinforcement that will increase the baby's vocalizations. When a baby says "wawa" and her parents give her a drink of water, saying the word "wawa" is being learned using positive reinforcement. When a toddler reaches for a book and brings it to her parent, who immediately stops whatever else he or she is doing and reads the book with her, book reading is being positively reinforced.

Negative reinforcement also works in parenting. Let's say that when a child is told to eat her vegetables, she cries and pushes the vegetables away. And let's also say that the consequence of her behavior is that she doesn't have to eat her vegetables because her parents don't want to hurt her feelings. Guess what will happen to the frequency of crying to get her way? It will *increase* as a result of negative reinforcement. The behavior (crying) increases while the consequence of not eating vegetables—or of not doing other things that her parents think she should do—decreases (or is prevented altogether). This learning process is the same for the baby as it was for the rat encountering a blinking light. The parent teaches the child—and the child learns—that crying prevents undesired (from the child's point of view) consequences, such as eating vegetables, from being delivered. Learning theory tells parents that, having learned that crying got her out of eating vegetables, this child will also cry (or, depending on her age, have tantrums, "talk back," storm out of the house, etc.) to get out of doing other activities she may not like, such as cleaning her room or washing dishes—unless her parents address the unintended consequences of what she learned by refusing to eat vegetables!

I encounter this a lot in my work with children. Parents worry that if they insist that vegetables be eaten rather than child-preferred foods such as pizza, French fries, chicken nuggets, or dessert, their child's feelings will be hurt. The children I work with often have very strong tantrums, and many of them have been able to use negative reinforcement to shape their parents into giving them the foods they want—or else.

On the face of it, both positive and negative reinforcement have the same outcome because both increase the target behavior. However, an animal's physiological responses, including the brain chemicals associated with stress, are higher when a learning process involves negative reinforcement. Preventing an aversive consequence (a flashing light) is much more stressful than receiving a food pellet. This is true for humans too. Physiological markers for stress, including increased heart rate, sweating, and increases in a stress hormone called cortisol, all occur when trying to avoid an aversive event (negative reinforcement).[6] Positive reinforcement activates the pleasure/reward centers in the brain, whereas negative reinforcement activates the stress/fear centers. Of course, there are times when negative reinforcement is a useful part of learning in humans. For example, "Wear your coat outside or you'll get cold" is a practical example of negative reinforcement. The target behavior is wearing a coat outside when it is cold and the consequence is getting frostbite, or at least being cold. In this case, the target behavior *increases* (coat wearing) while the consequence is *prevented* (not being cold). We must all do things to prevent bad consequences (e.g., we have to work to earn money in order to prevent bankruptcy), and we certainly want our children to learn that as well. But in general it is better to help a child learn using positive reinforcement. If there is a choice, try to use appropriate rewards such as earned praise and natural positive consequences rather than aversive negative reinforcement.

The same is true with adults. A boss who praises good work, and gives raises to those who work hard, can improve productivity—and job satisfaction. In contrast, a boss who yells and threatens workers with job loss can also increase productivity—but will also succeed in increasing stress and lowering job satisfaction, which may lead to unintended negative business consequences.

Learning Theory: Decreasing Target Behavior

Positive and negative reinforcements inform parents about factors that increase target behaviors, but what about decreasing target behaviors? Sometimes we may wish to limit or eliminate our children's unwanted behaviors, such as spitting food, hitting a sibling, or throwing a tantrum.

Again, animal learning models are helpful. Imagine that a rat that has previously learned to lever press by receiving a food pellet now gets a slight electric shock, instead of a food pellet, whenever it presses the lever. What will happen to the target behavior? It will decrease, of course, and rather quickly. This kind of decrease is called "punishment," a word that has taken on negative connotations in today's society; parents hearing it may conjure up images of severe beatings and other inhumane practices that, sadly, are in the news today all too often.[7] However, in learning theory, *any* consequence that results in a decrease in the target behavior is called punishment.[8] Practical examples of punishment include a time-out, during which a child is required to sit in a chair for a specified amount of time after misbehaving, or having to do an aversive chore. Getting yelled at when you hit your brother is another form of punishment. Note that these are examples of punishment *only* if they actually reduce the target (unwanted) behavior. And what is an effective punishment for one child may not be for another. My youngest daughter would absolutely melt when I sent her to her room, but some of my other children seemed to consider staying in their room a reward! My youngest son liked to draw, so going to his room was no big punishment at all. But a time-out worked for him if it meant sitting in a corner in the dining room—and not being able to draw to pass the time.

Another way to decrease behavior is through what we call "extinction." Extinction occurs when a behavior that was previously learned is no longer rewarded. When its trainer stops delivering food pellets to our lever-pressing rat, given that lever pressing is not an instinctive activity for rats, the frequency of lever pressing will slowly decrease to zero again, just as it was before training. A behavior is said to be "extinguished" whenever it decreases and ultimately ceases after the reward is removed.[9] In extinction, unlike punishment, no aversive stimulus is delivered. Rather, the reward is taken away.

Let's look at how punishment and extinction play out in human behavior. One of the things I do in my work is to teach children who are having trouble learning to talk how to speak more clearly. That is, I help them learn how to pronounce their words more accurately, rather like the character Henry Higgins in *My Fair Lady* (although unlike Professor Higgins, I do *not* put stones in the children's mouths as Rex Harrison did to Audrey Hepburn in the film!). I once worked with a boy who was struggling with the "l" (as in Lego). Using positive reinforcement learning methods, whenever this child produced a correct "l" sound, I gave him a sticker. Over time, the child's production of the "l" sound and his speech in general improved, thanks in large part to the positive consequence of the sticker.

The next semester, however, the child went to work with another clinician, who told me that his correct pronunciation of "l" was decreasing. I asked her what approach she was taking, and she said the consequence of his correct "l" during speech practice was to give him a sticker, just as I had done. So what had changed?

When I asked the child about what he thought was happening, the actual nature of the learning reinforcement came to light. It turned out that I had been giving him stickers from a popular children's cartoon called *Teenage Mutant Ninja Turtles*. The next clinician thought these cartoon characters were too violent, so she was giving him stickers from another cartoon, *Barney*. Barney was a meek and goofy purple dinosaur who taught preschool children positive lessons about manners, and for the boy, getting stickers from this show (when questioned, the child reported that Barney didn't have weapons like the Ninja Turtles) not only didn't provide positive reinforcement, it seemed like a punishment.

Despite the clinician's good intentions, from a learning perspective, she was actually *punishing* correct "l" production. Though she *thought* she was using positive reinforcement, because the behavior was decreasing, it could not have been positive reinforcement. For this boy, Barney stickers were not rewards like the Ninja Turtle stickers were. Sure, other children may increase their target behavior when Barney stickers are a consequence, and that may have been the clinician's previous experience. But in this case these stickers were not reinforcing, they were punishing—to this child. The target behavior (a correctly pronounced "l") decreased when the consequence (a Barney sticker) was provided.

In the example of sending my daughter and my son to their rooms as a form of punishment, it was actually a punishment only for my daughter. The unwanted behaviors *decreased* when she was sent to her room. But, for my son, being sent to his room had no effect on his unwanted behaviors. Therefore, it wasn't a punishment. It didn't matter that I thought it would be a punishment for him; it was not. We had to use a different consequence, in this case, sitting in a chair in the corner of the dining room, to effectively decrease his undesirable behaviors.

These examples illustrate what can happen when *beliefs* about the nature of learning and the reward value of consequences overwhelm the actual data. Whether you view something as positive or negative does not necessarily mean that the learning paradigm follows those beliefs. Be sure to see if your child is actually learning the way you think—it may not be working out quite like you thought.

This happens all the time when parenting. We have a preconceived view or bias about what the consequence is supposed to do and assume that learning is happening in the way we imagine. But reality intrudes all too often. What we think is a reward may be a punishment, and what we think is a punishment may be a reward. The only way to know for sure is to actually observe the *results* of our teaching. If the target behavior is increasing, it is being reinforced; no matter what we think should be happening, it *has* to be because of either positive or negative reinforcement. If the behavior is decreasing, it *has* to be due to punishment or extinction, no matter what we believe.

I remember another example from my experience treating a child who has autism. I used behavioral learning principles to get his tantrums under control so he could join the regular classroom. By the time he started school, his home tantrums were a thing of the past. But at school his tantrums started up again and began increasing. When I visited the school and completed what is called a "functional behavioral analysis," I learned that the consequence for his tantrums in school was to be taken out of the classroom and put in a separate "time-out" room. The teachers told me that the purpose of the time-out was to reduce the frequency of the tantrums.

The time-out was designed to be a consequence for the target behavior (tantrums) that they were attempting to decrease. Because other children may find being removed from the classroom and placed in a time-out to be an aversive consequence, the teachers assumed that that is what would happen for this child as well. My data showed that, in reality, the time-out was functioning as a *reward* for his tantrums. The target behavior was actually increasing following the imposition of the consequence. Because children with autism usually display a reduced motivation for social interaction, it is perhaps not surprising that he learned that throwing tantrums would get him away from social situations he did not like—via the time-out. In short, the time-out was a *desirable* consequence for him and acted in the same manner as a food pellet does for a rat learning to press a lever: It was positive reinforcement.

No matter what the parent or teacher believes is happening, if tantrums are increasing, they are being reinforced. Similarly, if vocabulary learning is decreasing, it is being punished (or extinguished). All behaviors that are increasing are, in some way, being positively and/or negatively reinforced, and all behaviors that are decreasing are being punished or extinguished. It is often useful to check our assumptions about learning and to carefully observe what is happening to the target behavior. If we wish to teach a child to read, is our encouragement increasing this behavior? If not, a different consequence (reward) is needed. Is our child's problem solving decreasing? If so, how is it being punished or extinguished? How can we get a child to clean his room? Remember, the only way to increase a target behavior is through positive or negative reinforcement. We can shape (teach) and reward a clean room with praise or some other reward (positive reinforcement) or by preventing an aversive activity from happening: "If you clean your room, you can skip doing the dishes." Or "If you clean your room, you don't have to eat Brussels sprouts for dinner tonight." I happen to like Brussels sprouts, but some of my children did not.

To make things even more interesting for parents, individual children within the same family may have very different responses to exactly the same consequence. I've already mentioned that this was true for time-outs, but here's another example: For my youngest child, a disapproving look was an effective punishment; the behavior that generated this consequence usually decreased. In some of my other children, a disapproving look definitely was not a punishment because it seemed to have no impact whatsoever on their behavior. And in one child, who was a bit on the defiant side, disapproving looks from me seemed to actually reinforce the mischief. For this child, I had to find other consequences in order to decrease unwanted behavior.

The Power of Intermittent Consequences

A question that is bound to come up in your mind, if it hasn't already, is how often a reward or a punishment has to be delivered in order to increase or decrease a target behavior. As a parent, do I have to carry around large bags of M&Ms or other rewards like an animal trainer at Sea World in order to teach my children? Do I have to give them a reward every time they do a desired behavior? Learning science provides answers to these questions, and, thankfully, these answers are not problematic for intuitive parents. Let's return to the lever-pressing example again to illustrate those answers.

There are literally infinite ways of scheduling food pellet delivery in rats. A trainer can deliver a food pellet every single time the rat lever presses. The trainer could give a pellet every other time the rat lever presses, every third time, every fourth time, and so on. This schedule, wherein food pellets are delivered according to a predetermined, consistent pattern, is called "fixed interval" and allows the rat to predict precisely which lever press will deliver a food pellet. But the best food delivery schedule for maintaining a learned behavior such as lever pressing is a "variable interval," in which the rat *cannot* predict precisely which lever press will deliver a food pellet. A variable reward schedule turns out to be an optimal learning condition.

This is great news for parents. It means they do not have to "helicopter" over their child to deliver a reward every single time the child demonstrates a desired behavior, nor count up to a specific number of times the child demonstrates the behavior to deliver a reward on a fixed schedule. Just so long as rewards that maintain or increase the target behavior are provided intermittently, the reinforcement will be effective. In fact, a variable and intermittent schedule is actually beneficial. Rewards can be delivered in a reasonable manner using a flexible schedule that does not have to be slavishly followed.

This is not the case when it comes to punishment. Because punishment produces a stress response rather than a pleasure response (as is the case with a reward), delivering the consequence *consistently* is more effective (and humane) than using a variable, inconsistent schedule. Common sense also tells us that if a child's undesirable behavior is producing some kind of reward (as was the case for the child whose crying produced the reward of not having to eat vegetables), consistent consequences will be required to decrease it. Otherwise, the child will still intermittently be rewarded for her undesirable behavior (e.g., she still sometimes doesn't have to eat vegetables), which as I've explained above, will maintain or even increase the unwanted behavior. Also, it is extremely stressful for a child not to be able to predict when a behavior will result in an aversive consequence, and stress can have negative unintended consequences extending well beyond the particular targeted behavior. Parents need to think through which of their children's behaviors they want to increase using positive reinforcement, and then must be sure to reward them periodically. Likewise, parents should think through which behaviors they are hoping to decrease, and then be vigilant in ensuring that whatever consequence they impose is delivered consistently.

In two-parent homes, it is also important that the parents agree upon the target behavior to be rewarded or to be decreased, and to make sure they are consistent both in delivering rewards and imposing consequences. Children will learn more efficiently and display lower stress responses, both behaviorally and neurologically, if parent responses to target behaviors are *predictable*. Plus, some children are clever at playing parents against each other in order to derail the learning process.

If my wife and I could not agree on the importance of diminishing a target behavior or on the consequence for a target behavior, we set that behavior aside and went on to another behavior where we were in accord. Although it is impossible even for one parent to be 100 percent consistent, parents should strive to develop a mutually agreed-upon game plan for responding to unwanted behaviors and to rewarding learning goals. This not only reduces their children's stress, it reduces their own. By having a unified game plan, parents are prepared to respond to their children's needs in a calm and rational manner, and can avoid some of the conflicts that can arise in the heat of a challenging parenting moment or situation. If parents do not agree on what to reward— or to decrease—it is better to work together on a different target behavior wherein there is agreement about what should be taught and what the positive or negative consequence should be. You can always teach the discordant behavior after each of you has had a chance to think through the other parent's perspective and, when ready, tackle that behavior with a united front.

What about rewards? Do we need to carry around treats and candy (and contribute to the ongoing childhood obesity epidemic) in order to consistently reward children and properly wire their brains? Of course, the answer is no. There are all different kinds of consequences that stimulate the reward centers in the human brain. Parental approval, smiles, attention, verbal praise, access to toys, hugs, trips to the park or pool or grandparents' house are all potential rewards that can serve as positive reinforcers. To be sure, food treats are powerful rewards too, and there is no harm in occasionally delivering these to a child when he or she has earned them.

The caution here is that a frequent delivery of ice-cream cones or indeed any other reward will produce satiation in addition to delivering empty calories, such that the child will no longer engage in the target behavior in order to earn the reward. Or worse, she might demand the reward even though it has not been earned and emit screams, have tantrums, or indulge in other unwanted behaviors in order to obtain the reward. *Never* reinforce any unwanted behavior such as a tantrum, because it will only increase in frequency and intensity if it is rewarded even very intermittently. If a child receives a reward as a consequence for a tantrum or any other unwanted behavior, it may calm her down in that moment and get you out of the store without causing a scene or staunch the fury of fellow airplane passengers, but be aware that your child will be much more likely to pitch an even worse tantrum in the near future and that the meltdowns will increase in intensity—at the worst possible times. You, not your child, will experience the negative consequences!

In essence, the child in this situation has turned the tables on her parents and has become the trainer. She is cleverly, but of course not maliciously, using negative reinforcement to increase access to rewards such as candy or toys and using her own aversive behavior to control her parents' behaviors. Think it through: From the child's perspective the target behavior is your delivery of a piece of candy or a chicken nugget or a desired toy. To induce you to provide the target behavior, she screams or cries. Then she trains you to prevent or reduce the duration of her screaming and crying—which is aversive to you—by delivering the treat! You have now become the rat that was pressing a lever to turn off a flashing light.

Don't let your child become the trainer! Parents do best to extinguish tantrums right from the get-go and to reward the child with hugs and soothing words only *after* the tantrum has run its course. You want to be sure to reward the child for calming down, not for having the tantrum. (I'll discuss tantrums further, the important things children learn from them, and my own experiences dealing with tantrums while raising my own kids, in Chapter 10.)

Another important principle is that responses can be conditioned and consequences transferred to other rewards as well. This is the positive version of the kind of conditioning that Watson used in the Little Albert experiment, and it occurs naturally in babies. For example, when a mother feeds her baby, she is at the same time holding the baby close and probably talking soothingly. Whereas Watson used a rat paired with a loud clanging noise to elicit Little Albert's fear response and then conditioned him to associate his fear of the rat with white furry things in general, including a fur coat, the mother is conditioning the baby to associate the pleasure of eating with being held close and hearing her soothing words and tone of voice.

This kind of natural learning is important in humans because pairing the primary reward (in this case, food) with secondary rewards (hugs and soothing talk) means that hugs and soothing talk can then also produce the physiological responses that the primary reward itself produced. This is just like what happened to Little Albert and Pavlov's dogs but in a happy and special way that also builds emotional bonds between mother and baby.

Because this powerful form of conditioning occurs naturally in the course of caring for a baby, its significance is easy to overlook. But in truth, the natural, intuitive act of cuddling and talking to a baby while feeding him or her, and what that teaches the baby, lays the foundation for a lifetime of learning. It is far more important than trying to wire a baby's brain for rote learning, or trying to accelerate the acquisition of knowledge. When you feed your baby and hold him or her close and talk in the sweet, special way that mothers (and fathers too) talk to their babies, be sure to pat yourself on the back: You are also laying the groundwork both for learning and (in terms of neural circuitry) for a lifetime of positive learning for your baby in a way that educational DVDs, flash cards, computer programs, and even the most brilliant professional educators, child psychologists, or child development specialists never could.

- A developing brain needs authentic and accurate input—and so does your child. Always be nurturing, humane, and positive, but do not deceive your child by telling him or her that they are right when they are not.
- Learning principles, when properly understood, are very helpful to an intuitive parent. Be observant and check to see whether your parenting is working as you hoped. Always consider what the child is learning.
- Bear in mind that what is rewarding—or punishing—to one child may not be for another. Just because a parent thinks something is a reward or a punishment doesn't mean it will work that way. Being sent to her room was a punishment for my youngest daughter—but not for my youngest son.
- Think about the results of a child's undesirable behaviors. If she cries to get out of eating her vegetables—or throws a tantrum to get out of doing a chore—and is successful, she is being *rewarded* for crying and throwing tantrums. Children need to learn from an early age that these behaviors will not get them what they want.
- Positive reinforcement, negative reinforcement, and punishment (and extinction) are all effective learning techniques. But, when possible, it is better to use positive reinforcement than punishment or negative reinforcement because these latter forms of learning increase stress levels.
- However, it is not possible to avoid all forms of negative reinforcement or punishment. There are times when negative consequences must be part of an intuitive parent's tool kit. These should always be humane—neither verbally nor physically abusive—and a parent should deliver them in a calm, low-key, neutral tone.

- Don't add shame to the punishment or consequence. A child may indeed experience your shaming tone as a negative consequence, which may be effective in changing a target behavior in the short term. But shaming can have many other unintended and damaging consequences on your child's emotional development and on the parent-child relationship. Remember that your child is misbehaving because he or she has not yet learned how to behave, not because he or she is "bad" or undeserving of your unconditional love.

- Catch them "being good" and praise that—when they resist a tantrum, notice it and compliment them.

- If you are angry, as will happen, wait until you are calm before delivering a consequence (easier said than done but always the desired goal).

- Don't try to work on every behavior at the same time. Prioritize, then target only one or two high-priority behaviors at a time. And balance increasing good behaviors and reducing unwanted behaviors so that your child hears praise for good behavior at least as much—and ideally much more—than he receives feedback and consequences for undesired behaviors. After progress is made, add the next behavior on the list. If you try to reduce too many unwanted behaviors at the same time, a child may get the mistaken impression that you view him as a bad child with many faults.

Have a game plan. Anticipate a child's behavior so that you are ready to respond. If you are shopping and you pass the candy or toy aisle, be ready for a tantrum and know ahead of time how you will react.

chapter 8

Intuitive Parenting, Education, and Schools

Kindergarten Then and Now

I started kindergarten in the fall of 1961. The first day of school, I caught a Bluebird school bus on the corner of a busy street near our house, proud that I walked the two hundred yards or so on my own. My fifth birthday was still more than a month away, so I was by far the youngest in my class. Most of the other children were five years old, and some were even six. Even the girls were bigger than I was. And because I didn't start talking until I was nearly three and a half, I was still behind in my speaking and under-standing ability, and a bit shy as well.

Our school day was not complicated: I caught the bus at 8:00, arrived at school at 8:30, and left at 11:30 in order to be home in time for lunch. I attended the morning kindergarten; a similar program ran in the afternoon, from noon until 3:30. Because this was during the tail end of the American baby boom, classes were crowded. There were nearly thirty children in my kindergarten class, and the national average for student-teacher ratio in 1960 across all grades in public schools was slightly under twenty-six students per class.[1]

At school, a kind teacher greeted us and showed us where to hang our coats and sweaters. In her classroom, there were no desks or tables and chairs. Instead, there was a tile floor with a big oval rag rug. There were bookshelves along the walls, with only a few books (mostly picture books)—and no chalkboards. A mural depicting the alphabet in large letters and Arabic numerals from 1 to 10 ran around the top of the bookshelf.

Instead of books, the shelves held many wondrous things: seashells, nuts and seeds, leaves of various kinds and colors, and lots of glass rectangular terraria that held gopher snakes; hamsters; guinea pigs; mice; a flat, round horned lizard we called a horny toad; and, best of all (at least for the boys), a live tarantula. There were aquaria too, one with fish and one with frogs and tadpoles.

The kindergarten itself was located in a small, fenced-in area apart from the rest of the school, which held classrooms through sixth grade. There were two kindergarten classrooms, designated "A" and "B," arranged side by side like a duplex, in the yard. We had our own playground with small swings, teeter-totters, a slide, and a small merry-go-round. There were plenty of tricycles, wagons, and scooters too. The playground was in a hard-packed-dirt area, circled by a sidewalk about four feet wide where we could ride, push, or pull the wheeled toys.

The program of study included two recess times as well as a nap time, a snack time, and a reading time. We also had a time when the teacher would stand by a terrarium or an aquarium and tell us about the animals or fish inside. Snack time included cookies or square pieces of cake along with small cartons of milk.

After nap time, we children would gather in front of the teacher while she read us a very short story. But having to sit still in a circle and listen to the story was not compulsory, so some of us, including me, walked around and looked at the animals and fish while she read. So long as we were quiet while she was reading, this was not a problem. After reading each page, she turned the book to show the picture on that page.

We were not required to read or write or complete work sheets. We did draw and make things with paste and construction paper and sometimes craft "art" out of Popsicle sticks, and when we brought these items home, our mothers seemed to treasure them. We also had plaster of Paris and cast small statues in molds the teacher gave us.

The main focus of kindergarten in those days was on acclimating children to school and exposing them to academic instruction and topics, such as reading and numbers, that would be taught explicitly in *later* grades. The guiding educational philosophy was to nurture every child's latent curiosity as a foundation for the more structured education that would come later in grammar school, middle school, and high school. Exploration and learning to think were considered far more important than rote memorization. Indeed, there were no tests, and the only memorization was learning one's address and phone number, which was drilled into each of us in case we got separated from our class or from our families. And this approach to early education was by no means unique to my own experience;[2] it was a standard model for kindergarten for more than a century.[3]

Things have changed dramatically for young children today. I regularly visit kindergarten classrooms in my work as a child development specialist, and the transformation is striking. All the classrooms I visit have tables and chairs, or desks, regardless of reasonable expectations of what four- or five-year-olds are developmentally ready for. Children spend much time sitting at desks completing written work sheets on numbers and letters. The culture has changed right along with the furniture: Learning activities are compulsory, so that sitting still and listening while the teacher reads a story is not optional. And unfortunately, because these are part of my fondest memories of kindergarten, the terraria and aquaria are nowhere to be found. Heaven forbid that a teacher would keep a live tarantula in a classroom! And by the end of the academic year, today's kindergartners will be expected to read, write, and complete math problems that were end-of-the-year goals for first-graders as recently as 1980.[4]

In a teacher survey published in the late 1980s, the following example of "exit skills" were reported for kindergartners: label body parts (head, nose, mouth, etc.), label primary colors, label primary shapes (triangle, square, circle), count from 1 to 20, order three items according to size (big, bigger, biggest), hold a pencil correctly, name the letters of the alphabet, use paste or glue, and name days of the week. With regard to work habits, the students finishing kindergarten were expected to sit appropriately in a group, focus attention on the teacher, not disrupt peers, and to wait appropriately.[5] (Perhaps as a harbinger of the oncoming push for acceleration in the 1990s and 2000s, this survey also showed that the prevailing kindergarten exit skills were increasingly being taught by preschool teachers, essentially extending these expectations to a younger age.)[6] Now, it seems that many three-year-olds starting preschool are expected to know what exiting kindergartners knew only a generation earlier.

Reading through these data, I couldn't help wondering whether charging high tuition for day-care placements hasn't been at least a contributing reason for the dramatic push for accelerated academics. Schools competing for tuition may have been marketing the higher academics to middle-class parents. From a scientific viewpoint, it is difficult, if not impossible, to test this hypothesis, but there are indirect hints that this may have contributed to the trend.[7]

In contrast, a sample list of modern kindergarten items includes, in addition to identifying shapes and naming letters, counting from 1 to 50, writing numbers from 1 to 50, counting 10 objects, adding and subtracting by 1s, 2s, 3s, 4s, and 5s, printing one's first and last name, reading high-frequency words, and writing written text from a model. Many of these latter items appeared in earlier decades as first-grade material. To make matters even more daunting for today's kindergartners, they must also "read and comprehend at the .75 reading level as measured by classroom assessment tools (e.g., DIBELS, SM, AR, STAR Reader, Wright Group) and/or MAP test." (These are all standardized tests children have to take.) These poor souls are also expected to "have a math level of .75 as measured by SM, MAP, and/or classroom assessment tools." And the school district from which these criteria were taken requires that parents read and sign a paper stating that they have reviewed these exit criteria for their children.

Kindergarten is now a regimented, highly organized enterprise, often set up in conformance with the Common Core curriculum. The Common Core sets forth universal benchmarks for students to attain at each grade level in mathematics, social sciences, science, and English and language arts.[8] Kindergarten is not spared. According to the Common Core Mathematics Standards in Kindergarten, "Instructional time should focus on two critical areas: (1) representing and comparing whole numbers, initially with sets of objects; (2) describing shapes and space. More learning time in kindergarten should be devoted to numbers than to other topics."[9] The general focus of the Common Core curriculum is consistent with what I experienced in my own kindergarten many years ago: My teacher would count tadpoles, leaves, rocks, and so on, and would show us various objects and tell us about their shape. But in those days, this material was not introduced or "taught" through drill-based instruction; we were simply *exposed* to the concepts in the context of a concrete narrative.

Today, the nurturing, intuitive orientation we experienced has been replaced with didactic instruction and an expectation that kindergartners "master" the material on a written test. Common Core standards for "Grade K" have replaced the old-school, generic orientation to whole numbers using sets of objects and describing shapes in space. The standards define specific "knowledge modules" that each child is expected to learn, including "counting and cardinality," "operations and algebraic thinking," "numbers and operations in base 10," "geometry," and "mathematical practices."[10] These topics are further segmented into instructional content that supports each module.

FOR EXAMPLE, "MATHEMATICAL PRACTICES" *MANDATES* THAT CHILDREN SHOULD ATTAIN THE FOLLOWING EIGHT COMPETENCIES:

1) make sense of problems and persevere in solving them,

2) reason abstractly and quantitatively,

3) construct viable arguments and critique the reasoning of others,

4) model with mathematics,

5) use appropriate tools strategically,

6) attend to precision,

7) look for and make use of structure, and

8) look for and express regularity in repeated reasoning.

These competencies are far beyond the skill level of even many advanced four-, five-, and six-year-old children. To be sure, by using coercion and drill, it is certainly possible to induce children at this age level to parrot these skills, but few will actually master the underlying reasoning behind the concepts. When state-mandated testing is the measure of success, however, teachers are required to emphasize rote memorization for test items rather than the independent thinking and thinking abilities underlying the content being taught.

Parents reading this might be thinking: "But the modern world, relative to 1960, is much more complex! In order to compete in a global society my child must be ready to take on this information in kindergarten," or "I know this is unreasonable, but this is what the other children in kindergarten are doing and I must prepare my child to excel in this context."

It is important to address both of these issues head-on. First, in 1961, when I started kindergarten, the *Apollo* moon landing was nearly a decade away, and items such as the Internet, desktop and laptop computers, smartphones, and tablets either had not been invented or were decades away from being widely available. We didn't even have calculators! No kindergarten teacher could have devised a "common core" curriculum to explicitly prepare us for inventions and information beyond her imagination. But what we did see in action in education in the 1960s was an optimistic awareness that the world would be a more complicated place in the future—and a conviction that young minds had to be nurtured and shaped for thinking and reasoning ability so that children would be able to *learn* about new inventions and readily incorporate them into their lives in that more complex future. In addition to encouraging students to develop problem-solving skills, educators made an explicit effort to encourage independent thinking, which likely accounts for the fact that, despite the scornful looks from my teenage and twentysomething children, I can and do use my smartphone and laptop and other modern technological devices productively both in my work and in leisure activities. And, thankfully, I no longer have to use a slide rule for complex mathematical computations!

In the 1960s, we also knew that learning to read was the key to accessing all the wonderful knowledge that was out there, both in terms of what was known in 1961 and in terms of ideas yet to be discovered and written about. National testing data show that children in kindergarten in 1961 had much higher reading comprehension rates by the time they reached high school than children have today, even though there were no "preliteracy" lessons and formal reading instruction was not initiated until second grade.[11] Further, while young children were expected to recite fewer facts, they were expected to understand concepts thoroughly. And children were not permitted to progress in school until they had mastered the core knowledge the next learning steps were founded on.

Kindergartners educated in 1961 in the United States would be at the top of educational achievement among developed countries, but those educated more recently, using rote learning and through misguided attempts to accelerate learning beyond all reasonable expectations for four-, five-, and six-year-olds, have fallen to eighteenth place in world rankings of developed countries. And this precipitous drop in ranking has occurred within the last twenty to twenty-five years, precisely coinciding with a shift in American teaching philosophy pushing these skills earlier and earlier.[12] If you teach your children to reason and focus on building their math and reading skills at a reasonable, developmentally appropriate pace, they will be very well equipped indeed to compete with their peers who are being force-fed "knowledge" their young brains are not yet ready to learn.

The Education Assembly Line

Just as expectations for what children should learn in kindergarten today have risen precipitously, so have expectations at each subsequent grade level through elementary and middle school—regardless of the very natural differences in children's development and readiness. You'd think, given the nationwide push to teach children more and more complex concepts at earlier and earlier ages, that there surely must be an extensive scientific literature to support these efforts. Not only does no such data exist, but an emerging body of research indicates that attempts to accelerate intellectual development are in fact counterproductive. Recently, a lead editorial in one of the most prestigious scientific journals in the world, *Science*, questioned why middle school children were being taught college- and even graduate-school-level cell biology concepts when their developing minds were not yet ready to receive this complex information. How meaningful was rote memorization of features such as the Golgi apparatus, the editorial asked, if the children had not been taught the knowledge foundations and acquired problem-solving abilities in the underlying areas of cell structure, chemistry, and biology?

This problem is captured eloquently in an essay entitled "Trivializing Science Education" by Dr. Bruce Alberts, editor in chief of *Science*. In addition to being the editor of this publication, Dr. Alberts is a professor emeritus in the Department of Biochemistry and Biophysics, University of California, San Francisco, and an accomplished scientist in his own right. He has served on science education review boards for the State of California and is certainly well qualified to comment on current methods of teaching science to children. Professor Alberts writes:

> Few people are aware of what has been learned from research about the teaching of complex scientific concepts to young people, and there is a strong tendency to assume that the best science curricula are the most "rigorous." Although rigor might appear to be a worthy goal, the unfortunate result of this persistent view is that difficult concepts are taught too early in the science curriculum, and they are taught with an overly strict attention to rules, procedure, and rote memorization. . . . [F]or my grandchildren, "science" includes being able to regurgitate the names of parts of the cell in 7th grade, after memorizing terms such as Golgi apparatus and endoplasmic reticulum. Those of

us who are passionate about science have thus far failed to get *real science* taught in most of our schools. Is it time to regroup with a different strategy [emphasis added]?[13]

The answer to Dr. Alberts's question is a resounding *yes*. It is indeed time to regroup, because this is not only happening in science education, it is endemic to the entire educational enterprise, starting with preschool. Worse, the emphasis on "an overly strict attention to rules, procedure, and rote memorization" has extended even into the cradle, manifesting as "helpful guidance" to parents about how to "prepare" babies for future academic demands.[14] Worse, the approach is displacing commonsense, intuitive nurturing time with "schoolwork" at home and in preschools across the country at ever younger ages.

Unfortunately, several factors are coalescing in modern society to change the emphasis in education from the development of reasoning to increased rote learning. Foremost is the ongoing pressure to "prepare" a baby's brain to participate in traditional school-style learning at ever earlier ages.[15] Many have questioned the wisdom of doing this, and a number of leading scholars have publicly worried about whether these efforts are damaging our children and stunting their intellectual growth.[16] But so-called success in school is a high-stakes enterprise that weighs on the minds of parents from the time the baby is born, or even sooner.

I noticed one day that a colleague on the faculty at Vanderbilt University School of Medicine, who usually has a low-key, even personality, was visibly agitated. I asked him what was wrong and he said that his son was taking an entrance exam that day—not for college or even for a "magnet" high school—but for kindergarten! This particular kindergarten is in a prestigious private school where many wealthy Nashvillians and faculty members from local universities send their children. These parents evidently compete fiercely for the opportunity to pay more than $18,000 per year for kindergarten, in the hopes of later paying more than $20,000 per year for a well-regarded private high school so that their children will get into the "right" college to the tune of $40,000 or more per year. The demand for places in this kindergarten is so high that the administrators can afford to cherry-pick the most "advanced" children and, in essence, inadvertently misuse a popular kindergarten readiness test as an entrance exam. And because parents are busy teaching their children the answers to the test, it takes a better score every year to get in.

It seems absurd that any parent should need to be anxious about his or her preschooler being tested for "eligibility" for kindergarten. But my colleague genuinely (and unfortunately) believed that his child's entire future was riding on whether he scored well enough on the test that day to get into this prestigious school. Although the school is indeed excellent, there were plenty of other great options in the Nashville area. But it didn't seem to help when I pointed out that a number of high schools, including some public schools, had college placement statistics that equaled and in some cases exceeded those of the school his son was "applying" for. It was clearly not the end of the world if his son wound up at another school; it might even be a blessing for the boy to attend a school that understood the diversity of developmental patterns among bright, capable children and that would give him more time to mature in those aspects of learning where he simply needed more time.

I also pointed out that many of the parents seeking enrollment in the school my colleague so wanted his son to attend were "redshirting" their children for a year, meaning that they were applying for kindergarten entry for their children at age six rather than age five, the usual age for entry. Simply being older than other children entering kindergarten worked to these families' advantage; also, his son was competing with older children on a test that did not take age into account. I then learned that my colleague and his wife, also a faculty member at Vanderbilt, had been drilling their son for nearly a year on how to take this test.

The whole episode struck me as tragic. But it is by no means an unusual example of misguided attempts to artificially accelerate learning—and of the artificially created but nonetheless real stress parents face. Do you think this poor child was unaware of his parents' anxiety about whether he would "make the grade" on the test? How would not getting into the school color his perspective on education and learning? (Ironically, although he did get into that kindergarten, his parents left the school two years later.)

In contrast, I recently tested a high school student from the very same school who had not been accepted there for kindergarten. She "failed" the kindergarten entrance exam, went to another, less selective school, and transferred into the school in ninth grade. I'd first met this student when she was entering middle school and was struggling in some subjects. Her parents are both professionals and were a bit concerned about her academic future. My testing showed that her memorization skills were average but her reasoning ability was very high, far above average. It was only because grade school and middle school had to that point emphasized rote learning that she *appeared* to be unintelligent; her real struggle had to do with the mismatch between how she was forced to learn in school and her real potential.

I persuaded the parents—and the school—to quit forcing her to fill up endless work sheets and perform rote memorization and to instead have her focus on reasoning, problem solving, science, and reading for pleasure. The transformation was dramatic! Her grades improved significantly right away because her ability to think through test items was enhanced. Now a high school junior in the very school she could not get into in kindergarten, she is one of the top students in her class, with a high grade point average in all subjects and high scores on standardized tests. She is also confident and happy—a big change from what I saw in middle school. By having her shift away from rote learning toward thinking ability, her parents activated meaningful learning and empowered her to succeed in the very exclusive high school. No doubt these newfound skills will continue to serve her in college and for the rest of her life.

Entrance exams and high-stakes testing for kindergarten are a relatively new development.[17] Professors Lorrie Shepard and Mary Smith from the University of Colorado were already lamenting this accelerating trend in the late 1980s, pointing out that academic demands in kindergarten and first grade had risen considerably higher than they'd been twenty years prior and were continuing to escalate, despite the fact that "narrow emphasis on isolated reading and numeracy is detrimental even to the children who succeed and is especially harmful to children who are labeled as failures."

Since then, the situation has accelerated to the point where, across the nation, parents are delaying kindergarten entrance in order to boost their child's entrance test scores, just as happened at the exclusive private school my colleague wanted his son to attend. In 2006, Dr. Ashlesha Datar, a social scientist at the RAND Corporation, conducted a study comparing children entering kindergarten "on time" to those whose parents held them out for a year. Professor Datar reported: "I find that entering kindergarten a year older significantly boosts test scores at kindergarten entry. More importantly, entering older implies a steeper test score trajectory during the first 2 years in school."[18]

Consider the implications of this research. Simply waiting until a child is older dramatically increases scores on kindergarten entrance exams. Is the child more intelligent? Does she have a higher potential than she had the year before? No! It is simply a matter of schools trying to teach too much too soon. Parents are responding by simply waiting until their child is more mature and his or her brain is more fully developed in order to take on academic material that should be taught to older children.

The impact of accelerated testing has had a disproportionate impact on boys. Studies have shown that the highest scores on kindergarten entrance exams are attained by older females.[19] Although it is certainly true that both boys and girls show significantly higher entrance scores if they test when they're older compared to those who've entered kindergarten at the usual age, this difference is even more pronounced when comparing older females to younger males entering on time. When a boy who is perfectly intelligent and on target in terms of physical and mental development attempts to enter kindergarten at the usual age of five years old, he will be at a significant disadvantage relative to the older boys and especially relative to the older girls that parents have held out of kindergarten for a year.

I can only imagine what would have happened to me in a modern kindergarten: I began attending before my fifth birthday! In today's educational situation, my mother would have been wise to hold me out for not one but two years so that I would be entering kindergarten at the age of six rather than four. That is a huge difference in development and is a sad testimony to what a high-stakes operation kindergarten has become.

Worse, as professors Smith and Shepard predicted back in 1989, efforts to "teach to the test" in preschool to prepare children for an impossibly accelerated kindergarten program have derailed natural learning processes at an age when a child should be feeling positive and excited about discovery and learning and should be allowed to learn at his or her own pace.[20]

The very idea of using any kind of intellectual test in kindergarten to predict long-term intelligence is absurd. It has long been known that preschool and early-school-age intelligence tests are relatively inaccurate predictors of a person's later intellectual abilities.[21] More than thirty-five years ago, professors Ken Hopkins at the University of Colorado and Glenn Bracht at the University of Minnesota studied the stability of IQ scores in the same children by testing them each year over a ten-year period, from when they entered first grade through eleventh grade (junior year of high school). The results showed that the scores of the kids in their sample were highly variable—meaning unstable—from year to year in first, second, and third grade, and were relatively variable until after a child finished fourth grade. Only after that, when the children were around age ten or eleven, did the scores become much more stable.

This finding that IQ scores obtained in kindergarten and early grammar school are not very stable has been repeatedly replicated.[22] Professor Michael J. Roszkowski, at American College in Pennsylvania, completed a study designed to examine whether the earlier results would be the same if different kinds of IQ tests were used. His findings were highly similar to those reported earlier: There was considerable variation in IQ scores when children were retested. He noted that 68 percent of the students had higher IQs in fourth grade than they had in first grade, with the highest gain being 27 points! In simple terms, this child went from average (IQ of 103) to gifted (IQ of 130) after only three grades. Consider what this means for kindergarten testing: A school would miss out on some very talented students if they mistakenly believed that early testing provides an accurate estimate of a child's long-term potential.

But schools continue to use entrance testing regardless of its unreliability, and the pressure some parents feel to secure places in prestigious schools by the time a child reaches kindergarten has induced them to push their children to be "successful" test takers at ever younger ages, reaching down even into infancy. Parents themselves begin "teaching to the test" by drilling their toddlers on vocabulary, numbers, letters, and other items usually encountered on kindergarten readiness tests, well before babies' and toddlers' minds are ready to appreciate and integrate this knowledge.

Intuitive Solutions to Educational Challenges

In a nutshell, there are two primary difficulties parents must address in modern education: 1) an increasingly irrational, accelerated curriculum that pressures children to learn material—and parents to teach it—long before their developing minds are ready; and 2) a one-size-fits-all assembly-line process based on age level rather than ability level.

There are a number of potential solutions to these challenges, and they fall into two broad classes. First, parents can work within the existing public or private school system and with individual teachers to adapt the classroom—and its curriculum—to meet their child's needs. The second solution is to seek an alternative education. Both solutions can be successful: The truth is that all good teachers naturally and intuitively meet their students where they are intellectually. Unfortunately, however, increasing federal, state, and district-wide micromanagement of curricula in many public schools and spillover of this approach into some private schools is making it difficult for even the best teachers to follow their own instincts about how to best engage and teach individual children. But it can still be done, and my wife and I got involved to ensure it was done with our children in the schools they attended.

For example, when our youngest child, Jane, was in grade school (kindergarten through fourth grade), in Nashville public schools, a new superintendent had mandated district-wide standards and curricula. One of the new requirements involved mandatory, specific homework assignments, which dramatically increased the "sheet work" sent home with Jane each day. Worse, the lessons contained in these work sheets made no sense whatsoever from a developmental perspective. For example, in second grade, assigned math work sheets covered diverse concepts including telling time, number lines, and addition and subtraction as well as multiplication and division. These work sheets were given out in no cohesive order and without any seeming rationale—other than attempting to boost test scores.

At that time, Jane was ready to learn addition and subtraction, and I knew that it made no sense for her to move on to multiplication and division until she was proficient in addition and subtraction. So I met with the teacher and requested modification of the work sheets and homework so that it would focus on what she needed at that time without confusing her. Because the district required that the mandated homework be turned in, after Jane had completed the addition and subtraction problems, I completed the remaining problems on the work sheets and signed them so that there was no pretense about who was doing what.

I certainly wasn't the only parent in the district—or the nation—to do some of my daughter's homework. At least I made it completely clear that I was doing so! Multiple studies indicate that some parents are currently completing up to 75 percent or even *all* of their child's homework, practically speaking, for the same reasons I did.[23] There is simply too much homework being assigned in today's schools, and the content is hopelessly confusing, so parents are standing over their children and either directly or indirectly giving them the answers.

Fortunately, by using intuitive parenting, I was able to work with the teacher in order to ensure that Jane got the math education she needed. This approach paid dividends. By high school, Jane was able to complete the overwhelming majority of her math lessons without my help, and her skills were outstanding. An informal query of other parents in her classes indicated that many of them were still having to help out much more extensively.

The point here is to interact with the teachers and do your best to individualize your child's lessons. A helpful strategy is to observe your children doing their assigned work and to notice which items they can easily complete, which are a bit more difficult for them, and which ones they simply cannot do. Work with the teachers so that your child is responsible for the easy items and the ones that are of moderate difficulty. Try to negotiate holding off on the impossible items until your child is ready.

A second strategy for intuitive parents seeking to address the mismatch between current educational practices in their child's educational needs is to seek alternative programs. These can take the form of Montessori, Waldorf, or other schools that overtly and automatically individualize their curricula to meet each child's developmental needs. Many public school districts offer charter schools or magnet schools that provide alternatives to a one-size-fits-all educational approach, and there are private options as well in many cities. Several of my children went to public magnet schools, and these were outstanding.

Other intuitive parents take on homeschooling as a potential alternative solution. Historically, homeschool programs were often organized around concerns that religious beliefs and values were not being included in public school curricula. More recently, many more homeschool programs have been developed specifically to foster academic achievement based on each child's individual learning style. Homeschooling is not for everyone, and it can be difficult to distinguish between the roles of parent and teacher at home! On the other hand, for parents who are on board with it, homeschooling can be an excellent alternative to other kinds of education. We homeschooled several of our children for limited amounts of time when there simply wasn't a reasonable match for them in the educational system. I handled geography, math, and science lessons, and my wife was the primary homeschool instructor teaching all the other subjects including history, literature, social studies, and so on. We purchased a homeschool curriculum, which was very helpful in guiding our lessons. For us, this was a last resort and not our primary educational method. However, it was great to have this option and curriculum available when there simply weren't any good choices for schools at those times in our children's development.

Other alternative schools can be private schools or schools that are faith affiliated—Catholic schools, Quaker schools, Jewish schools, and so on. But be forewarned, some of these may stress assembly-line learning and "learning by work sheet" as much or even more so than public schools, so be sure to find out what they are teaching and how they are teaching. Do not assume that private or faith-based schools automatically will be the best fit for your child.

Regardless of which solution is right for you, the key is to be actively engaged in your child's education. Unfortunately, simply turning your children over to the local school district and having a high degree of confidence that they will emerge on the back end well educated is risky at best!

- Early education has become a high-stakes, stressful experience for all too many parents—and their children!
- Be prepared to be an engaged partner in your child's school experience, and do not be afraid to request modifications—especially for homework—if that is what your intuition and common sense suggest.
- The American education system and Common Core are designed to boost test performance, not to ensure your child has a positive or successful learning experience. "Teaching to the test" results in a scattered, nonsensical presentation of academic subjects. Make sure your child has mastered and is confident in a basic skill (e.g., addition, letter names) before moving to the next step.
- If your child is ready to learn the next step, don't hold her back. Most children will move more quickly in one subject (e.g., reading) while taking longer in another (e.g., math). In

third grade, one of my children was reading at a second-grade level but could do fifth-grade math. It is rare for a child to be precisely at grade level in every subject. Let him or her work at the proper level whether it be below—or above—his or her grade-mates.

- If you cannot find a public school that works with and for your child, do not hesitate to enroll in an alternative school such as Montessori or Waldorf or a private or faith-affiliated school if your family can afford it, or consider homeschooling.

chapter 9

The Perils of Too Much Too Soon: ADHD, Autism Spectrum Disorder, and Learning Disabilities

One can hardly turn on the news or read a newspaper these days without encountering alarming stories and statistics about the rise in developmental and learning disorders afflicting our children. In the spring of 2014, headlines from across the United States proclaimed that one in sixty-eight children has been identified with an autism spectrum disorder (ASD).[1] The news on attention-deficit hyperactivity disorder (ADHD) is even worse. In March 2013, the *New York Times* reported that 11 percent of all school-age children had received a medical diagnosis of ADHD;[2] for high-school-age boys, the rate was reported to be 13.2 percent—representing a 40 percent rise in just the past decade[3]—and it is not uncommon for boys to be taking some kind of ADHD medication during school in the United States.[4]

Autism, developmental and learning disabilities, and attentional issues are real, and children may be born with disabilities, mild to profound, that will require extra dedication from intuitive parents and at times from specialists who can help to remediate the impact of such disabilities on a child's life. Later in this chapter I will discuss when parents should worry or seek outside advice or help and how to apply the principles of intuitive parenting if your kids do face serious developmental challenges. But first, I want to address the reason why this phenomenal rise in rates of children with ASD and ADHD diagnoses should concern all parents.

There are likely several reasons for the astronomical rise in rates of ASD and ADHD; in the case of ADHD, there is on ongoing debate about whether it is being overdiagnosed in the United States.[5] But in addition to better detection in children who were formerly missed, the subjective nature of the diagnosis, the escalation in the amount of time young children spend in front of TV and video screens, and the impact of pharmaceutical company marketing campaigns may be significant factors as well. But isn't it also time that we took a hard look at the potential downside of pushing babies' and young children's immature brains into doing things they are not ready for? In this chapter we will take a more detailed look at autism, ADHD, and other learning disabilities in order to explore the notion that pushing the limits of development may involve risks, side effects, and unintended consequences.

In our society today, the prevailing notion when it comes to learning seems to be that any form of accelerated specialized training in babies, toddlers, and preschoolers will simply provide an added "value" to other kinds of learning and, at worst, will have a benign impact or no impact at all. In other words, attempts to push skills such as phonics training into preschool—or even infancy—are considered either potentially effective or harmless. But there are several clues in the scientific literature exploring these intellectual get-rich-quick schemes that suggest otherwise.

Parents using vocabulary training videos or DVDs with their infants are hoping to convey an advantage to their babies when they later enter school. Who could fault this? After all, many studies over nearly a hundred years have shown that a larger vocabulary often translates into better academic performance, better reading,[6] and higher[7] IQ.[8] And if showing a child a video, DVD, or software program names objects or pictures in the hopes of increasing their vocabulary, what harm could that cause?

A study by Judy S. DeLoache at the University of Virginia and her colleagues published in the journal *Psychological Science* in 2010 yielded some intriguing results on this topic. Professor DeLoache studied the amount of vocabulary learned by twelve- to eighteen-month-old toddlers who watched vocabulary DVDs and compared that to a control group that did not watch them. Toddlers in this age group often learn new words at a rapid rate, displaying a "vocabulary burst," making them an excellent group for scientists to study the effects that video or computerized vocabulary learning have on word learning.

Many people were surprised by the results of DeLoache's study: It turned out that the toddlers who watch vocabulary DVDs do *not* learn more words than those who don't watch the educational DVDs, meaning that attempting to accelerate vocabulary learning by having toddlers watch them provided no benefit. But, even more surprising, it turned out that "*the highest level of learning occurred in a no-video condition in which parents tried to teach their children the same target words during everyday activities*" (emphasis added).[9] In other words, the children watching the vocabulary DVDs ended up learning *fewer* words than those who simply interacted with their parents in a normal, natural, *intuitive* fashion. This finding is in direct support of the primary thesis of this book: Children learn best in everyday naturalistic activities while interacting with their parents or caregivers.

In addition to counting the number of words each child learned, Professor DeLoache also surveyed the parents, asking them how many words they *thought* their child had learned. Dr. DeLoache reported: "Another important result was that parents who liked the DVD tended to overestimate how much their children had learned from it."[10] Parents *believed* that their children were learning more from the vocabulary program than they actually were. One can imagine that these parents were also letting other families know how much their toddlers were learning from the DVD, even though the truth was that they were learning *less* than children who were learning in the natural, intuitive way. One can further speculate that some parents who heard about the word-learning DVDs felt peer pressure to provide them for their own children, or at least felt some guilt that they were not providing this special training. But it turns out that parents' beliefs did not match the actual outcome for their children.

Georgene Troseth and her colleagues at Vanderbilt University's Peabody College have long been studying what children learn from DVDs. In addition to supporting the findings reported by Dr. DeLoache—namely, that on average, toddlers learn less from video than they do in everyday interactions with their parents or caregivers—Dr. Troseth has also reported that children learning from DVDs rather than everyday interactions tend to be *less social*.[11] If toddlers are spending their time watching DVDs or looking at computer screens, they are not spending as much time interacting with people. So it is not surprising that these toddlers do not develop socially at the same rate as children who have less exposure to video, computers, or DVDs and more interaction time with their parents, siblings, and peers.[12]

Combining the results of these studies indicates that well-meaning but misguided attempts to accelerate neural development in the form of vocabulary DVDs could have the unintended consequence of slowing both vocabulary development and social development. And at the same time, parents nevertheless tended to think that their children were learning more from the DVDs than they actually were. Might it then also be possible that in our efforts to artificially accelerate development in our society in general, we are potentially producing unintended negative consequences in any number of other domains as well—while thinking that our methods lead to better outcomes than they are actually producing?

Lessons from Hyperlexia

As you may recall from Chapter 4, hyperlexia is a disorder in which children can read words, sometimes to a precocious degree, but don't comprehend their meaning. This disorder is often seen in children who have autism. Children with autism often have a special fascination with letters and can spend hours and hours each day looking at letters and learning the sound symbols that each represents. I have known children with autism who could literally read aloud nearly any word in English; some as young as two could "read" words such as "elephant," "roller coaster," "dinosaur," "caboose," "peninsula," and just about any other typewritten form I presented to them. Often, their parents thought their child was remarkably gifted. To some extent this was true because most two-year-olds cannot read these words at all; in fact, most two-year-olds do not yet know sound-letter associations, so their children were quite precocious for reading words aloud. Later, though, the parents' initial excitement faded as they realized that their child, by spending a majority of his or her learning time focusing on letters and numbers, was missing out on many other important learning opportunities, as is so often the case in autism. The time spent learning letters at a young age had a cost, in terms of social development and in terms of developing many other aspects of cognitive ability.

These parents had not forced their children with autism to spell or read. Rather, in the natural course of reading books to their children, they realized that their child had a special affinity for letters. The child would always demand that the parent say the letters over and over again, and may have brought blocks decorated with letters to the parents to name them. Of course, parents will naturally comply with these kinds of requests, and no one should ever be critical that they did so. In cases of autism, the parents were simply responding to their child's interests. And because children with autism tend to have restricted interests and to be less social than other children, it is not surprising that many of the interactions between the child and his or her parent centered around the things the child preferred: in this case, letters.

But what about children who do not have autism? What would happen if letters were drilled before children showed an interest in them? What would happen if the letters were presented before the children knew the meanings of the words that the collection of letters represent? Might this *induce* hyperlexia in these children? There are some intriguing data that suggest that drilling letters early, and taking them out of a meaningful context, could interfere with reading comprehension in a process that is eerily similar to the hyperlexia seen in autism. The children can say their letters and read words but may not know the meaning of what is being read.

How do fluent readers, who read with comprehension, process text? Because meaning drives comprehension, fluent readers scan the page and rapidly form hypotheses about meaning based on the content and context of what they are reading. More important, they do not read letter by letter! L o o k a t e a c h l e t t e r a n d b e s u r e t o r e a d e a c h o n e. O n e a t a t i m e. Pretty laborious and slow. And reading each letter, making its sound, and then assembling these bits of sounds into words makes it hard to keep track of what the words mean and to assemble them into meaningful sentences. But because these are in English, if the reader knows this language, the meaning can be deduced by using reasoning.

As this example illustrates, reading letter by letter by letter is very slow and inefficient. But what if children are forced to "read" before they know the language in terms of the meanings of words—before they have naturally acquired vocabulary or have developed the neural infrastructure necessary to map letters onto word meanings? Is the brain then biased toward laboriously identifying and unconsciously pronouncing each sound in the mind in order to read the words? Children with learning disabilities associated with reading problems are often inefficient at comprehending what they read. And there appears to be an ever-increasing number of children in the United States with these kinds of learning disabilities,[13] a number that now includes at least 5 percent of school-age children.[14]

This is a conundrum because educational reform, and exposing children to phonics and text at earlier and earlier ages, is supposed to increase reading ability and, by inference, decrease learning disabilities. One cannot help wonder whether attempting to impose a letter/phonics–based symbol system before the underlying language structures have been learned is at least in part contributing to learning disabilities. According to the 2013 edition of the *World Factbook* produced by the Central Intelligence Agency, the Scandinavian countries of Finland, Sweden, Denmark, and Norway, which start teaching reading quite late by American standards, all have higher overall literacy rates than those of the United States.[15] Although making direct comparisons can be difficult because of the different ways various countries classify disabilities, surveys show these Scandinavian countries also appear to have much lower incidence rates for learning disabilities.[16] A conservative interpretation of these data from Scandinavian countries (as compared to the United States) indicates that starting reading instruction early does *not* necessarily translate into better literacy rates, nor is it associated with reducing the incidence of learning disabilities. But further study is needed to determine whether starting reading later—after language skills have more fully developed—will actually reduce the odds of developing a learning disability.

For intuitive parents teaching reading, if individual children are precocious in their language acquisition and wish to read with comprehension, there is no reason to stop them from doing so. On the other hand, it is clear that forcing children to read early does not necessarily convey any advantage with regard to long-term literacy as they become adults and that forcing reading on an immature brain may in fact have the unintended consequence of making that brain inefficient at processing text and translating the symbols into meaning.

Attention-Deficit Hyperactivity Disorder (ADHD)

In a letter to the *New York Times* responding to an op-ed on the subject of ADHD and pre-K education, veteran teacher Lynn Hughes opined:

> As an elementary school teacher for the past 47 years, I find much of the debate about attention deficit hyperactivity disorder narrow-minded and disturbing. Do I have students who fit the description of ADHD? Some, and medication has helped them dramatically from their first days of taking it.
>
> But I have lots of kids who just wiggle, who observe and exclaim over things the rest of us miss (such as a new bird at the feeder outside our window or the emerging of a monarch butterfly in our classroom habitat), would rather stand than sit when they work, who need to take a break from sustained activity (a drink of water will often suffice), and who are perfectly all right.
>
> We are not all the same, and traditional classroom expectations fit only some of us, especially when we are young and have less self-control. We need to look not only in our children *but also at the setting in which we place them. Preschool is not the place for workbooks, being quiet, and holding still.* It is the time to explore the world, *ask a million*

questions and create a seamless day in which work and play blend into one *self-directed* adventure [emphasis added].

Young children need a rich and stimulating environment, and permission to bounce around in it. The few who are actually in need of evaluation and perhaps intervention will stand out even in that setting.[17]

Like so many dedicated teachers, Ms. Hughes knows what children need to learn and how to teach them. She also understands that no one-size-fits-all curriculum will ever succeed, and that it is completely unrealistic to expect preschoolers to sit still and learn passively. Most important, she raises the possibility that at least a portion of the "epidemic" of ADHD is a consequence of misguided attempts to force too much onto a normally (and naturally) developing mind.

The fifth edition of the *Diagnostic Statistical Manual of Mental Disorders* (DSM-5) of the American Psychiatric Association defines ADHD as the inability to inhibit distractors and focus attention (ADHD, predominantly inattentive type); the inability to inhibit the impulse to move (ADHD, predominantly hyperactive-impulsive type); or a combination of both (ADHD, combined). As mentioned at the beginning of this chapter, the incidence of ADHD, and the number of children medicated for ADHD, has been increasing at alarming rates.

What are the reasons for this increase?[18] Specific causes are not known, but recent research has indicated that disruptions in certain chemicals in the brain that are responsible for carrying neural impulses from one nerve cell to another via the synapses are implicated. These neurotransmitters are hypothesized to be present in higher or lower amounts in the synapses, which, as we saw in Chapter 2, is the space between nerve cells across which information is carried from one cell to the next.

There can be no doubt that ADHD is a real condition and that some children do indeed have difficulty paying attention and/or inhibiting the impulse to move—and that these children can sometimes be helped by medication. Children with the hyperactive-impulsive form of ADHD literally bounce off the walls and cannot stay with even a highly motivating task for more than a few minutes. They come into a room and move from toy to toy without playing very long and trash the room pretty quickly. The key diagnostic marker is that the child cannot inhibit movement in *preferred* activities, not just during boring, less interesting activities. In practice, this is easy to recognize because the child will be playing with a toy that is really interesting but will constantly get up and move around for a few moments before returning to continue playing. They get up and come back, get up and come back, get up and come back; it is exhausting even to watch. Similarly, those with ADHD-inattentive type cannot inhibit distractors. They will be playing with an interesting favorite toy but cannot continue playing when there is movement somewhere else in the room or an extraneous noise. These children are easily distracted and also cannot maintain attention on *preferred* activities.

In contrast, *all* people have difficulty focusing on boring, repetitive tasks.[19] Some have more motivation to do so and will comply, but others will simply quit paying attention unless their minds are actively engaged.[20] This effect can be seen in tasks requiring rote memorization versus fluid reasoning. In a study of boredom in students, scientists William Mikulas and Stephen Vodanovich reported that task complexity has a direct bearing on attention; in this case boredom was associated with reduced attention levels.[21] It should surprise no one that the more thinking skills are engaged, the more attentive people are. Unfortunately, memorization is not an active thinking task and is associated with increased levels of boredom (and hence less attention).

We can see that this finding potentially extends to teaching.

Professors Lannie Kanevsky and Tacey Keighley interviewed gifted students and found that "all of the students in the study mentioned the need for complexity in their learning experiences. They sought novel, authentic, abstract, open-ended experiences and felt the familiar, artificial, concrete, decontextualized, simplistic nature of most assigned work contributed to their boredom." This is best captured in a quote from one of the students in the study: "The only thing you do at school is memorize. That's all they expect you to do. They don't expect you to understand. They just want you to remember that 2 + 2 = 4 and not tell you why. We're never asked, we were never questioned, never inspired to ask why does this work? It was just, you know, do the work, hand it in, I'll mark it. You'll get a grade. That was it."[22]

Research on brain circuitry dedicated to attention is quite fascinating.[23] Scientists have identified two interacting systems that involve multiple brain centers and multiple levels of information processing. One system is dedicated to filtering the mass of information the brain receives each minute to identify the important signals. Imagine that you are walking in a jungle. A myriad of sights and sounds greet your eyes and ears: There are monkeys chattering in the treetops, the sound of the wind blowing in the trees, birds are calling; there are beautiful flowers, broad tree trunks, ferns growing, vines streaming down from the branches overhead, and insects buzzing about. There is a tremendous amount of information flowing into the brain that has to be processed and interpreted. But what happens when there is a faint noise in the trees above—the sound a leopard makes before she drops down on her prey? Your brain had better detect and pay attention to that signal and give it a high priority or it is very unlikely your DNA will be passed on to the next generation! This attention circuitry monitors the ongoing information stream and quickly focuses attention when a high-priority signal comes in. The brains of children with ADHD give a high priority to the wrong signals. Harmless background sounds get the attention that should have been reserved for very important signals. In the case of the leopard in the jungle, the brain responds to the overhead tree-rustling signal by raising stress levels and prompting the whole body to get ready to move. But what if the brain responded this way every time a bird chirped? The mind and the body would constantly be on "red alert"—and a child with this brain would be jumpy and stressed out.

The second attention system is designed to enable us to volitionally focus attention on objects or activities of interest so that we can harness our mind to pay attention to the particular stimuli we choose. For example, perhaps when we are back in the jungle we hear an unusual bird call and want to learn more about its source and nature. Our brain can suppress the surrounding "background" noises and sights so that we can devote attention to listening for the bird call of interest and to locating the signal in the hope of catching a glimpse of the bird making it. Now, imagine that the neural circuits usually responsible for this task cannot filter out distractors. I want to find that interesting bird but I cannot inhibit my attention to the monkeys chattering or the wind blowing. This makes it much more difficult for me to sort out the bird call from other signals and therefore also difficult for me to listen to and locate the bird.

It is not surprising that children with ADHD have trouble learning in the usual way and often miss important information. They cannot attend to relevant input in the classroom (or at home) unless distractors are minimized, and lessons must be provided over and over again so that the key information can be gleaned over multiple encounters. Their attention is elsewhere or they are moving around rather than paying attention. But there are important caveats. Many children who end up being diagnosed with or labeled as ADHD are perfectly fine in most situations but seem to struggle only when they are in school. It is important to bear in mind that the basic definition of ADHD explicitly states that symptoms *must* occur in *multiple settings*. So, if a child is "wiggly" or inattentive only at school and nowhere else, this should *not* meet the diagnostic criteria for ADHD. Stated directly, teachers and schools should not be the sole source of an ADHD diagnosis. Many parents I work with report that teachers and other school personnel often push ADHD as the diagnosis and medication as the solution; but modern schools may be structured in a way that actually induces ADHD-like symptoms both in terms of movement and in terms of inattention. Let's see how schools may inadvertently push children—especially boys—into looking like they have ADHD when they may not have it.

Imagine you are learning a new language, let's say German. What would happen if you were put in a classroom where the teacher spoke only fluent German in long sentences and many of the other students could also speak German, but you had only limited comprehension of German? It is easy to understand that a student attempting to learn in this context might be "wiggly" and inattentive. On the other hand, if the teacher started off with simple German vocabulary words and short phrases you could understand and tailored the lessons to your speed of learning, your attention would be focused and you would tend to move a lot less—and pay attention a lot more. The same could be true for lessons in your native English with subjects such as chemistry, physics, and mathematics when these are unfamiliar topics. If the teacher tried to present information that was far above your skill level, you would tend to wiggle more and pay less attention. You might really want to learn, and try hard to pay attention for a while, but if as the minutes passed you understood less and less, rather than more and more, you might at some point give up trying. You would then start watching the clock, looking outside, wiggling, and paying less attention.

One cannot help wonder whether many of our children are experiencing the same thing when they go to school. There are many different, quite normal learning styles, but a particular child's style may not quite match up with the method a teacher is using in his or her lessons. For example, if one watches typically developing two- and three-year-olds, they are very active and tend to naturally move from one play activity to another fairly quickly. These children are not hyperactive or inattentive relative to what one could reasonably expect in a toddler.

Now what would happen if we tried to teach them as if they were middle-school learners? Is it reasonable for rambunctious but otherwise normal little boys and girls to sit still at a desk or in a circle and listen to a teacher for more than a few moments at a time? What if a child isn't ready to read in preschool and is forced to sit and complete lessons that are far beyond her skill level? Or to complete written work sheets? Is it fair and reasonable to label a young child who can't yet do these things as having ADHD and put her on psychoactive medication? This is akin to saying that you have ADHD if you cannot pay attention to a teacher speaking in German in long sentences when you have only a very limited German vocabulary, and that the solution to your problem is not for the teacher to step back and make the lesson simpler, but for you to take medication so that you will comply with classroom expectations by sitting still and listening.

Could it be that attempting to teach preschoolers using grammar or even middle school techniques and grammar or even middle school content is contributing substantially to the rise in diagnoses of ADHD and the increase in the amount of stimulant medication being dispensed to children in the United States? The answer is currently unknown but is certainly worth examining scientifically.

The way that children are being taught using DVDs, video, and computers at younger and younger ages is another possible contributor to the ADHD epidemic. One cannot help but speculate that children's brains are becoming wired to learn using a modality that is two-dimensional, mechanistic, and offers predictable learning routines that facilitate rote learning but not fluid reasoning (problem solving). What happens when a child who has spent hours and hours learning from a computer in a passive way with canned programs is put into a school that requires listening to and interacting with a human teacher, is conducted in three-dimensional space, and requires novel problem solving? A child whose brain has been shaped since infancy to learn from the computer program or DVD may have difficulty adapting and adjusting to the new learning environment. That child may also be lagging in development of some social skills. It is certainly worth examining whether the increased amount of time children spend in virtual reality is also contributing to the increased rates of ADHD in our classrooms.

Lessons from Autism and Autism Spectrum Disorder (ASD)

Every year, we hear more and more about autism and autism spectrum disorders, and how these conditions are increasing dramatically in the United States. As with ADHD, the number of new cases appearing over the last few decades is truly astounding. The following are data from the Centers for Disease Control (CDC), which monitors the rates of ASD over time. In 1978, the overall incidence was estimated at about 3 in 10,000 children.[24] In 1990, the rate of autism was still approximately 3 children in 10,000. But by 1996 the rate had climbed to 34 in 10,000. By 2004 it more than doubled to 80 in 10,000.[25] This year, the CDC figure is 147 in 10,000, which translates to 1 in 68.[26] This nearly fiftyfold increase since 1990 may be small potatoes compared to the overall numbers in ADHD, but it is stunning nevertheless. And the CDC is also reporting that more than 2 in every 100 boys has autism (actually 1 in 42).[27] The way things are going, I predict the ASD rate will double (or better) in the next five years.

To be sure, it is clear that as standards for diagnosis change and attempts are made to diagnose the condition earlier and earlier, it is difficult to know how much of this increase is simply due to new standards and how much is due to more accurate diagnostic practices. It is also important to bear in mind that the definition of autism has been expanded, so that children who would not have been diagnosed in the 1970s, '80s, or even '90s are now being identified on a broad autism spectrum. On the other hand, it is also likely that the core rate of autism is indeed increasing in the United States.

Autism is a developmental disability that includes a reduced motivation for social interaction with other human beings, a rigid adherence to routines (so that a child has tantrums or a meltdown if a routine is not followed), and, in most cases, language disorders. Also, many children with autism have intellectual deficits to some extent. The condition was portrayed in the movie *Rain Man*, which starred Tom Cruise and Dustin Hoffman, with Mr. Hoffman winning an Academy Award for his amazingly accurate portrayal of a high-functioning autistic adult.

Children with autism are very difficult to raise. And because they often lack the social motivation seen in typical infants, toddlers, and preschoolers, they may not communicate even when they know how. Mothers in particular can become guilt-ridden if their child has autism, perhaps as a vestige of a theory, widely accepted by medical professionals and the public in the 1950s and early 1960s, that autism was a result of parents—particularly mothers—not providing their baby with sufficient emotional warmth. This theory has been thoroughly discredited; it is very clear that parents do not cause autism. But because the subject is still a sensitive one, I want to be very careful in talking about the relationship between autism and attempting to teach a child too much too early. I especially want to be sure that no mother reading this will mistakenly jump to the conclusion that she somehow caused her child's autism by attempting to teach her child to read or because her child had a special affinity for computer games. Rather, I am simply trying to show that children with autism are perhaps particularly vulnerable to learning from DVDs or computers; that the reduced social demands and restricted social interactions of these learning situations can produce the kind of splinter skills and rote learning described above; and that this can be exacerbated in autism because these children have a special affinity for these kinds of learning activities.

Children with autism love routines and will perform activities over and over again to a much greater extent than other children. They also prefer predictability and sameness in what they do and see. For example, I work with children with autism who love letters, especially typewritten letters. Look at all the letter "o's" on this page. They all look the same and are perfectly predictable, as is every other letter. This predictability and sameness seems to be pleasing to a child with autism, who will spend hours and hours staring at letters (or whatever else they find fascinating). This means that young children with autism will become experts at recognizing letters; unfortunately, it also means that the learning they would have gotten by interacting with other people or by looking at other kinds of objects will be missed.

Also, children with autism love to listen to the same things over and over again. It may be music, particular songs, or listening to the dialogue on video or DVDs. Many children with autism are echolalic, which means they will repeat things that they've heard even though what they've heard may have little or nothing to do with the current topic of conversation. The reason they listen to the same things over and over again, particularly with a recording or a video, is because these sounds, musical notes, or phrases are consistent. When I say the phrase "The ball is rolling" more than once, I will not say it precisely the same way every time. One time I may use a contraction—"The ball's rolling"—and another time I may emphasize the word "is": "The ball *is* rolling." Or I may use rising intonation to ask a question: "The ball is rolling?" But when a child with autism watches a DVD or listens to a recording, the words and phrases are precisely the same every time they are repeated.

Now consider the nature of DVDs and computer games and why they are especially attractive to a child with autism: The child can learn to activate the DVD player or the computer on his own and does not need to interact with his parents or others to get access; the video and audio material is exactly the same every time he plays it, so that it falls within his preference for routines and sameness; and another human being, whom he would rather not interact with, is not involved in learning the material (if learning is the goal of the activity). Also, although sound quality has improved in the last decade or so, the "voice" on many computer games continues to have a rather robotic or monotonic quality, which many children with autism also seem to prefer. Taken together, it is clear that an infant or toddler who already has a propensity to become autistic will be particularly drawn to canned learning programs and will be less likely to prefer natural interactions with their parents and siblings.

But what about the broader "autism spectrum"? Is it possible that children who otherwise do not have autism and in no other way behave like the *Rain Man* may mistakenly be identified as being on the broad autism spectrum if their brains were wired when they were babies to learn from machines instead of people? Bear in mind that a skilled clinician would never diagnose autism in children who simply preferred computers or DVDs but were otherwise socially adept and developing normally. On the other hand, the results of the studies looking at vocabulary learning using DVDs or computers found that the infants and toddlers learning from these media tended to be less social, which of course is a feature of autism. These games and educational materials are specially designed to attract and hold a baby's attention: They are colorful, loud, and visually interesting—certainly much more so than a mother or father. Because of this, one wonders whether the increase in the "spectrum" children who do not meet the traditional definition of autism but nonetheless are a bit less social than other children may have had the condition exacerbated by early and prolonged exposure to educational DVDs and computers.

Introducing these new technologies to ever younger children, coupled with efforts to push academic learning earlier and earlier, has created a "natural experiment" on whether these technologies are altering development in ways that exacerbate the symptoms of conditions such as ADHD, learning disabilities, and autism. Clinically, I have worked with parents to increase social interaction, reduce shallow learning, and improve performance in these children by reducing both the nature and the amount of time they are plugged in to these technologies.

In addition, it is clear that Baby Genius DVDs, educational programs for memorization, and other rote learning exercises especially diminish reasoning and problem-solving abilities in these children, especially those who have autism. Carefully observe your baby or toddler. If he or she gets sucked into the videos or games and reduces his or her attachment to people, it may be wise to put away the tablets, computers, and videos. It may also be helpful to increase human contact and natural interactions while adopting a responsive interaction style. Of course, if you suspect your baby is developing autism, ADHD, or any other clinical condition, be sure to discuss it with your pediatrician or family physician right away.

Whether shifting to rote learning at earlier ages and introducing electronic learning before a baby's brain has been imprinted for human interaction is associated with the rising trends in these kinds of cases in our society is an open question. However, parents should be sensitive to how and what their children are learning and to whether educational products and, later, educational goals and techniques are meeting their child's learning needs and are in harmony with their child's learning style.

What If a Child Really Does Have ASD, ADHD, or a Learning Disability?

I have been on the faculty at Vanderbilt University School of Medicine in Nashville, Tennessee, for nearly twenty-five years. Part of my clinical work and research is focused on helping children with disabilities learn. This work has included patients with ASD, patients with ADHD, and some with a learning disability. Quite a number of young children I have seen for difficulties developing speech and language subsequently display learning disabilities—including reading problems—after they enter school.

One of my own children had difficulty understanding what people were saying when he was in preschool and, like so many of the patients that I treat, also received special support when learning to read. Not surprisingly, his reading lagged behind his classmates until he reached high school. By the time he entered college, however, he was an excellent reader and graduated on time. In sum, I have familiarity with all these conditions as a clinician—and have been on the other side of the table as a parent as well. Finally, because I also conduct research on how to help these children learn, and serve on numerous research review panels evaluating studies on this topic, I am fortunate to be in a position to see what helps these children—and perhaps more important, what does not!

The fundamental aspects of intuitive parenting already discussed in this book are perhaps even more important when it comes to raising children who learn differently from their peers. But parents of children with developmental disabilities, learning disabilities or delays, attention-deficit challenges, or a combination of these conditions are especially vulnerable to questionable treatments and to teaching techniques that may be worthless—or, worse, detrimental to their children. It is especially heartrending when I encounter a case wherein valuable learning time and scarce family resources have been squandered on an ineffective fad "treatment," given the remarkable discoveries and great strides that have been made in better understanding and treating these disorders. There are in fact quite a number of healthful treatment choices, but parents have to be both informed and skeptical to be sure their children are getting the right kind of help.

One of the key principles of intuitive parenting is that there are no shortcuts or "silver bullets" that trigger learning. As we saw earlier in the book, children will learn what you teach them. This simple-sounding statement is actually quite profound—especially for children with disabilities. If your child is having trouble learning to read, the treatment should focus on reading tutoring. Of course, parents and clinicians working together have to be creative in determining the best way to teach a child with dyslexia or some other form of reading problem.

For example, quite a number of children I've treated have difficulty with phonemic awareness, which is the ability to efficiently assemble letters into meaningful words. These children read very slowly and have great difficulty comprehending what they read. As you can imagine, this difficulty becomes quite debilitating as a child finishes elementary school and enters middle school; and the consequences are even worse if the condition persists into high school. My clinical work and the scientific literature indicate that many of these children can be effectively taught to read in whole word units. That is, the process of sounding out words using phonics is minimized and a child is instead taught to read in larger "chunks."[28] To be sure, many children do learn to read using phonics-based approaches, but for children who are having difficulty learning to read using standard instruction, alternatives are needed. Of course, the general proviso that reading instruction should include reading comprehension as well as phonics and/or decoding is true for all children, but children with learning differences need modifications to the curriculum and often need tutoring or special instruction that is tailored to their learning.

What could make more sense—and be more intuitive—than saying that children who are learning differently need to be taught the concepts and content they are struggling with—the *actual information* they need to learn—in this case, how to read?[29]

On the other hand, desperate parents may have "special skills," tools, or training programs pushed on them and their children that have little to do with reading, despite the lack of evidence to support the use of such programs, and even despite evidence that suggests that they are less than helpful.[30]

One such example is prism glasses, which are sometimes prescribed for children with reading-related learning disabilities and often coupled with "eye-tracking" exercises. This purported treatment seems to persist even though a number of studies have shown that the prism glasses not only do not improve reading but also don't even improve eye convergence insufficiency, which was what the glasses were designed to do in the first place and why they were thought to be effective. A clinical trial in the UK published in 2005, for one example, showed that "prism reading glasses were found to be no more effective in alleviating symptoms, improving the near point of convergence . . . than placebo reading glasses for the treatment of children age 9 to 18 years with symptomatic CI [convergence insufficiency]."[31] In plain English, the special glasses were worthless for improving CI! Nonetheless, my patients' parents routinely report that prism glasses have been recommended or even pushed on them as something they should be using to help their child who has a reading-based learning disability.

Because phonics are such an integral part of reading, there are also quite a number of instructional and computer-based training programs that teach sound discrimination, letter identification, phonic-based sequencing, and other phonic "processing" skills thought to improve reading.

Quite a number of schools have purchased these kinds of software for use in "resource" rooms or special reading classrooms. As with prism glasses, however, scientific studies show that this kind of training does not improve reading. And as with prism glasses, clinical trials that put this approach to the test directly contradict the promises made by the manufacturers and by clinicians who seem to have great faith in these kinds of products. For example, a clinical trial published in 2004 testing listening software designed to facilitate better speech processing concluded that although children did learn to discriminate and sequence sounds (they learned what they were taught by the software), "it does not appear that these gains translate into a broader measure of language acquisition or *into actual reading skills*" (emphasis added).[32]

Intuitive Parenting, Common Sense, and Snake Oil: What NOT to Do

An intuitive parent has a large storehouse of common sense and recognizes that some approaches seem downright bizarre when viewed with a critical eye. As an example, there is a software program called Interactive Metronome being heavily marketed to clinicians that purports to improve ADHD, dyslexia, autism, reading disorders, auditory processing disorder, Parkinson's, and other conditions.[33] The actual "treatment" includes teaching patients to clap their hands and/or tap their feet in time with a computer-based metronome. I have no doubt that hand clapping and/or foot tapping will teach a child to clap her hands and/or to tap her feet in time with the metronome. But how in the world is this going to teach a child how to read, to be more social, or how to talk and understand? Hand clapping and foot tapping have nothing to do with learning to read, social skills, or learning to talk!

The claims for autism are, if anything, even worse.[34] The Interactive Metronome Web site claims that "while the cause of autism is not fully understood, it is clear that early intervention can make a world of difference for children. Traditional therapy has produced wonderful results for many families, *but IM training will take your sessions to the next level*" (emphasis added). This claim is heartrending because I know firsthand, as a clinician helping families of children with autism, how desperation makes parents easy prey for such a dubious assertion. The fact is that there are hundreds of studies showing that behaviorally based treatments—essentially, teaching a child with ASD how to talk, how to comprehend what is said to him, how to reduce his tantrums, how to be social, and how to ameliorate all the other challenges he may have—are effective.[35] In contrast, there is *not one clinical trial* showing that Interactive Metronome teaches these skills. In fact, one could hypothesize that IM training could potentially make at least one symptom of autism *worse*. Many children with autism engage in repetitive behavior, including some who move their hands the same way over and over again. One can't help wonder whether the hand-clapping practice in IM may actually reward—and exacerbate—repetitive behaviors. This has not been tested, but it is a plausible hypothesis that should be studied.

If someone promised you a pill that improves ADHD, apraxia/dyspraxia, autism spectrum disorders (including Asperger's syndrome and PDD—pervasive developmental disorder), brain injury, brain tumor (following surgery or chemotherapy), auditory processing disorder, cerebral palsy, dyslexia and other reading disorders, "language-learning disabled," limb amputation, nonverbal learning disorder, stuttering and stroke in children, and MS, Parkinson's, stroke, and spinal cord injury in adults, you would probably be very skeptical and, I hope, think "snake oil." But the IM Web site indeed claims that their product—not a pill this time but a computer-based learning program—will benefit people with all these conditions.[36]

Why would anyone believe in, much less purchase and subject their child to, such a scheme? As was the case with actual snake oil, a tiny kernel of fact is wrapped in a much larger rubric without any supporting evidence. According to a 2013 story on National Public Radio,[37] the original snake oil was derived from a Chinese water snake and was rich in omega-3 fatty acids. It could have been effective as a topical ointment for reducing inflammation from arthritis or bursitis. Of course, over time, "snake oil" was promoted as a cure-all for many other conditions that had nothing to do with the original use. Hence the term came to refer to products or treatments that were cure-alls of dubious value. Sound familiar?

In the case of Interactive Metronome, the "germ of truth" does *not* extend to treatment. Rather, the approach is based on the solid scientific finding that timing and rhythm are a bit slow and/or a bit erratic in many populations with disabilities or, in people with motor conditions such as Parkinson's disease or cerebral palsy, very slow and/or very erratic. But this scientific fact is *not* evidence that teaching someone to tap to a metronome will improve the disease— or anything else (other than their tapping skills). In autism, some children have excellent rhythm and timing, although many do not. And teaching them to clap is really beside the point because the primary issues in ASD are reduced social interaction and restricted interests (including repetitive behaviors). Brain studies and behavioral studies have turned up many things children with autism do not do as well as other children, but there is no one "skill" or silver bullet or computer program that will cure autism—or ADHD, or learning disabilities. Certainly not Interactive Metronome!

But there is no shortage of testimonials touting the benefits of snake oil. There are all kinds of snake-oil treatments pushed on parents, and when their child does make progress, even if it is not due to the "treatment," it is only natural for them to attribute gains to the snake oil—even in situations when all kinds of other, proven treatments were being delivered at the same time. A story published in the February 18, 2015, *New York Times* described sensory-based treatments being given to children with disabilities in New York City public schools.[38] These included weighted and pressure vests that teachers—and parents—reported helped the students to "focus" and "attend" better. These kinds of treatments are all too often prescribed for a host of conditions, including ASD, ADHD, and learning disabilities thought to arise from a "sensory integration" disorder.

But what does clinical science have to say about sensory integration "diagnoses" and "treatments"? In June 2012 the prestigious medical journal *Pediatrics* included a policy statement on "sensory integration" diagnosis and treatment:

> Sensory-based therapies are increasingly used by occupational therapists and sometimes by other types of therapists in treatment of children with developmental and behavioral disorders. Sensory-based therapies involve activities that are believed to organize the sensory system by providing vestibular, proprioceptive, auditory, and tactile inputs. Brushes, swings, balls, and other specially designed therapeutic or recreational equipment are used to provide these inputs. However, it is unclear whether children who present with sensory-based problems have an actual "disorder" of the sensory pathways of the brain or whether these deficits are characteristics associated with other developmental and behavioral disorders. *Because there is no universally accepted framework for diagnosis, sensory processing disorder generally should not be diagnosed* [emphasis added].[39]

The statement on treatment arising from these sensory "diagnoses" indicated that "parents should be informed that the amount of *research regarding the effectiveness of sensory integration therapy is limited and inconclusive*" (emphasis added).[40]

Our knowledge on weighted vests and their impact on focus and attention is even more straightforward: A number of studies show that they do not work! That is, a review of scientific studies (rather than testimonials or case reports) on weighted vests concluded

> Therapists who use sensory integration therapy may recommend that children wear weighted vests as an intervention strategy that they claim may assist in remediating problems such as inattentiveness, hyperactivity, stereotypic behaviors and clumsiness. Seven studies examining weighted vests are reviewed. While there is only a limited body of research and a number of methodological weaknesses, on balance, *indications are that weighted vests are ineffective* [emphasis added].[41]

Notice that like Interactive Metronome, proponents of this approach tout it for a plethora of conditions—and the treatment is far removed from the actual skills a child with ASD, ADHD, or learning disabilities needs to be taught. In sum, despite the headlines, and widespread (and increasing) implementation in New York City schools, there are no accepted diagnostic standards—and no credible evidence—that these techniques actually improve the core symptoms of ADHD, ASD, learning disabilities, or any other learning difficulty.

There are also snake-oil causes promoted for learning differences—sometimes with tragic consequences. This is particularly problematic in conditions such as ASD and ADHD because we do not yet know the cause of these learning differences. This provides an opportunity for snake-oil salesmen to promulgate and publicize spurious causes to go along with their dubious cures.

A rather dramatic example can be seen in the now-discredited theory that vaccines cause autism promoted by British physician Andrew Wakefield. He was lead author on a scientific article published in the prestigious medical journal *The Lancet* in 1998 that examined—and supported—the link between the measles, mumps, and rubella (MMR) vaccine and autism.[42] This report had a profound impact on families in the United States and Europe that is still evident today: Parents became concerned that getting their child the MMR vaccine would put them at greater risk for autism, and in many countries vaccination rates decreased so that in some places these serious, life-threatening diseases have been on the rise, even in countries where they had become quite rare.[43] Several celebrities, most notably actress and model Jenny McCarthy, also took up the cause and generated publicity for the claim, and many parents continue to express fear over having their children vaccinated—or worry that their child's autism was caused by the MMR vaccine he or she received as a toddler. It turned out that the article was so flawed that it was removed from *The Lancet*, which published a retraction.[44] In addition, Dr. Wakefield's medical license was revoked (in the UK) and the *British Medical Journal* reported that the research was fraudulent.[45] It is now abundantly clear that the vaccine-autism story was simply snake oil of the worst kind. But the impact this false report had—and continues to have—should be instructive to intuitive parents of children with learning differences.

Intuitive Parenting, Common Sense, and What *Should* Be Done for ASD, ADHD, and Learning Disabilities

As with so many aspects of intuitive parenting, the overarching principle for helping children with disabilities learn is very straightforward and makes intuitive sense: Find out what a child does well, and use this strength to address the weaknesses. Parents should seek out a clinician who has a can-do attitude and is willing to do the detective work to find the unique aspects of the child's aptitudes. I can honestly say that I have *never* encountered a patient who could not be taught if the clinician was willing to get into that child's individual learning patterns. To be sure, I have worked with children with severe disabilities who have a slow learning curve. Despite this, with a focused learning plan and the help of the parents and other family members, even these patients will learn and make progress. There is always hope and a positive way forward!

The many children with ASD, ADHD, and some forms of learning disability can learn quite rapidly when using a common-sense, intuitive approach. Indeed, in so many cases the learning "problems" were exacerbated by an educational system that employed a one-size-fits-all approach to teaching, and this inflexibility actually worsened the problems. But when the teaching approach was switched, for example, to a "learning by doing" rather than a "learning by listening" approach, the child made great strides. In general, parents should seek out clinicians and teachers who enjoy teaching their child and who are willing to problem-solve to find answers to the learning differences rather than insisting that a square peg be forced into a round hole. A meeting with these professionals should include not only the "red flags" that are barriers to learning but also the "green flags" that indicate areas of strength. In short, for everything a child can't do, there should be at least one thing mentioned that a child can do— and a plan for linking learning to what a child is doing well.

When a parent is concerned about whether his or her child has ADHD, ASD, an intellectual disability, a learning disability, or any other developmental difference, there are a number of steps to take. First and foremost—and I cannot stress this enough—the parent should complete a medical evaluation with the family physician or pediatrician. It is vitally important to consider whether any medically related conditions may be causing or contributing to the learning difference. Although routine physical and diagnostic tests such as neurological scans may not locate a specific cause for the learning difference, no one should *assume* that there is nothing wrong from a medical standpoint. Brain tumor, seizure disorder (epilepsy), celiac disease (wheat allergy), and traumatic brain injury are just a few of the medical conditions that have turned up when I referred some of my patients with learning differences for a medical examination.

Several years ago, I was working with a patient from New York who another clinician had diagnosed as having ASD. I insisted that the boy be seen by the family doctor, who then scheduled a neurological examination. Shortly thereafter, his mother called and thanked me for saving his life! It turned out that his ASD symptoms were the result of a brain tumor that would have been life threatening if left untreated.

Because many of the clinicians diagnosing and treating learning differences have master's degrees—or, like me, PhDs—we are neither trained nor qualified to conduct a medical evaluation. This can be confusing for parents because physicians who have completed MD training and clinical psychologists and other developmental specialists who have completed PhD training are both called "doctor" but have different types of expertise. Both types of expertise are needed to gain a proper perspective on learning differences. The physician can evaluate a child's medical condition, and the psychologist, learning specialist, or developmental specialist can test a child's thinking ability and learning patterns. Also, with rare exceptions, only a physician can prescribe medication.

After checking with the physician to ensure that no medical conditions are causing or contributing to the learning difference, a comprehensive evaluation by a psychologist or developmental specialist should be scheduled. The latter category may include speech and language pathologists (if a parent concern relates to a child's speaking and/or listening abilities) and special educators, such as reading specialists. Occupational therapists are often included when a child has difficulty with fine motor skills such as writing. Be sure to discuss your concerns with the clinician who will be seeing your child in advance of the diagnostic session. Most important, ask what tests will be given and what kinds of learning differences will be considered during the evaluation. Unfortunately, it is not uncommon for these evaluations to simply "confirm" a preordained outcome. Many parents report that the clinician or center they visited was focused on finding ASD or ADHD and did not test for alternatives. Following the confirmatory evaluation, the child was steered into a prepackaged intervention program. Please be careful when seeking evaluations—and answers!

The test battery should *always* include measures of *nonverbal* cognitive ability because tests with a heavy verbal component such as complex verbal instructions may underestimate a child's actual learning potential. The battery should also include measures of listening comprehension and vocabulary in addition to the cognitive skills presented previously in this book. There should also be tests of achievement—namely, reading, writing, and math. Finally, there should be clinical tests, such as the Autism Diagnostic Observation Schedule (ADOS-2) for autism, that evaluate a child for the particular symptoms of ASD, ADHD, or learning disability. Then all the information—cognitive ability, achievement, and clinical barriers to learning—can be integrated to develop a proper learning plan. The assessment should *never* simply be designed to confirm a preordained diagnosis such as ASD, ADHD, learning disability, or a controversial diagnosis, such as sensory integration deficit (mentioned previously). Nutritional imbalance, auditory processing disorder, or other diagnoses are not in the DSM and are all too often an entrée into questionable or worthless treatments such as Interactive Metronome, weighted vests, or sensory brushing, or expensive special diets or vitamin treatments with limited or no support from clinical studies.

Most important, insist on a differential diagnosis from the developmental specialist. Some clinicians diagnose virtually all children with learning differences as having the same condition and then recommend a one-size-fits-all treatment program. Perhaps a parallel situation will illustrate this point. If you went to your physician with a high fever, what would you think if she said, "You have a high fever and I'm going to give you aspirin," because in her experience, high fevers respond to aspirin treatment. This might be fine if the high fever is otherwise benign, but a high fever could be a symptom of many different conditions, from a simple cold or flu to more serious conditions including meningitis, appendicitis, strep, ear infections, or even staph infections. It could even be Ebola! Meningitis could require hospitalization and aggressive treatment using powerful antibiotics whereas appendicitis could require surgery; Ebola requires quarantine and different drugs than meningitis, and so on. You would hope and trust that the physician would consider all these alternatives in making a *differential* diagnosis and then prescribing treatment that fits your particular health condition.

Unfortunately, the diagnostic process for learning differences often focuses on establishing eligibility for placement of special education or for a particular program, rather than on considering alternative explanations for the symptoms. I have encountered this one-size-fits-all approach in a variety of clinicians, including some physicians, so parents need to do their homework before visiting a clinic. On the other hand, there are also many excellent clinicians including most physicians, as well as special educators, psychologists, speech pathologists, occupational therapists, and learning specialists. The key is finding one who avoids simply putting a label on all children who display a particular symptom.

For example, late onset of speech (late talking) can be a symptom of conditions including autism, intellectual disability, hearing loss, language disorders, and so on.[46] However, it is not uncommon for parents seeking explanations about the late talking to have their child tested *only* for placement in an autism classroom or autism treatment program. Indeed, parents coming to our clinic have expressed confusion over going to a specialist who ruled out autism and then being told that their child is being placed in an autism program at school. How could this happen? The reason is that the specialized assessment may have used a widely used—and validated—process such as described in the DSM-5 manual to perform a *differential diagnostic evaluation*, whereas the school or other agency used a checklist to establish eligibility based on broader confirmatory qualifications. Most late-talking children can be made *eligible* for an ASD program, and children who have difficulty understanding spoken language can easily be made eligible for ADHD programs if a differential diagnosis is not performed properly. And this despite the fact that the children *do not* meet the DSM diagnostic criteria for ASD or ADHD.

Many years ago, local pediatricians were referring patients to me for an intervention study I was conducting for children who talk late. The head of a large group practice told me that they were impressed with the fact that different children I had seen received individualized diagnosis and treatment recommendations. Some of the children had speech disorders, others had difficulty understanding, others had autism, others had generalized intellectual disabilities, and so on. This physician then told me that some of the other clinicians the practice referred to evidently diagnosed all children with the same label—and prescribed the same treatment even when they did not have identical symptoms.

So what can an intuitive parent do? The most straightforward answer is to ask questions prior to the evaluation. What kinds of things are you testing for? What kinds of tests will you be using? If my child has trouble understanding what is being said, how will that affect the results of testing? Please tell me about the different kinds of diagnoses your center makes: Are you testing for program eligibility for ASD, ADHD, intellectual disability, or learning disability? What percentage of the children who you see at your center (or in your practice) receive these diagnoses? You can also ask what kinds of treatments are recommended. If the center diagnoses all children as having "processing disorder," "sensory integration deficit," or disruptions of rhythm and timing and funnels patients into these prepackaged programs regardless of their symptoms, seek out a different evaluation that doesn't use a one-size-fits-all diagnosis and treatment package.

The clinician should provide a written report with all the

tests, results, and recommendations and also be willing to discuss their diagnosis with the parents and inform them of the reasons for their conclusions. If, for example, a diagnosis of ASD or ADHD is given, the clinician should say what behaviors and traits were identified and what tests were given. Parents should be invited to ask questions and should be treated with respect even when they disagree! Sometimes, when I have had to tell parents that their child has intellectual disabilities, the parents disagree. Parents in this situation may tell me about all the things their child knows—and can do—so I would never try to contradict or in any way denigrate this narrative. Rather than trying to browbeat them into accepting my conclusions, I do my best to answer questions and tell them how and why I reached this conclusion. If they continue to disagree, I do not push the point but rather focus on areas where the parents do see challenges for their child. This could be in speaking and/or understanding spoken language. I say, for example, "Let's teach your child how to talk and how to understand because we agree that he needs help with those skills." If I am correct in my diagnosis, it will become clear over time that the child does indeed have intellectual disability and will learn more slowly than other children in multiple aspects of learning.

A few years ago, I saw a three-year-old boy whose parents were both professionals. They were quite upset when I told him that their child had autism, and they told me why I was mistaken. They did see that he was behind in his speaking ability and so accepted intensive intervention designed to teach him how to talk. I followed up with the family a year later, and the little boy was speaking in short sentences. But it also had become clear that he displayed both the reduced social motivation and the restricted interests that are the hallmarks of autism. His father told me that they were very grateful for my help in improving his speaking ability, but while I thanked him for that, I again told him the truth: that it was now even clearer than it had been earlier that their son did indeed have autism. Whether he was more ready to hear that information or not, I don't know, but I was very grateful that he had at least accepted my recommendation for verbal intervention. There was no need for me to ram my opinion down their throats and risk alienating this family! In general, clinicians evaluating learning differences should be open-minded and supportive of the families they work with.

What Should the Treatment Be?

After a differential diagnosis has been performed and the clinician has discussed the reason for his or her diagnosis, a treatment program will likely be discussed. Again, parents should ask questions—and get answers. In general, the treatment should be focused *directly* on improving a child's learning weaknesses and on empowering the child to learn compensatory strategies. For example, a child with learning disabilities in reading should be taught to read and to understand (comprehend) what she reads. She should not be taught to clap her hands in time to a metronome, tolerate deep pressure, jump on a trampoline, or do anything else that does not focus on reading. To be sure, if a child cannot tolerate noise, desensitizing her could be a worthwhile goal. But this should be done using desensitization procedures rather than through dubious techniques like sensory brushing or wearing a weighted vest.

A number of years ago, I worked with a family whose son had autism and who was deathly afraid of the noise made by the air conditioner when it came on. His reaction was so strong that he literally tore holes in the drywall at the house whenever the air-conditioning unit turned on. Another clinician had diagnosed him with sensory integration deficit and prescribed wearing a weighted vest and brushing his arm with a soft brush in order to improve the condition. Neither so-called treatment was effective at all. In contrast, I recorded the noise of the air conditioner turning on and gradually desensitized him. This was done by playing the noise softly when he was engaged in one of his favorite activities—playing video games. He tolerated the noise at low volume. After several weeks, I gradually increased the volume until it reached the same level as the actual air-conditioning noise. By this time, the noise no longer bothered him because he had been desensitized. I also (along with my colleagues at the clinic) taught this child how to talk, but the parents seemed much more grateful to be able to turn the air-conditioning on during the hot, humid summer months in Nashville! Scientific studies have shown that desensitization of this kind, because it focuses directly on the particular sensitivity that the child has, can be effective.[47] Similarly, intuitive parents will identify exactly what they want their child to learn and teach that *directly*.

If a teacher or other learning specialist pushes for ADHD medication—and they should *not* be—ask whether their real concern is to improve the child's behavior in the classroom, and also be sure to ask whether alternative strategies have been tried. I have worked with many, many children with ADHD and taught them to reduce movement and increase attention using behavioral self-monitoring—without medication. I am not opposed to medication when it is warranted. It is clear that medication benefits many children with ADHD.[48] The scientific literature also clearly shows that behavioral interventions such as self-monitoring can be highly effective as well.[49] Be aware, though, that just as is the case with ASD and learning disabilities, indirect training programs such as Interactive Metronome, "executive function training," or short-term-memory drills are unlikely to be effective. An analysis of studies looked at these forms of training and concluded that "studies training short-term memory alone resulted in moderate magnitude improvements in short-term memory . . . whereas training attention did not significantly improve attention and training mixed executive functions did not significantly improve the targeted executive functions."[50] In other words, the short-term-memory drills improved short-term memory (children learn what you teach them!), but not the broader "executive function" skills. In contrast, a review of school-based treatments that, for example, taught children how to sit still for longer periods of time, focus on listening during class, write down their assignments, complete homework, and so on found that attention was improved and movement was decreased.[51] An intuitive parent intuitively knows that this is true: Teaching a child with ADHD how to monitor and improve their ADHD symptoms improves their ADHD!

If you do decide to try medication treatment for your child, be sure to discuss what to expect, as well as any potential side effects, with the physician. Parents should never feel pressured into accepting a treatment they do not agree with or that has not been thoroughly explained. Parents also have a right to know what the expected outcomes are and how long it will take (or may take) to achieve those outcomes. Questions to ask may include: How will I know if the treatment is working? If the treatment doesn't work, what are the alternatives I can try with my child? Is there a plan for transitioning away from the medication in the future?

Finally, parents should be treated as partners in the intervention process rather than as impediments—or adversaries—and invited to participate in the treatment in whatever ways they can. Some parents are not able to provide tutoring or other kinds of interventions themselves, and this is fine. Parents should never be handed a guilt trip when a home treatment program is not feasible; there are lots of reasons why this could be the case. On the other hand, parents should always be *offered* the opportunity to assist with the treatment plan. In my experience, some parents can be very engaged in intervention while others cannot. The overall majority, though, are eager to help and are awesome supporters—and advocates—for their child with learning differences. Regardless, a clinician, tutor, or teacher should always keep parents informed about goals, activities, and progress and should support parents' efforts to implement home programs to the extent that they are able. This is not just my opinion; numerous scientific studies have supported parent training as an excellent intervention for children with learning differences.[52] If the parents are able, they should be sure to offer assistance to the clinician and set up a process for regular consultation with the people involved in helping their child learn.

- Rates of ASD, ADHD, and learning disabilities are skyrocketing in the United States today. One cannot help wondering whether the least part of this increase is due to pushing learning on children before their developing brains are ready to receive the information.
- Other countries, such as Finland, have much lower rates of these disabilities and have much better learning outcomes. Coincidentally, Finnish educators are also more patient with when things are taught and do not subscribe to an "earlier is better" mentality.
- If your child is struggling with her lessons or if a teacher suggests ADHD—or any other learning problem—it is important to determine whether the problem is arising from a mismatch between the child's developmental level and learning style in a one-size-fits-all modern classroom, or whether it is indeed ADHD, ASD, or another learning problem. Ask yourself whether the problem can be solved by simply changing the teacher, classroom, or school. Many of my patients have had their "ADHD" "cured" simply by switching to a curriculum that better fits their own style.
- No parent should automatically assume that there is nothing wrong when their child displays a learning difference, such as a language disorder, ADHD, or ASD, or is behind on a

developmental milestone, such as beginning to speak. They should discuss their concerns with their pediatrician or family physician.

- If an educational and/or psychological evaluation is scheduled, parents should be sure to insist that this be a *differential diagnosis*—one in which various explanations for the learning difference are considered—rather than simply a *confirmatory* evaluation wherein a child is made eligible for services under a preordained category such as ASD or ADHD.

- The evaluation should include not only clinical tests but cognitive assessment and achievement tests, with the goal of identifying not only weaknesses (red flags) but also specifying a child's strengths (green flags) so that an individualized learning plan can be developed.

- The clinician conducting the evaluation should provide a written report and be willing to discuss the reasons for his or her conclusions with parents and should also be willing to answer any and all questions the parents may have. If parents disagree with the clinician, they should not be made to feel that they are in denial or that the conclusions are being rammed down their throat. The clinician should seek areas of consensus as a starting point for intervention.

- The intervention itself should directly target deficit areas rather than being a generic or tangential plan. For example, a child with reading-based learning disabilities should be taught to read so that reading comprehension and/or phonics are emphasized in tutoring rather than "auditory processing," "executive functioning," "sensory integration," or other indirect methods or packages.

- Be aware that there are many "snake-oil" solutions being pushed on desperate parents. If a special diet, software-based computer learning program, or learning "package" touts cures

for many different conditions, it is unlikely to actually be effective. Effective treatment is individualized and specific to a
child's unique patterns of strengths and weaknesses.

- Finally, do not get caught up in the educational rat race and
  lose sight of what is important for your child. Intuitive parents
  value not only educational achievement but also a positive,
  interactive relationship with their child. Never lose sight of
  this, whether or not your child has ASD, ADHD, intellectual
  disability, or another type of learning difference.

chapter 10

Follow Your Intuition to Enjoy the Journey

One of the real tragedies of parenting in modern society is that stresses and expectations end up robbing parents of the joys and triumphs of one of the most profound experiences of their lives: raising a child.

Today, advances in public health and modern medicine have dramatically increased the odds that a baby will be born healthy and will avoid many of the diseases that struck down so many children in previous generations. A child born in the United States today has a life expectancy of seventy-nine years, whereas just prior to World War II, less than seventy years ago, a child born in the United States had a life expectancy of sixty-two years.

My mother-in-law was born in the early 1920s. In addition to an older sister, she had two brothers, both of whom died before they reached kindergarten age. That was not at all unusual in those days. Essentially, her parents lost half their children to childhood disease. I can only imagine the pain and loss they felt. What would my life be like if three or four of my children had died when they were babies or toddlers? Even the thought of this brings tears to my eyes. Although the 50 percent death rate in my mother-in-law's family was higher than average, infant mortality statistics in the United States from 1920 indicate that more than 100 out of 1,000 babies born in the United States that year—or 10 percent—did not celebrate their first birthday. In 2012, fewer than 6 per 1,000— much less than 1 percent—did not make it to their first birthday. Now, 6 per 1,000 is still too many infant deaths, and the United States ratio is higher than a number of other places, such as Monaco, Bermuda, Singapore, Japan, Sweden, and Hong Kong, all of which have infant mortality rates of less than 3 per 1,000. But in general, having babies in countries with a reasonably developed public health infrastructure is much safer than it used to be.

Childhood diseases such as polio, measles, pertussis (whooping cough), and tetanus that ravaged many families in the past became significantly less prevalent in the twentieth century, thanks to effective vaccines. In addition, medical science now can often save babies born prematurely, even when they weigh less than one pound at birth. And when a baby gets sick, pediatricians and other child specialists are well equipped to treat diseases and other health conditions that even a few generations ago meant lifelong disability or even death. I am profoundly grateful that my children and grandchildren are the beneficiaries of these discoveries and advances in medical knowledge and medical technology.

At the same time, the complexity of the same modern society that conveys so many benefits to babies today appears to cause ever-increasing stress in many parents. It is hard for anyone to know how to navigate in this global, wired, fast-paced, and fast-changing world, and perhaps our collective anxiety about that fact has given rise to the mistaken notion that parents need to fine-tune their parenting in order to ensure the best possible outcome for their baby. Every year, there are new studies on nutrition, learning, and brain development. How can anyone possibly keep up with all the new research? In addition, in many families there is either only one parent or two working parents, and both are working longer hours, leaving less time to spend with their children. This either consciously or unconsciously raises the importance of the time parents do get to spend with their babies, and the sense that "quality time" is at a premium may lead a parent to feel that everything his or her baby needs to know has to be packed into a smaller amount of time. And given the importance attributed to getting into the "right" school in our ever more competitive educational environment, it is tempting to skip ahead to academic training right from the start, or at least as early as possible. It just seems like there is not enough time to let a baby grow up at his or her own natural pace. After all, preschool and kindergarten are just around the corner!

Fortunately, although the stresses of parenting are real, and it is certainly true that the demands of modern society leave us less time to spend with our children, quality time doesn't have to be micromanaged to be effective. In fact, because the baby's brain comes prewired to be a highly efficient learning organ, micromanagement and focusing on pushing a child to reach developmental milestones at precisely the right time or ahead of schedule are completely unnecessary. Letting go of the panic and responding to your baby and toddler in natural, playful ways is precisely what they need, both in terms of neural development and in terms of confidence.

There is nothing in life more rewarding—and fun—than raising a child. From an evolutionary perspective it is the most important activity any person can engage in because, in a broad sense, parents are perpetuating the species. But the belief that so much must be learned in so little time all too often means that parents sacrifice precious moments and precious memories to misguided attempts to accelerate learning and thinking through hyperfocused teaching activities.

Slow down! Taking care of your children's basic needs, feeding them, holding them, talking to them, playing with them, and laughing with them is what they really need. Your child's life, like yours, will be fast paced, high pressured, and goal oriented soon enough. Now, rest assured that there is nowhere you or your child needs to get to, that you won't get to just by being present and interacting in natural ways. Mother Nature has given you a great gift: time in which the only thing you need to do, to do a perfect job, is to be with and care for your baby. There is nothing better than watching a baby while he or she is asleep, holding him or her and smiling together, or playing peekaboo over and over again. Please don't miss the opportunity to enjoy these and other wonderful moments in the mistaken belief that such things are trivial or pointless and not an efficient way to wire a baby's brain.

BRINGING IT ALL TOGETHER

ENJOYING YOUR BABY

Babies are the coolest invention ever. They are completely dependent on their parents for survival and are ill-equipped to talk back or otherwise criticize the care they are being given. To be sure, they do come equipped with the ability to let you know when they are hungry, tired, or otherwise out of sorts. And of course, because their needs often require immediate attention both day and night, mom and dad are often sleep deprived, which can make some opportunities to enjoy the baby easy to miss. On the other hand, babies do sleep quite a bit—usually, anyway—so there are fairly long stretches when parents can catnap or attend to the myriad of non-baby responsibilities in their lives. Single parents who have essentially 24/7 solo child-rearing responsibility do not have the luxury of "tag teaming" to care for their babies and so must be especially on the lookout for opportunities for rest and respite.

Many families seek out additional caring for their infants. This could be in the form of grandparents or other family members or arranging for child care for part of the day. I have talked to many parents, especially mothers, who worry that because their baby is receiving care from someone else during much of the day, "mommy time" must be heavily dedicated to "teaching." Parents appear to experience some degree of panic that the regular care that meets their child's physical needs is somehow inadequate to meet their educational needs. Actually, observing quality time does not mean that a parent needs to morph into a "tiger mother" on steroids to pack a day's worth of learning into one or two precious hours. In fact, regular child care, both by parents and other caregivers, does plenty to ensure that an infant's brain is being properly wired. Ironically, insecurity about whether one or two hours of time with their baby is sufficient for learning leads some parents to mistakenly believe that they have to plug in to special software or video learning in order to maximize their baby's intellectual development. Sadly, this myth ends up reducing bonding time and fun time with mommy and daddy even further.

The truth is that, even given the sheer amount of work taking care of a baby entails every day, there are still plenty of opportunities for watching and enjoying infant development. This is true even if parents share part of their child care with others. Remember that parents do not need to build an adult brain in one year—or even three years! Please do not let guilt or insecurity, especially over having limited time during a busy day, derail your intuition and common sense about how to take care of and interact with your baby. Playing Little Piggies, Itsy-Bitsy Spider, or Patty-Cake with your six-month-old is every bit as valuable, if not more valuable, than putting her in front of an "educational" DVD. The whole key is to spend whatever time you can afford totally immersed in communicating and playing with your baby.

A baby comes into the world with a set of prewired reflexes to help her survive. No one has to show the baby how to suck, and if you put your finger or something else in their little hands, they will naturally hold on very tightly. They also can cry and make "comfort" sounds while eating. Because having a baby, especially a first baby, is such a physically challenging task for new mothers, the exhaustion and recovery from childbirth may render these moments a bit of a blur. However, many mothers I have talked to over the years have fond memories of the first moments and first weeks of holding and feeding their new baby.

I was fortunate to be present during the birth of all seven of my children. After each one was born and my wife was resting after the exhausting effort she exerted during labor and delivery, I took them from the nurse and sat rocking and talking to each for hours. It didn't really matter what I said, although it was always about how they were born into a family that loves them very much and that their father was very excited to have them join the menagerie. Indeed, after my fifth child was born, I later learned that the terrific physician who delivered him went home and told his wife that the parents having this fifth child seemed even more excited with their baby than did many couples having their first. I suspect that he got that impression because we were indeed extremely grateful to have this child join our family; even with four "priors" we had learned to focus on treasuring the moment and experiencing the joy of having a baby and creating a new person. Any given day may feel exhausting and endless, but a child is changing minute to minute, and the time between birth and the first birthday is unbelievably fleeting.

It is amazing how much development occurs in that short time. Although the baby does not talk in words until around her first birthday, plenty of communication emerges en route. Although an infant is an amazingly helpless creature, before long she is moving, looking, and communicating in her own way. This first year will see her go from undifferentiated crying, to making different non-crying noises, to babbling that sounds like talking, to first words. The first year will also see her going from barely able to move, to rolling over, to crawling, and perhaps to taking her first tentative steps. The baby will also be limited to mother's milk or infant formula for the first part of the first year but will be able to have some cake (if her parents wish!) on her first birthday—and will be eating a variety of foods (in addition to mother's milk and/or formula) by then. Of course, this remarkable progress co-incides with foundational development of the baby's brain as it becomes ready for a lifetime of learning and thinking.

But the relatively slow and incremental day-to-day nature of this development makes it easy to miss. I recently had a young mother remark that her infant was boring because he wasn't changing what he did very much. In truth, he was probably making changes every day, but such small changes that they could be easily overlooked. Only after her child reached about four months of age did this young mother begin to notice lots of changes and to get very excited about them. I wouldn't want anyone to misconstrue her comment as a lack of interest or attachment to her baby. Rather, she didn't notice all the small changes he made as an infant—in part, perhaps, because she was sleep deprived and overwhelmed by the many adjustments that come with new parenthood.

But it is worthwhile to train yourself to notice small changes in your baby. For example, listen to the small changes in how they sound when they cry and when they babble. Try to imitate the sounds they make. Notice subtle changes in how they reach out and grab objects and how they play with toys. Again, imitate their movements and talk to them about what they are doing. Your baby won't understand all your words, but their brain will process this information as well as the social interaction itself. Routines such as bedtime, bath time, and feeding are important, and babies will also follow regular patterns in their behavior and in their speech. These routines will be augmented as the baby gets older and their brain learns more and more about controlling and coordinating their sensory and motor systems. Indeed, routines are the very foundations upon which development, and brain architecture, are built.

It is fine if it turns out that you can only spend an hour or two with your baby. Try to avoid feeling like each of the steps the baby learns must be guided or, worse, hurried along. Learn to tune in to your baby's unique temperament, traits, and routines. If you do so, responding to your baby will come naturally. Some babies are more analytical and cautious: They seem to watch for a while and then make rapid progress after they decide to try something new. One of my children was perfectly capable of walking by the time she was twelve months old but waited until she was sixteen months old before she stopped crawling. But after she started walking, she did not toddle at all and walked perfectly. She was running one or two months later. She was just more naturally cautious and analytical than some of my other children. Other babies are adventurous. They are more active and push the envelope of development. One of my nieces started walking when she was nine months old. She fell a lot and bumped her head, but she was determined to explore everything as quickly as she could.

Your goal is to watch a baby so as to learn about his or her unique abilities and then to respond to and nurture these, rather than trying to accelerate development or micromanage them into a cookie-cutter path. There was no need to hurry my niece, she walked early anyway; and there was no point in hurrying my daughter, even though her first birthday passed without her walking. She caught up quickly when the time was right. My mother indicated that I also walked late. She reported that I would walk in my playpen when I was a year old, but not outside. Perhaps I was cautious, like my daughter. Interestingly, my oldest granddaughter started walking when she turned sixteen months and, like her mother, was running less than one month later.

Developing powers of observation is not only fun but also serves as the foundation for responding to your baby; later, you will apply what you've observed to your growing child in ways that will help her learn. Another technological advance that is a boon to parents is the wide availability of relatively inexpensive cameras and video cameras, including smartphone versions. I can assure you that images of your baby as she grows up will be highly valued as you grow older. It may even be helpful to use smartphone video to record things your baby does every day. At the end of the day, when baby is asleep, these can be shared with a spouse or partner who missed all the exciting moments. In addition, it can be instructive to watch what your baby was doing last month, last week, or even yesterday. You'll be amazed, in retrospect, how much your baby is developing and how much interaction is going on while you are meeting your baby's needs. Don't forget to send these to grandma and grandpa as well (who love getting them, believe me!).

Most babies learn to walk and talk during this first year, but it is all too easy to overlook the magic as it unfolds. That immobile, inarticulate infant will be walking and talking before you know it. Be sure to notice what is happening along the way, and try not to let the relative sameness of day-to-day caregiving obscure your baby's successes. Take lots of pictures and videos! Do not let worry and panic fundamentally alter the way you interact with your baby or, worse, replace or displace natural interaction with "educational" activities that are not designed to properly teach a baby. Adapting "brain games" or reading programs that teach a school-age child will not match an infant's or a toddler's natural learning style and will not activate their brain properly to engage thinking and reasoning. It is far better to simply react to your baby's gaze, grasp, and vocalizations than to strap them into a baby seat and push the "on" button on the computer or DVD player. Learn to push your own "on" button for social interaction and play instead.

ENJOYING YOUR TODDLER

After a baby's first birthday, development comes fast and furious. That one-year-old who took her first steps will be running by the time her second birthday arrives. Those first words will turn into short phrases and her vocabulary will go from a few words to two hundred or more. And "What's that?" questions will emerge as well as the toddler seeks new information and is curious about nearly everything. In addition, most toddlers are reasonably good-natured; the temper tantrums of the "terrible twos" (and into the threes and fours) have not yet arrived. This is the time when the developing child is highly focused on her parents. She will imitate gestures, sounds, and words and is constantly looking to her parents for guidance and reassurance. Of course, there is plenty of exploring going on as well, and parents need to be vigilant to keep their baby safe as her sense of danger will likely not be fully developed yet.

This is precisely the wrong time to sit down and drill a child on schoolwork. A toddler's natural learning style is to move around, exploring objects while getting her parents' input. She will touch an unfamiliar object and look at mom for information about the object. Mother should name the object and pause, then provide additional information in a short sentence. For example, when the toddler grabs the kitty's food bowl, you could say "Bowl . . . That is the kitty's bowl." This is also a time to show the toddler what the object is used for and to provide information on how to play with the object. In this case, mother could meow like a cat and pretend to eat from the bowl. After that, daddy can spin the bowl, bang on it with a spoon, or roll it on the floor. If the toddler picks up the bowl and spins it, mother and father can imitate the toddler's action, which many toddlers find to be hilarious.

Remember that no two-dimensional vocabulary lesson could replicate this kind of natural, spontaneous, playful, three-dimensional, information-dense interaction. A video clip of a cat eating from a bowl has no idea, of course, whether a toddler is watching it; and if she is watching it, whether she's looking at the bowl or at the kitty. A video doesn't involve any encounter with an actual bowl, so the child isn't touching or moving that bowl in ways that activate motoric and sensory centers in her brain. The video doesn't know that there is also a bowl on the viewer's own kitchen floor that her cat eats from, so it can't inspire her to make that contextual connection. Neither can the video engage the baby emotionally, encourage social interaction, or help her forge and deepen relational bonds. Nothing about the video creates an experience of learning as a fun, pleasurable, possibly even funny activity. Finally, the video couldn't "happen" as an immediate consequence of her having expressed interest in, being attentive to, or being motivated to learn about the bowl. It doesn't *know with a high degree of certainty* that this toddler is ready to receive the information it contains and is not able to deliver it at precisely the right time to develop the child's brain.

Only parents and caregivers can provide the kind of multifaceted, interactional learning that wires a child's brain for learning, continued development, and life in the real world.

PRESCHOOL: PERSONALITY PLUS AND CURIOSITY GALORE

Between the ages of two and four, children wear their emotions on their sleeves. They don't call them the "terrible twos" for nothing! Development in these years, both in terms of a child's brain and in terms of what the child says and does, is simply astounding.

With regard to verbal development, a two-year-old will be using short phrases such as "go bye-bye," "want more cookie," "me love mommy," and so on. A four-year-old can easily produce five- and six-word sentences and will often use complex syntax. "I know where we can go," "What's for dinner tonight?" "Why is the sky blue?" and "You are the best mommy in the world!" are examples of what a four-year-old might say. (I should note that he might also say "You are the worst mommy in the world!" if he's unhappy with something you have or haven't done; but don't worry, most parents hear the same critique at some point or another!)

Play patterns develop from exploring objects and simple play routines in a two-year-old to simple card games, board games, pretend games, and other socially oriented play in a four-year-old. To be sure, four-year-olds have not developed sophisticated peer interaction skills nor the ability to play complex team sports, but they are far more capable of relatively sophisticated interactive play than are two-year-olds. Pretend play evolves from using objects in imaginative ways (e.g., pretending to drink from a cup or using a fork to pretend to brush her hair), to role-playing and "dress up" with favorite dolls or action figures, and the ability to generate imaginative stories. Of course, four-year-olds love to be told fairy tales and other imaginative stories as well as making them up.

The neuroscience of imagination is remarkable. Simply put, imagination activates the same centers in the brain that would be activated if the events were real. If I imagine I am eating an apple, the motor (movement) areas of the brain responsible for bringing the apple to my mouth, biting, and chewing all get activated. As an example, the motor strip at the top of the brain that is responsible for moving my hand will get activated whether I actually eat an apple or just imagine doing so. The cerebellum, which is responsible for routine motor activities such as chewing, will also get activated during imagining as if the apple were actually being chewed. But in addition, even *more* brain activation occurs when we are imagining doing something than when we actually do it. When I am actually eating an apple, the visual centers at the back of my head in the occipital lobe monitor only whether my hand is on the apple and whether it is being properly guided toward my mouth. I will notice what color the apple is, but visual processing of this action is relatively minimal. On the other hand, if I imagine I'm eating an apple, the visual centers in my brain light up just as if I were watching a video of someone eating an apple. Imagining eating an apple also activates language centers responsible for meaning that aren't activated by actually eating an apple. That is, the meaning centers in the front of the brain that conjure up words such as "apple" and "eating" also light up under brain scans when someone is asked to imagine eating an apple. (I only wish that imagining I am exercising, which does "light up" my brain as if I were actually exercising, had the same physical benefits!)

Moreover, imagination, like fluid reasoning and problem solving, involves multiple centers in the brain. The key here, in terms of physical and mental development, is that there are no "brain games" or special programs that can take the place of a toddler's real-life 3-D experiences because these are the *foundation* for subsequent imagination. In short, I cannot *accurately* imagine eating an apple unless I have actually eaten one. Watching a DVD or an educational program showing someone eating an apple will only provide the watching and listening part of the experience. The motor experience, the taste, the smell, and all the other nuances of eating an apple cannot be conveyed within the context of a DVD or educational computer program. This, in turn, means that the neural pathways connecting these various centers of the brain will be underdeveloped and so, therefore, will their integration. On one hand, "hard-wiring" rote answers to vocabulary questions in a toddler can be impressive and get them a good score on developmental checklists. On the other hand, this artificially accelerated memorization process short-circuits reasoning, visualization, and the other aspects of actually knowing multiple and subtle characteristics of the vocabulary word and will likely have a long-term cost in terms of fluid reasoning, problem solving, and imagination. Given a choice between playing with a toddler with objects they are interested in versus focusing on rote learning of educational items, it is far better to spend the time nurturing and responding to a toddler in the real world with objects and activities that are relevant to her current state of mental, physical, and emotional development.

THE INTUITIVE PARENT KNOWS HOW TO RESPOND TO TANTRUMS

Nearly all children, when they are toddlers, throw tantrums when they don't get their way. There are lots of reasons for this, including that they often do not have the words to express what they want. And because their time sense is pretty much restricted to the here and now, deferred gratification or the failure to immediately satisfy the request can result in a meltdown. Not surprisingly, tantrums have been the subject of many studies over the last hundred years. And it is remarkable how consistent the results of these studies have been.

Tantrums are not the result of poor parenting. Rather, they are a natural part of development. Parents should not be alarmed or upset when their child has tantrums. Actually, tantrums in toddlers are an important part of development: These episodes teach her how to regulate emotions and how to deal with being upset. Given that the world will not always conform to a toddler's wishes, getting upset is unavoidable.

As we've discussed in Chapter 7, parents play a vital role in helping a toddler to cope with frustration, in part by serving as role models. The best thing parents can do when a tantrum occurs is to remain calm and wait for the child to work things out on his or her own. Some parents have been influenced by a popular myth that any adversity or negative emotion a child experiences may constitute harm and be detrimental to the child's emotional development. When their baby or toddler gets upset, or they feel he or she might become upset, they rush in to talk the child out of it, or to distract him or her with toys or food or a change of activity. This teaches the toddler that it is the parents' job to ensure that he or she is happy at all times and that adversity is to be avoided at all costs. At the least, the parent deprives the toddler of the opportunity to gain control of his or her own moods—and mental health.

This is problematic from several perspectives. First, a toddler needs to learn how to calm himself and how to deal with adversity. Every human being is going to have to face frustration at some point in their life. As with learning and problem solving, the brain must be wired to cope with frustration; distracting a child away from a tantrum or "fixing" the frustration that is gathering into one derails this important developmental process.

In addition, as we've seen, distracting or deflecting the tantrum using food or a toy will actually increase the tantrums, because any behavior that is rewarded will increase. This fundamental principle of operant conditioning is easily forgotten in the heat of the moment and the desire to calm the child down when he's upset. One time my youngest son wanted a toy at Walmart. Not surprisingly, it was a dinosaur. When his mother said no, he immediately laid on the floor and started screaming and kicking his feet. If his mother had given in and bought the toy, or given him juice or some other food to calm him down, he would've learned that screaming, lying on the floor, and kicking is an effective way to control his mother's behavior and to get rewarded. Guess what would happen the next time he wanted something?

So, how should the situation be handled? Because this particular child was my sixth, we had learned to go to the store in pairs. That is, I went shopping along with my wife and young children. When the meltdown occurred, I didn't say a word; I simply picked my son up and took him out of the store while my wife continued shopping. I sat with him in the car and waited until he calmed down and then took him back into the store. To be sure, while I was carrying my screaming child out of the store, I got my share of looks from other people. I can only imagine what they were thinking. But I really wasn't worried about that because it seemed more important to me to help my young son learn how to deal with frustration. The key here is to ignore the tantrum as best as you can and wait until the child calms down. Then, it is equally important that he be *rewarded* for calming down. In this case, the reward was to return to the store, which he liked. Note that we did not buy him the dinosaur or try to distract him by using food or another toy. We simply let the tantrum run its course.

What is happening in the brain during all this? When any of us are upset, our brain becomes saturated with neurotransmitters. This is important in terms of responding to highly stressful situations: If a predator is about to eat us, we have to tune up our brains to move as quickly as possible. And the emotions associated with the stress take precedence over any other activities—it's a matter of survival. This is exactly what happens with toddlers, except that instead of confronting a predator, they are not getting a toy they want, hearing the word "no," or having to sit in their car seat when they don't want to. These upsets seem rather minor to an adult but are every bit as real to a toddler as the threat of being eaten by a predator. Toddlers having a tantrum are very upset, are under a great deal of stress, are flooded with neurotransmitters, and don't know how to control their heightened emotions. In nature, after the danger has passed, the neurochemicals associated with the fight-or-flight response are pumped out of our brains and we become rational again. The same neurochemical "cool-off" will happen with toddlers if we let the process take its natural course.

Unfortunately, it can be really hard to be patient with

tantrums in public, because people looking on may be judgmental. The notion of having a "happy" childhood and the peer pressure that parents seem to put on one another to be the "perfect" mother or father derails this natural process. I recall another time when this same child, my youngest son, had a relatively severe meltdown in Target. Don't you hate it that there are attractive toys and candy in front of the cash register at so many stores? These can really stress out parents and induce tantrums in toddlers. Waiting in a long checkout line only adds stress to the situation. My son was in the shopping cart in the checkout line and wanted one of the toy cars on display. When my wife said no, he lost it worse than usual, screaming very loudly. My poor wife was embarrassed as the other people in the checkout line began giving her dirty looks, but she didn't want to simply leave the shopping cart and take him out of the store. I had another cart (with six children at that time, we sometimes had to use two carts to get our groceries) and could not pick him up and take him out as I usually did. And on this particular day I had ended up being several places behind her in the checkout line with two of our other children in the cart.

Fortunately, I could see the stress she was under and felt bad for her. In order to deflect the embarrassment from her, I remarked, "Hey, lady, can't you take care of your kid? See how good my children are being?" This had just the effect I was hoping for: Everyone in line took their attention off my wife and looked at me with astonished disapproval. Now they directed their scorn to the rude man who was picking on the poor lady whose child was having a meltdown. Of course, they didn't know that I was actually the father and husband. I thought it was hilarious, and I didn't mind that these strangers now consoling my poor wife, taking her side against me, thought that I was a jerk. The point is, there was a lot of pressure on my wife to give in during the tantrum because it was embarrassing and because people nearby were clearly questioning her abilities as a mother.

What would the consequences have been if she'd given in? Because the tantrum was severe, and other, relatively more minor, tantrums had been ignored, my son would have learned that throwing a severe tantrum was a great way to get what he wanted and that if he simply ratcheted up the intensity in public places he could control his mother's behavior. On the other hand, if a parent understands that having tantrums is a normal part of development and in fact is essential for developing emotional regulation and dealing with frustration, he or she is prepared to react calmly and positively to the meltdown. The reason I did not mind all the scorn from the other parents in the Target checkout line was because I knew that the fact that my son was having a severe tantrum was in no way a negative reflection on my wife's parenting skills.

Because tantrums will occur, it is important to have a game plan in place and think through in advance what your response will be. It is difficult to be rational when a child is having a tantrum because their crying and anger actually produce a stress response in the parent, so that the parent's own brain is now also awash in the neurotransmitters generated in emotionally charged situations. Having a game plan and a response ready to go will actually reduce the parent's stress response in addition to providing the opportunity for the child to learn how to deal with adversity and their own emotional responses.

A key point here is that a toddler will eventually calm down on his or her own. Some toddlers are so strong willed that it may take a while, and patience is required. It is especially important for parents to avoid rewarding tantrums in strong-willed toddlers as they will continue to increase the intensity of their meltdowns until they get what they want. Be prepared to wait them out. After the tantrum has run its course, a toddler will usually seek reassurance and consoling from his or her parent. And while it may not feel like it during these years, if you behave consistently, your child will "get it" and tantrums will eventually taper off.

Few children enjoy being in a car seat, but of course it is important that they learn to accept this as a matter of safety. My youngest daughter, our seventh child, became very agitated once when I strapped her in her car seat. Because she had only recently become large enough for a front-facing seat, I hypothesized that she was upset about the change in direction and change of position this entailed. Regardless, what ensued was one of the worst tantrums she ever displayed. Fortunately, she could not hold a candle to some of her older siblings on that score, but for her this was a relatively severe tantrum. Naturally, I waited her out, and after about ten minutes she stopped screaming and simply was crying (a sad cry). She then said to me tearfully, "Need a hug!" Of course, I took her out of her car seat and gave her a big hug while telling her how much I loved her. Soon she was smiling again, and there was no problem putting her back in the car seat. On the way to the store, I praised her for being such a good girl in the car.

I must say that it is hard to be the seventh child. By the time she came into the family, her older siblings had pretty much succeeded in introducing their parents to just about every conceivable twist and turn on the parenting road map, and we were well prepared to respond to her antics. For example, when she was two and displayed her first tantrum, I simply smiled at her and walked out of the room. She looked at me as if to say, "Hey, Dad, this should be tearing your heart out, I am doing a full-body layout and crying my lungs out!" She was even banging her little fists on the floor and kicking her feet. Very cute! I now wish I had shot video of the whole thing. Of course, by this time I'd gotten used to the hysterics of her older sister, who held the family record for the worst tantrums. And our sixth child, the young man who delighted in having severe meltdowns while in Target and Walmart, had prepared us to deal with the worst a toddler could generate. So, by this point, my wife and I had a lot of experience and confidence in how to deal with tantrums and were not in the least concerned or adversely impacted by anything our seventh child could conjure up.

Understanding the nature of tantrums, and learning how to deal with them, is extremely important because tantrums of a different sort will resurface during the teenage years. As with toddlers, it is very important to be patient and emotionally sensitive, even with teenagers. Stay calm and be sure to listen, but do not try to talk them out of their emotions. Let them learn how to regulate their moods and emotions in the face of all the hormonal changes and new social pressures they are experiencing. The skills parents learn when dealing with their toddlers' tantrums will serve them well when teenage years arrive. And if a child has learned how to deal with her emotions as a toddler, her brain is already wired to self-regulate. Consequently, dealing with teenage emotions will be much easier on both parents and teens. They will have the confidence and the experience to understand that being upset is natural, normal, and a passing condition that can be waited out and dealt with in a positive way.

To be sure, as in most families, our teenagers had their share of crises. I recall one episode wherein one of the girls yelled at me at the top of her lungs that I had ruined her life. If I recall correctly, this had to do with the fact that my wife and I had a firm rule that although our young teenagers (regardless of gender) were allowed and even encouraged to go out on group dates (with an adult chaperone), they were not permitted to go out alone on a one-on-one date until passing their sixteenth birthday. Well, naturally, this child had been asked out on a "real" date at the age of fifteen and a half, and I was holding firm to the rule. So when she indicated, at her maximum vocal output, that I had permanently derailed what had heretofore been her promising future life, I calmly responded that this was unfortunate because she had so much of her life still in front of her.

After this episode passed, a few months later something else came up and she once again informed me that I had ruined her life. To this I responded that there was no need to update me on this sad state of affairs. Alas, having ruined her life previously, and accepting full responsibility for this tragic state of affairs, I could see no point in her reiterating my folly on that score: I was in complete concurrence that I had ruined her life and that ruined means ruined. But I did let her know that if her life had become un-ruined in the interval between these capricious and no doubt malicious applications of paternal guidance with regard to her life (or lack thereof), I certainly wish I'd been informed as to the events and timeline associated with the un-ruining process.

Teenagers, like toddlers, have ups and downs in their emotional regulation. If they have learned as toddlers that unhappiness is not a normal state and that a parent's job is to prevent anything unpleasant from happening to them at all costs, then their brain has not been properly wired to cope with the exponentially greater stresses of adolescence. Worse, they will have learned that whenever their parents have failed to prevent them from feeling unhappy or experiencing discomfort, it is the parent's job to then come to the rescue. It is far better to teach a toddler how to regulate his or her own emotions internally and also to teach him or her that unhappiness and discomfort are a natural part of life that will pass. These lessons will not prevent the emotional roller coaster that is often an integral part of adolescence, but will provide them with the behavioral tools and neural wiring to better deal with these ups and downs. Because I knew that these feelings were not an unnatural part of teenage behavior, I was well prepared to respond calmly and positively when they occurred. I am not saying it was always easy, or that I never lost my temper, or that my teenagers always made the choices I would have liked to see, but I can say that I thoroughly enjoyed watching my teenagers develop. I was able to enjoy the journey. And I am enjoying them even more as adults.

My wife and I have a wonderful storehouse of memories

associated with watching our children grow up. And I am genuinely saddened that few of our friends—and seemingly even fewer
of the young parents we know or who I've met through my work—
have the same experience. They seem to be in a near constant
state of panic, stress, and worry about whether they are raising
their children in a way that maximizes their potential. Their
homes are stocked with the latest educational gadgets and whatever other DVDs, apps, games, or learning programs happen to
be the current fashion. Their poor children, though perfectly intelligent and capable, are enrolled in after-school drill classes so
they can better memorize test items. And I have seen the same
things happening in an ever-increasing number of families with
preschool-age children. Education seems to be more and more
focused on work sheets that seem like busywork at best and pointless at worst. I call this intellectual gambit "death by work sheets."

The Joys of Intuitive Parenting

Because having children is basically what human beings have done
for thousands of years by so many people, it is easy to forget how
awe inspiring it is to be a parent. All different kinds of people have
children, and no advanced degrees or special training are required
to have them. People become parents who have never gotten a
driver's license, graduated from high school, or even finished elementary school. Indeed, it is far easier to start a family than to get
a driver's license or to finish high school (or even elementary
school). And after all, all of us were born and we all had parents of
one kind or another. What is so special about that? The answer is
that it is tremendously special for every child and every parent.

Some religions teach that each of us was created in God's image
and likeness. Regardless of whether or not one believes in God, it is
certainly true that having a baby is creating someone in our own
image and likeness. What could be more profound and more

rewarding than that? And what else in our lives, whether it be making a lot of money, building a better mousetrap, or writing the Great American Novel could possibly be more important and satisfying? To raise a child is to take a direct hand in shaping and contributing to the future of humankind. Even more important, it is a very personal, profound, life-changing, and life-enriching experience.

The decision to have a baby and raise him or her over approximately twenty years from infancy to adulthood is rather like bungee jumping off a bridge: One can only hope that things will turn out OK in the end! But raising a child is also among the most rewarding things anyone can do. Barbara Bush, the wife of President George H. W. Bush and mother of President George W. Bush, wisely observed that parenting was full of long days and short years.[1] And this is exactly right. There is an unbelievable amount of work to do every day just taking care of a baby or young child. And it is a round-the-clock enterprise. I spent hundreds and hundreds of nights rocking and talking to my infant children while my hardworking and weary wife got some much-needed shut-eye. And she was by far the one who carried the overwhelming majority of the child-rearing load at our house.

As hard as any given moments, nights, or developmental stages were, I can honestly say that my most treasured memories are of the time I spent with my children. Though I was also trying to remain employed in a competitive medical-school academic environment within the context of a Darwinian "publish or perish" job culture, I do not regret one moment of the time I spent being a fully engaged and involved father, and I can honestly say that nothing in my life has been more rewarding or more important. Now that I am an empty nester, I am all the more grateful I did not lose so many great and memorable moments to stress and worry or derail the good times by pushing "academics" 24/7.

The key to accessing the sheer joy of parenting is to live in the moment with your child. Take all those fears and all those anxieties about whether you are making the grade as a parent and lock them away. These feelings will only steal those precious, all-too-fleeting moments with your baby and will in fact undermine your efforts to be a natural, confident parent. Know, and believe in your heart of hearts, that you have everything you possibly need to be exactly the parent your child needs.

acknowledgments

Of course, there are many people who have contributed—either directly or indirectly—to this book. I deeply appreciate the unfailing and patient support from Niki Papadopoulos, who is my editor at Current/Penguin Random House. She recognized the important elements of intuitive parenting and—through numerous drafts and phone conversations—helped me bring them to life. I count myself fortunate to have benefited from her experience and wisdom. The rest of her team, including Kary Perez, Linda Cowen, and Taylor Fleming, were also so very helpful—and kind. Lisa Kaufman also merits special thanks, because she was crucial in transforming my earlier "professor speak" drafts into ideas and examples that are accessible to intuitive parents.

Professor Steven Pinker at Harvard University also deserves special acknowledgment: the idea for this book arose from a number of conversations—and lively discussions—we had on our photographic jaunts. He was steadfast in his encouragement and was so very helpful in showing me the ropes. My agent, Max Brockman, was also very helpful in guiding me through the steps needed to bring this project to fruition.

Of course I would be remiss if I failed to mention my own wonderful children and grandchildren who continue to inspire me and are the source of so much joy and love and all the other wonderful things associated with being an intuitive parent. I also deeply appreciate their forbearance in providing the terrific examples of intuitive children and grandchildren herein! I am so very proud of each and every one of them. My wife, Mary, has simply been tremendous: a prototypical intuitive parent, who has been supportive and also inspirational. I'm very fortunate indeed that she joined me on embarking on our own amazing journey together as intuitive parents nearly thirty-six years ago.

Finally, I am indebted to all the families I have had the privilege of serving in my work at Vanderbilt University School of Medicine. These families, many of whom have children with developmental challenges such as autism, ADHD, Down syndrome, learning disabilities, or other development disabilities, are simply amazing in the heroic efforts they make every day helping their children learn and grow. They've also been an important source of inspiration and motivation for this book. It is my sincerest wish that the words herein empower these families—and all families— to trust their common sense and be amazing intuitive parents!

notes

Introduction: What is Intuitive Parenting

1. James Boyce, "Parental Anxiety: Why Do Mums and Dads Feel So Guilty?," *Guardian*, August 5, 2014, http://www.theguardian.com/commentisfree/2014/aug/06/parental -anxiety-why-do-mums-and-dads-feel-so-guilty.
2. Ibid.
3. Amy Chua, *Battle Hymn of the Tiger Mother* (New York: Penguin Press, 2011).
4. Lenore Skenazy, *Free-Range Kids: Giving Our Children the Freedom We Had Without Going Nuts with Worry* (Hoboken, NJ: John Wiley & Sons, 2009).
5. Bharat B. Biswal, Maarten Mennes, Xi-Nian Zuo, Suril Gohel, Clare Kelly, Steve M. Smith, Christian F. Beckmann, et al., "Toward Discovery Science of Human Brain Function," *Proceedings of the National Academy of Sciences* 107, no. 10 (2010): 4734–39.

Chapter 1: Mother Nature's Instruction Manual

1. T. H. Clutton-Brock, *The Evolution of Parental Care* (Princeton, NJ: Princeton University Press, 1991).
2. Janine Beisson, and T. M. Sonneborn, "Cytoplasmic Inheritance of the Organization of the Cell Cortex in Paramecium Aurelia," *Proceedings of the National Academy of Sciences of the United States of America* 53, no. 2 (1965): 275–82.
3. Polar Bears International, "Polar Bear Mothers and Cubs FAQ," Polar Bears International, http://www.polarbearsinternational.org/sites/default/files/polar_bear_mothers _and_cubs_faq.pdf.
4. The Fox Website, "Do Foxes Hunt in Packs?" The Mammal Group, University of Bristol, http://www.thefoxwebsite.net/faq/foxecology#q3.
5. Robin W. Baird, "The Killer Whale," in *Cetacean Societies: Field Studies of Dolphins and Whales*, ed. Janet Mann (Chicago: University of Chicago Press, 2000), 127–53.
6. Polar Bears International, "Polar Bear Mothers and Cubs FAQ," Polar Bears International, http://www.polarbearsinternational.org/sites/default/files/polar_bear_mothers _and_cubs_faq.pdf.
7. David. C. Geary, "Evolution of Paternal Investment," in *The Handbook of Evolutionary Psychology*, ed. David M. Buss (Hoboken, NJ: John Wiley & Sons, 2005), 483–505.
8. Ibid.

9. Dorothy G. Singer, Roberta Michnick Golinkoff, and Kathy Hirsh-Pasek, eds., *Play = Learning: How Play Motivates and Enhances Children's Cognitive and Social-Emotional Growth* (New York: Oxford University Press, 2006).

10. Jennifer Kromberg, "How Dads Shape Daughters' Relationships: Dad Creates a Daughter's Conscious and Unconscious Relationship Expectations," *Psychology Today*, July 1, 2013, https://www.psychologytoday.com/blog/inside-out/201307/how-dads -shape-daughters-relationships.

11. Arnold Sameroff, "Transactional Models in Early Social Relations," *Human Development* 18, nos. 1–2 (1975): 65–79.

12. Ibid., and David A. Kolb, *Experiential Learning: Experience as the Source of Learning and Development* (Upper Saddle River, NJ: Pearson Education, 2014).

13. Weiyi Ma, Roberta Michnick Golinkoff, Derek Houston, Kathy Hirsh-Pasek, "Word Learning in Infant- and Adult-Directed Speech," *Language Learning and Development* 7, no. 3 (2011): 185–201. Douglas Quenqua, "Quality of Words, Not Quantity, Is Crucial to Language Skills, Study Finds," *New York Times*, October 16, 2014, http:// www.nytimes.com/2014/10/17/us/quality-of-words-not-quantity-is-crucial-to-la nguage-skills-study-finds.html.

14 Kim Parker and Wendy Wang, "Modern Parenthood: Roles of Moms and Dads Converge as They Balance Work and Family," Pew Research Center, March 14, 2013, http://www.pewsocialtrends.org/2013/03/14/modern-parenthood-roles-of-moms -and-dads-converge-as-they-balance-work-and-family/.

15. Ibid.

16. Common Core State Standards Initiative, "Home," Common Core State Standards Initiative, http://www.corestandards.org/.

17. Brent Gleeson, "3 Great Examples of Successful Mom Entrepreneurs," *Forbes*, June 12, 2014, http://www.forbes.com/sites/brentgleeson/2014/06/12/3-great-examples-of -successful-mom-entrepreneurs/.

18. Federal Trade Commission, "Ads Touting 'Your Baby Can Read' Were Deceptive, FTC Complaint Alleges," FTC, August 28, 2012, http://www.ftc.gov/news-events/press- releases/2012/08/ads-touting-your-baby-can-read-were-deceptive-ftc-complaint.

19. Ibid.

20. Judy S. DeLoache, Cynthia Chiong, Kathleen Sherman, Nadia Islam, Mieke Vanderborght, Georgene L. Troseth, Gabrielle A. Strouse, and Katherine O'Doherty, "Do Babies Learn from Baby Media?," *Psychological Science* 21, no. 11 (2010): 1570–74.

21. Heather L. Kirkorian, Ellen A. Wartella, and Daniel R. Anderson, "Media and Young Children's Learning," *The Future of Children* 18, no. 1 (2008): 39.

22. DeLoache, et al., "Do Babies Learn from Baby Media?," 1570.

23. David Crary, "Your Baby Can Read Company Going Out Of Business," HuffPost Parents, July 16, 2012, http://www.huffingtonpost.com/2012/07/16/your-baby-can -read_n_1677465.html.

24. Federal Trade Commission, "Defendants Settle FTC Charges Related to 'Your Baby Can Read' Program," Federal Trade Commission, August 22, 2014, https://www.ftc .gov/news-events/press-releases/2014/08/defendants-settle-ftc-charges-related-your -baby-can-read-program.

25. Your Baby Can Learn, Web site, http://yourbabycanlearn.com/.

26. Elizabeth L. Tighe and Christopher Schatschneider, "A Dominance Analysis Approach to Determining Predictor Importance in Third, Seventh, and Tenth Grade Reading Comprehension Skills," *Reading and Writing* 27, no. 1 (2014): 101–27.

27. Georgette L. Troseth and Judy S. DeLoache, "The Medium Can Obscure the Message: Young Children's Understanding of Video," *Child Development* 69, no. 4 (1998): 950–65.

28. Robert E. Owens Jr., *Language Development: An Introduction*, 9th ed. (Upper Saddle River, NJ: Pearson Education, 2014).

29. Gordon Wells, *The Meaning Makers: Children Learning Language and Using Language to Learn* (Portsmouth, NH: Heinemann Educational Books, 1986).

30. Steven Pinker, *Language Learnability and Language Development* (Cambridge, MA: Harvard University Press, 1996).

31. Ibid.

32. Marlene Sandlund, Suzanne McDonough, and Charlotte Hager-Ross, "Interactive Computer Play in Rehabilitation of Children with Sensorimotor Disorders: A Systematic Review," *Developmental Medicine and Child Neurology* 51, no. 3 (2009): 173–79.

33. Tristan Lavender, and Bernhard Hommel, "Affect and Action: Towards an Event-Coding Account," *Cognition and Emotion* 21, no. 6 (2007): 1270–96.

34. Bernhard Hommel, "Action Control According to TEC (Theory of Event Coding)," *Psychological Research* 73, no. 4 (2009): 512–26.

35. Martin S. Banks and Philip Salapatek, "Infant Visual Perception," in *Handbook of Child Psychology*, ed. Paul H. Mussen (Hoboken, NJ: John Wiley & Sons, 1983).

36. Patricia K. Kuhl and Andrew N. Meltzoff, "The Bimodal Perception of Speech in Infancy," *Science* 218, no. 4577 (1982): 1138–41, quote on p. 1138, emphasis added.

37. Robert Plutchik, *Emotion: A Psychoevolutionary Synthesis* (New York: Harper and Row, 1980).

38. Daniel S. Messinger, Alan Fogel, and K. Laurie Dickson, "A Dynamic Systems Approach to Infant Facial Action," *The Psychology of Facial Expression* (1997): 205–26.

39. Sylvie Rayna and Ferre Laevers, "Understanding Children from 0 to 3 Years of Age and Its Implications for Education," *European Early Childhood Education Research Journal* 19, no. 2 (2011): 161–72.

40. Lane Strathearn, Jian Li, Peter Fonagy, and P. Read Montague, "What's in a Smile? Maternal Brain Responses to Infant Facial Cues," *Pediatrics* 122, no. 1 (2008): 40–51, quote on p. 40.

41. Heather Bortfeld, Eric Wruck, and David A. Boas, "Assessing Infants' Cortical Response to Speech Using Near-Infrared Spectroscopy," *Neuroimage* 34, no. 1 (2007): 407–15.

42. Strathearn et al., "What's in a Smile?"

43. Daniela Perani, Ferruccio Fazio, Nunzio Alberto Borghese, Marco Tettamanti, Stefano Ferrari, Jean Decety, and Maria Carla Gilardi, "Different Brain Correlates for Watching Real and Virtual Hand Actions," *Neuroimage* 14, no. 3 (2001): 749–58.

44. Betty Hart and Todd R. Risley, *Meaningful Differences in the Everyday Experience of Young American Children* (Baltimore, MD: Paul H. Brookes Publishing, 1995).

45. Deborah L. Kaplan and Kristina M. Graff, "Marketing Breastfeeding: Reversing Corporate Influence on Infant Feeding Practices," *Journal of Urban Health* 85, no. 4 (2008): 486–504, quote on p. 486.

Chapter 2: Brain Science for the Intuitive Parent

1. Max R. Bennett, "The Early History of the Synapse: From Plato to Sherrington," *Brain Research Bulletin* 50, no. 2 (1999): 95–118.

2. John C. Mazziotta, Arthur W. Toga, Alan Evans, Peter Fox, and Jack Lancaster, "A Probabilistic Atlas of the Human Brain: Theory and Rationale for Its Development," *Neuroimage* 2, no. 2 (1995): 89–101.

3. Ibid.

4. Paul Broca, "Sur les mots aphemie, aphasie et aphrasie; Lettre a M. le Professeur Trousseau," *Gazette des hopitaux* 23 (1864).

5. Bryan Kolb, and Robbin Gibb, "Brain Plasticity and Behaviour in the Developing Brain," *Journal of the Canadian Academy of Child and Adolescent Psychiatry* 20, no. 4 (2011): 265–76.

6. Tom Feilden, "A golden age of discovery in neuroscience," BBC, September 5, 2012, http://www.bbc.com/news/health-19367832.

7. Thad A. Polk and Martha J. Farah, "The Neural Development and Organization of Letter Recognition: Evidence from Functional Neuroimaging, Computational Modeling, and Behavioral Studies," *Proceedings of the National Academy of Sciences* 95, no. 3 (1998): 847–52.

8. A. A. Zevenbergen and G. J. Whitehurst, "Dialogic Reading: A Shared Picture Book Reading Intervention for Preschoolers," in *On Reading Books to Children: Parents and Teachers*, ed. Anne van Kleeck, Steven A. Stahl, and Eurydice B. Bauer (Mahwah, NJ: Erlbaum Associates, 2003), 177–200, quote on p. 170; and David S. Arnold and Grover J. Whitehurst, "Accelerating Language Development through Picture Book Reading," *Developmental Psychology* 24, no. 4 (1988): 552–59.

9. H. Lodish, A. Berk, S. L. Zipursky, et al., "Overview of Neuron Structure and Function," section 21.1, in *Molecular Cell Biology*, 4th edition (New York: W. H. Freeman, 2000).

10. Alan Peters, Sanford L. Palay, and Henry deForest Webster, *The Fine Structure of the Nervous System: Neurons and Their Supporting Cells* (New York: Oxford University Press, 1991).

11. Bradley J. Molyneaux, Paola Arlotta, Joao R. L. Menezes, and Jeffrey D. Macklis, "Neuronal Subtype Specification in the Cerebral Cortex," *Nature Reviews Neuroscience* 8 (2007): 427–37.

12. Frederico A. C. Azevedo, Ludmila R. B. Carvalho, Lea T. Grinberg, José Marcelo Farfel, Renata E. L. Ferretti, Renata E. P. Leite, Roberto Lent, and Suzana Hercula no-Houzel, "Equal Numbers of Neuronal and Nonneuronal Cells Make the Human Brain an Isometrically Scaled-Up Primate Brain," *Journal of Comparative Neurology* 513, no. 5 (2009): 532–41.

13. Luciano Fadiga, Laila Craighero, and Alice Roy, "Broca's Region: A Speech Area?" in *Broca's Region*, ed. Yosef Grodzinsky and Katrin Amunts (New York: Oxford University Press, 2006), 137–52.

14. Karl Wernicke, "The Aphasia Symptom-Complex: A Psychological Study on an Anatomical Basis," in *Reader in the History of Aphasia: From Franz Gall to Norman Geschwind*, ed. Paul Eling (Amsterdam: John Benjamins, 1994), 69–89.

15. Margaret A. Naeser, Nancy Helm-Estabrooks, Gale Haas, Sanford Auerbach, and Malukote Srinivasan, "Relationship Between Lesion Extent in 'Wernicke's Area' on Computed Tomographic Scan and Predicting Recovery of Comprehension in Wernicke's Aphasia," *Archives of Neurology* 44 (1987): 73–82.

16. Christian Jarrett, "Why the Left-Brain Right-Brain Myth Will Probably Never Die," *Psychology Today*, June 27, 2012, http://www.psychologytoday.com/blog/brain-myths/201206/why-the-left-brain-right-brain-myth-will-probably-never-die.

17. Mister Numbers, "About Right Brain Math," Mister Numbers Pattern Play Math, http://www.patternplaymath.com/about.htm.

18. This quote comes from the Amazon description to Thomas Biesanz, *Right Brain Math*, (Growth Ink Publishing: 2011), http://www.amazon.com/Right-Brain-Math-Visual-Approach/dp/0979963621/ref=asap_bc?ie=UTF8.

19. Dianne Craft, "Teaching the Right Brain Child: Part I," Education Network of Christian Homeschoolers, http://www.enochnj.org/media/TeachingTheRightBrainedChild1.pdf.

20. Dianne Craft, "Teaching Your Right Brain Child," Dianne Craft Child Diagnostics, http://www.diannecraft.org/teaching-your-right-brain-child/.

21. Helmuth Steinmetz and Rüdiger J. Seitz, "Functional Anatomy of Language Processing: Neuroimaging and the Problem of Individual Variability," *Neuropsychologia* 29, no. 12 (1991): 1149–61.

22. Rosalind Arden, Robert S. Chavez, Rachael Grazioplene, and Rex E. Jung, "Neuroimaging Creativity: A Psychometric View," *Behavioural Brain Research* 214, no. 2 (2010): 143–56.

23. Arne Dietrich and Riam Kanso, "A Review of EEG, ERP, and Neuroimaging Studies of Creativity and Insight," *Psychological Bulletin* 136, no. 5 (2010): 822–48.

24. Karunesh Ganguly and Mu-ming Poo, "Activity-Dependent Neural Plasticity from Bench to Bedside," *Neuron* 80, no. 3 (2013): 729–41.

25. Fergus I. M. Craik and Ellen Bialystok, "Cognition through the Lifespan: Mechanisms of Change," *Trends in Cognitive Sciences* 10, no. 3 (2006): 131–38.

26. Nitin Gogtay, Jay N. Giedd, Leslie Lusk, Kiralee M. Hayashi, Deanna Greenstein, A. Catherine Vaituzis, Tom F. Nugent, et al., "Dynamic Mapping of Human Cortical Development during Childhood through Early Adulthood," *Proceedings of the National Academy of Sciences of the United States of America* 101, no. 21 (2004): 8174–79.

27. Ibid.

28. Michael M. Merzenich, Randall J. Nelson, Michael P. Stryker, Max S. Cynader, Axel Schoppmann, and John M. Zook, "Somatosensory Cortical Map Changes Following Digit Amputation in Adult Monkeys," *Journal of Comparative Neurology* 224, no. 4 (1984): 591–605.

29. Jon H. Kaas, "Neurobiology: Phantoms of the Brain," *Nature* 391, no. 6665 (1998): 331–33, quote on p. 331.

30. Ibid.
31. Elise Temple, Gayle K. Deutsch, Russell A. Poldrack, Steven L. Miller, Paula Tallal, Michael M. Merzenich, and John D. E. Gabrieli, "Neural Deficits in Children with Dyslexia Ameliorated by Behavioral Remediation: Evidence from Functional MRI," *Proceedings of the National Academy of Sciences* 100, no. 5 (2003): 2860–65.
32. Ganguly and Poo, "Activity-Dependent Neural Plasticity."
33. "Scientific Learning Products," Scientific Learning, http://www.scilearn.com/products.
34. "Science," BrainPro, https://brainsparklearning.com/brainpro/science/.
35. Paula Tallal, Steve L. Miller, Gail Bedi, Gary Byma, Xiaoqin Wang, Srikantan S. Nagarajan, et al., "Language Comprehension in Language-Learning Impaired Children Improved with Acoustically Modified Speech," *Science* 271, no. 5245 (1996): 81–84.
36. Stephen Camarata and Paul Yoder, "Language Transactions during Development and Intervention," *International Journal of Developmental Neuroscience* 20, no. 3 (2002): 459–65.
37. Ibid.
38. Wendy Cohen, Ann Hodson, Anne O'Hare, James Boyle, Tariq Durrani, Elspeth McCartney, Mike Mattey, et al., "Effects of Computer-Based Intervention through Acoustically Modified Speech (Fast ForWord) in Severe Mixed Receptive-Expressive Language Impairment," *Journal of Speech, Language, and Hearing Research* 48, no. 3 (2005): 715–29. Stephen Camarata, "Fast ForWord Does Not Significantly Improve Language Skills in Children with Language Disorders," *Evidence-Based Communication Assessment and Intervention* 2, no. 2 (2008): 96–98.

Chapter 3: "The Critical Period"

1. The State of the News Media 2011, Project for Excellence in Journalism, Pew Research Center, http://www.stateofthemedia.org/files/2011/01/magazine_audience_e.jpg.
2. Sharon Begley, "Your Child's Brain," *Newsweek*, February 19, 1996, 55–61.
3. Joan Beck, "To Shape a Life, We Must Begin before a Child Is 3," *Chicago Tribune*, April 21, 1994.
4. David Perlmutter and Carol Colman, *Raise a Smarter Child by Kindergarten: Build a Better Brain and Increase IQ up to 30 Points* (New York: Bantam Dell Publishing Group, 2006).
5. D. Purves, G. J. Augustine, and D. Fitzpatrick, eds., "The Development of Language: A Critical Period in Humans," in *Neuroscience*, 2nd ed. (Sunderland, MA: Sinauer Associates, 2001).
6. Robert DeKeyser, "Age Effects in Second Language Learning," *Language Learning* 63 (2013): 52–67.
7. Rod Parker-Rees and Jenny Willan, *Early Years Education: Curriculum Issues in Early Childhood Education* (New York: Routledge, 2006).
8. Jean Piaget, *The Origins of Intelligence in Children*, trans. Margaret Cook (New York: International Universities Press, 1952).
9. Lois Nelson, "Accelerating Cognitive Development: Harmful or Helpful to Children?," *Educational Leadership* 31 (1973): 255–58, quote on p. 257.
10. Guy Claxton, *Hare Brain, Tortoise Mind: Why Intelligence Increases When You Think Less* (New York: HarperCollins, 1997).
11. Larry Fenson, Elizabeth Bates, Philip Dale, Judith Goodman, J. Steven Reznick, and Donna Thal, "Reply: Measuring Variability in Early Child Language: Don't Shoot the Messenger," *Child Development* 71, no. 2 (2000): 323–28.
12. Stephen M. Camarata, *Late-Talking Children: A Symptom or a Stage?* (Cambridge, MA: MIT Press, 2014).
13. Stephen M. Camarata and Richard G. Schwartz, "Production of Object Words and Action Words: Evidence for a Relationship between Phonology and Semantics," *Journal of Speech and Hearing Research* 28, no. 3 (1985): 323–30.
14. David Crystal, "Towards a 'Bucket' Theory of Language Disability: Taking Account of Interaction between Linguistic Levels," *Clinical Linguistics & Phonetics* 1, no. 1 (1987): 7–22.
15. Constance Reid, "The Autobiography of Julia Robinson," *College Mathematics Journal* 17, no. 1 (1986): 3–21.

16. Jon Bardin, "Neurodevelopment: Unlocking the brain," *Nature* 487, no. 7405 (2012): 24–26, quote on p. 24, http://www.nature.com/news/neurodevelopment-unlocking-the -brain-1.10925.

17. Beth M. Iovanelli, "Q&A: What Are the Critical Periods in My Baby's Development?" Babble, 2012, http://www.babble.com/parenting/critical-periods-development/.

18. Christine Sterbenz, "The Heartbreaking Story of Genie, a Feral Child Who Will Never Learn to Communicate," *Business Insider*, October 9, 2013, http://www.busines sinsider.com/critical-period-for-language-acquisition-2013-10?op=1.

19. Inderbir Kaur Sandhu, "Early Brain Development: Critical and Sensitive Periods," Brainy-Child, http://www.brainy-child.com/expert/early-brain-development.shtml.

20. National Institute of Mental Health, *The Teen Brain: Still Under Construction*, NIH Publication no. 11-4929, 2011.

21. L. D. Selemon, "A Role for Synaptic Plasticity in the Adolescent Development of Executive Function," *Translational Psychiatry* 3, no. 3 (2013): e238.

22. David H. Hubel and Torsten N. Wiesel, "Receptive Fields, Binocular Interaction and Functional Architecture in the Cat's Visual Cortex," *Journal of Physiology* 160, no. 1 (1962): 106–54.

23. Martin S. Banks, Richard N. Aslin, and Robert D. Letson, "Sensitive Period for the Development of Human Binocular Vision," *Science* 190, no. 4215 (1975): 675–77.

24. Yuri Ostrovsky, Aaron Andalman, and Pawan Sinha, "Vision Following Extended Congenital Blindness," *Psychological Science* 17, no. 12 (2006): 1009–14.

25. John T. Bruer, *The Myth of the First Three Years: A New Understanding of Early Brain Development and Lifelong Learning* (New York: Simon and Schuster, 1999).

26. Patricia K. Kuhl, "Early Language Acquisition: Cracking the Speech Code," *Nature Reviews Neuroscience* 5, no. 11 (2004): 831–43.

Chapter 4: Enhancing Intelligence Using Intuitive Parenting

1. Ian J. Deary, Jian Yang, Gail Davies, Sarah E. Harris, Albert Tenesa, David Liewald, Michelle Luciano, et al., "Genetic Contributions to Stability and Change in Intelligence from Childhood to Old Age," *Nature* 482 (2012): 212–15, quote on p. 212.

2. Alan J. Gow, Wendy Johnson, Alison Pattie, Caroline E. Brett, Beverly Roberts, John M. Starr, and Ian J. Deary, "Stability and Change in Intelligence from Age 11 to Ages 70, 79, and 87: The Lothian Birth Cohorts of 1921 and 1936," *Psychology and Aging* 26, no. 1 (2011): 232–40.

3. Nancy Bayley, "Consistency and Variability in the Growth of Intelligence from Birth to Eighteen Years," *Pedagogical Seminary and Journal of Genetic Psychology* 75, no. 2 (1949): 165–96.

4. Thomas Sowell, *The Einstein Syndrome: Bright Children Who Talk Late* (New York: Basic Books, 2002).

5. Donna Beeston, "The Early Years of Albert Einstein: When Viewed through the Lens of Current Theory and Research, Were There Signs of Giftedness?," *APEX* 15, no. 4 (2009): 56–77. And Albrecht Folsing, *Albert Einstein: A Biography* (New York: Viking, 1997).

6. "Celebrating Edward Teller at 90," *Science & Technology Review* July/August (1998): quote on p. 4.

7. John Bruer, *The Myth of the First Three Years* (New York: Free Press, 2002).

8. "Gifted & Talented," NYC Department of Education, http://schools.nyc.gov/Choices Enrollment/GiftedandTalented/default.htm. Accessed on March 10, 2014.

9. Alfred Binet and Theodore Simon, *The Development of Intelligence in Children: The Binet-Simon Scale*, trans. Elizabeth S. Kite (Baltimore, MD: Williams & Wilkins Company, 1916).

10. Stephen Camarata and Linda Swisher, "A Note on Intelligence Assessment within Studies of Specific Language Impairment," *Journal of Speech, Language, and Hearing Research* 33, no. 1 (1990): 205–7.

11. Marlene Sotelo-Dynega, Samuel O. Ortiz, Dawn P. Flanagan, and William F. Chaplin, "English Language Proficiency and Test Performance: An Evaluation of Bilingual Students with the Woodcock-Johnson III Tests of Cognitive Abilities," *Psychology in the Schools* 50, no. 8 (2013): 781–97.

12. Oliver Sacks, *An Anthropologist on Mars: Seven Paradoxical Tales* (New York: Knopf, 1995).
13. David Wechsler, *Wechsler Intelligence Scale for Children: Manual* (New York: Psychological Corp., 1949).
14. Russell Graydon Leiter and Stanley David Porteus, *The Leiter International Performance Scale* (University of Hawaii, 1936).
15. McCay Vernon and Beth Daigle-King, "Historical Overview of Inpatient Care of Mental Patients Who Are Deaf," *American Annals of the Deaf* 144, no. 1 (1999): 51–61.
16. Kevin S. McGrew, "CHC Theory and the Human Cognitive Abilities Project: Standing on the Shoulders of the Giants of Psychometric Intelligence Research," *Intelligence* 37, no. 1 (2009): 1–10.
17. Randy W. Kamphaus, Martha D. Petoskey, and Anna Walters Morgan, "A History of Intelligence Test Interpretation," in *Contemporary Intellectual Assessment: Theories, Tests, and Issues*, eds. Dawn P. Flanagan and Patti L. Harrison (New York: Guilford Publications, 1997): 3–16.
18. Florence L. Goodenough and Dale B. Harris, "Studies in the Psychology of Children's Drawings: II; 1928–1949," *Psychological Bulletin* 47, no. 5 (1950): 369–433.
19. Dale B. Harris, *Children's Drawings as Measures of Intellectual Maturity: A Revision and Extension of the Goodenough Draw-a-Man Test* (New York: Harcourt, Brace & World, 1963).
20. John L. Horn, "Remodeling Old Models of Intelligence," in *Handbook of Intelligence*, ed. B. B. Wolman (New York: John Wiley & Sons, 1985), 267–300. John B. Carroll, "Psychometric Tests as Cognitive Tasks: A New 'Structure of Intellect,'" Technical Report no. 4, Educational Testing Service, Princeton, NJ, 1974.
21. Patricia K., Kuhl, Barbara T. Conboy, Denise Padden, Tobey Nelson, and Jessica Pruitt, "Early Speech Perception and Later Language Development: Implications for the 'Critical Period,'" *Language Learning and Development* 1, no. 3/4 (2005): 237–64.
22. Wolfgang Schneider and Michael Pressley, *Memory Development between Two and Twenty* (Psychology Press, 2013).
23. Kathy A. Lutz and Richard J. Lutz, "Imagery-Eliciting Strategies: Review and Implications of Research," *Advances in Consumer Research* 5, no. 1 (1978): 611–20.
24. Willem J. M. Levelt, "Models of Word Production," *Trends in Cognitive Sciences* 3, no. 6 (1999): 223–32.
25. Kevin S. McGrew and Jeffrey J. Evans, "Internal and External Factorial Extensions to the Cattell–Horn–Carroll (CHC) Theory of Cognitive Abilities: A Review of Factor Analytic Research since Carroll's Seminal 1993 Treatise," Carroll Human Cognitive Abilities (HCA) Project Research Report 2 (2004).
26. Jörg D. Jescheniak and Willem J. M. Levelt, "Word Frequency Effects in Speech Production: Retrieval of Syntactic Information and of Phonological Form," *Journal of Experimental Psychology: Learning, Memory, and Cognition* 20, no. 4 (1994): 824–43.
27. Steven Pinker, "Words and Rules in the Human Brain," *Nature* 387 (1997): 547–48.
28. Richard Murnane, Isabel Sawhill, and Catherine Snow, "Literacy Challenges for the Twenty-First Century: Introducing the Issue," *The Future of Children* 22, no. 2 (2012): 3–15.
29. *PISA 2009 Results: What Students Know and Can Do: Student Performance in Reading, Mathematics and Science*, Programme for International Student Assessment. OECD, 2011.
30. Anneli Niikko, "Finnish Daycare: Caring, Education and Instruction," in *Nordic Childhoods and Early Education: Philosophy, Research, Policy and Practice in Denmark, Finland, Iceland, Norway, and Sweden*, ed. Judith T. Wagner (Information Age Publishing Inc., 2006).
31. Wolfgang J. Arnold, "The Spiral Ganglion of the Newborn Baby," *American Journal of Otology* 3, no. 3 (1982): 266–69.
32. Scott Barry Kaufman, Colin G. DeYoung, Jeremy R. Gray, Jamie Brown, and Nicholas Mackintosh, "Associative Learning Predicts Intelligence Above and Beyond Working Memory and Processing Speed," *Intelligence* 37, no. 4 (2009): 374–82.
33. Robert Kail, "Speed of Information Processing: Developmental Change and Links to Intelligence," *Journal of School Psychology* 38, no. 1 (2000): 51–61.
34. Richard W. Woodcock, Kevin S. McGrew, and Nancy Mather, *Woodcock-Johnson III Tests of Cognitive Abilities* (New York: Riverside, 2001).

Chapter 5: Raising Lifelong Learners

1. Robin Goulden, Paul Nation, and John Read, "How Large Can a Receptive Vocabulary Be?," *Applied Linguistics* 11, no. 4 (1990): 341–63.
2. Steven Pinker, *The Language Instinct: How the Mind Creates Language* (New York: Harper Perennial, 1995).
3. "U.S. and World Population Clock," United States Census Bureau, https://www.census.gov/popclock/. Accessed February 27, 2014.
4. Douglas L. T. Rohde, and David C. Plaut, "Language Acquisition in the Absence of Explicit Negative Evidence: How Important Is Starting Small?" *Cognition* 72, no. 1 (1999): 67–109.
5. Jeanette Winter, *The House That Jack Built* (New York: Dial Books for Young Readers, 2000).
6. Mother Goose, "This is the House that Jack Built," http://www3.amherst.edu/~rjyanco94/literature/mothergoose/rhymes/thisisthehousethatjackbuilt.html.
7. Nancy D. Baker and Keith E. Nelson, "Recasting and Related Conversational Techniques for Triggering Syntactic Advances by Young Children," *First Language* 5, no. 13 (1984): 3–21.
8. Luciano Fadiga, Laila Craighero, and Alessandro D'Ausilio, "Broca's Area in Language, Action, and Music," *Annals of the New York Academy of Sciences* 1169, no. 1 (2009): 448–58.
9. Elizabeth A. Kensinger and Daniel L. Schacter, "Processing Emotional Pictures and Words: Effects of Valence and Arousal," *Cognitive, Affective, & Behavioral Neuroscience* 6, no. 2 (2006): 110–26.

Chapter 6: Confidence, Resilience, and Persistence

1. Robert A. Guth, "Raising Bill Gates," *Wall Street Journal*, April 25, 2009, http://www.wsj.com/articles/SB124061372413054653.
2. Evan Carmichael, "Before Microsoft: The Upbringing of Bill Gates," EvanCarmichael.com, http://www.evancarmichael.com/Famous-Entrepreneurs/556/Before-Microsoft-The-Upbringing-of-Bill-Gates.html.
3. Guth, "Raising Bill Gates."
4. Ibid.
5. Joan Freeman, *Gifted Lives: What Happens When Gifted Children Grow Up* (New York: Routledge, 2013).
6. Po Bronson and Ashley Merryman, *NurtureShock: Why Everything We Think about Raising Our Children Is Wrong* (Chatham, UK: Random House, 2009).
7. C. June Maker, "Giftedness, Diversity, and Problem-Solving: Multiple Intelligences and Diversity in Educational Settings," *Teaching Exceptional Children* 27, no. 1 (1994): 4–19.
8. Heidi Stevens, "Enough Already! Praise Gets Heavy, Why Can't We Stop?," *Southwest*, January 2015, 60–69, quote on p. 61.
9. Carol Dweck, *Mindset: The New Psychology of Success* (New York: Random House, 2006).
10. Bronson and Merryman, *NurtureShock*.
11. Ibid.

Chapter 7: Behavior—and Consequences

1. Arthur Robert Jensen, *The g Factor: The Science of Mental Ability* (Westport, CT: Praeger, 1998).
2. M. Alex Meredith and Barry E. Stein, "Visual, Auditory, and Somatosensory Convergence on Cells in Superior Colliculus Results in Multisensory Integration," *Journal of Neurophysiology* 56, no. 3 (1986): 640–62.
3. Tom Bartlett, "A New Twist in the Sad Saga of Little Albert," *The Chronicle of Higher Education*, May 20, 2015, http://chronicle.com/blogs/percolator/a-new-twist-in-the-sad-saga-of-little-albert/28423.
4. Randy L. Page, "Emotional and Rational Product Appeals in Televised Food Advertisements for Children: Analysis of Commercials Shown on U.S. Broadcast Networks," *Journal of Child Health Care* 11, no. 4 (2007): 323–40.

5. Arthur R. Jensen and William D. Rohwer Jr., "Verbal Mediation in Paired-Associate and Serial Learning," *Journal of Verbal Learning and Verbal Behavior*, no. 5 (1963): 346–52.
6. James H. Geer, Gerald C. Davison, and Robert I. Gatchel, "Reduction of Stress in Humans through Nonveridical Perceived Control of Aversive Stimulation," *Journal of Personality and Social Psychology* 16, no. 4 (1970): 731–38. Jens C. Pruessner, Dirk H. Hellhammer, and Clemens Kirschbaum, "Burnout, Perceived Stress, and Cortisol Responses to Awakening," *Psychosomatic Medicine* 61, no. 2 (1999): 197–204.
7. Associated Press, "Adrian Peterson Dodges Jail for Beating Kid," *New York Post*, November 4, 2014, http://nypost.com/2014/11/04/adrian-peterson-reaches-plea-deal-football-future-in-limbo/.
8. James M. Johnston, "Punishment of Human Behavior," *American Psychologist* 27, no. 11 (1972): 1033.
9. C. H. Graham and R. M. Gagne, "The Acquisition, Extinction, and Spontaneous Recovery of a Conditioned Operant Response," *Journal of Experimental Psychology* 26, no. 3 (1940): 251–80.

Chapter 8: Intuitive Parenting, Education, and Schools

1. Digest of Education Statistics, National Center for Education Statistics, http://nces.ed.gov/programs/digest/d11/tables/dt11_069.asp.
2. Hazel M. Lambert, *Teaching the Kindergarten Child* (Harcourt, Brace, 1958).
3. Patricia De Cos, "Readiness for Kindergarten: What Does It Mean?" California Research Bureau, California State Library, December 1997, 4–5. CRB-97-014.
4. W. Steven Barnett and Donald J. Yarosz, "Who Goes to Preschool and Why Does It Matter?" *Preschool Policy Matters*, no. 15 (2007).
5. Ann Higgins Hains, Susan A. Fowler, Ilene S. Schwartz, Esther Kottwitz, and Sharon Rosenkoetter, "A Comparison of Preschool and Kindergarten Teacher Expectations for School Readiness," *Early Childhood Research Quarterly* 4, no. 1 (1989): 75–88. Table 1 on pages 80–83.
6. Ibid.
7. Ibid.
8. Common Core State Standards Initiative, "Home," Common Core State Standards Initiative, http://www.corestandards.org/.
9. Common Core State Standards Initiative, "Kindergarten: Introduction," Mathematics, Common Core State Standards Initiatives, http://www.corestandards.org/Math/Content/K/introduction.
10. Ibid.
11. Jill Anderson, "Changing Readers, Changing Texts: Ed School Hosts Fifth Annual Jeanne Chall Lecture," News and Events, Harvard Graduate School of Education, February 12, 2010, http://www.gse.harvard.edu/news/10/02/changing-readers-changing-texts-ed-school-hosts-fifth-annual-jeanne-chall-lecture.
12. Jon Guttman, "Was the USA Ever No. 1 in Education?" HistoryNet, October 4, 2012, http://www.historynet.com/was-the-usa-ever-no-1-in-education.htm.
13. Bruce Alberts, "Trivializing Science Education," *Science* 335, no. 6066 (2012): 263.
14. "'Early Learning' Primer for Parents," International Parenting Association, http://www.internationalparentingassociation.org/Early_Learning/accelerate.html.
15. Lorrie A. Shepard and Mary Lee Smith, "Escalating Academic Demand in Kindergarten: Counterproductive Policies," *Elementary School Journal* 89, no. 2 (1988): 135–45, quote on p. 135.
16. Ibid.
17. Samuel J. Meisels, "High Stakes Testing in Kindergarten," *Educational Leadership* 46, no. 7 (1989): 16–22.
18. Ashlesha Datar, "Does Delaying Kindergarten Entrance Give Children a Head Start?" *Economics of Education Review* 25, no. 1 (2006): 43–62, quote on p. 43.
19. Sandra L. Crosser, "Summer Birth Date Children: Kindergarten Entrance Age and Academic Achievement," *Journal of Educational Research* 84, no. 3 (1991): 140–46.
20. Meisels, "High Stakes Testing in Kindergarten."

21. James M. Schuerger, and Anita C. Witt, "The Temporal Stability of Individually Tested Intelligence," *Journal of Clinical Psychology* 45, no. 2 (1989): 294–302.
22. Michael J. Roszkowski, "Stability of IQs from Group-Administered Tests: Some Further Data," *Psychological Reports* 54, no. 2 (1984): 482.
23. Jasper Copping, "One in Six Parents 'Do All the Homework,'" *Telegraph* (UK), January 16, 2014, http://www.telegraph.co.uk/education/educationnews/10578136/One-in-six-parents-do-all-the-homework.html.

Chapter 9: The Perils of Too Much Too Soon

1. "Data and Statistics," Autism Spectrum Disorder, Centers for Disease Control and Prevention, http://www.cdc.gov/ncbddd/autism/data.html.
2. Alan Schwarz and Sarah Cohen, "A.D.H.D. Seen in 11% of U.S. Children as Diagnoses Rise," *New York Times*, March 31, 2013, http://www.nytimes.com/2013/04/01/health/more-diagnoses-of-hyperactivity-causing-concern.html.
3. Patrick M. O'Connell, "ADHD, Medication Rates in U.S. Continue to Rise," *AAP News*, November 22, 2013, http://aapnews.aappublications.org/content/early/2013/11/22/aapnews.20131122-1.full.pdf+html.
4. David Rettew, "ADHD Medication Rates Across 50 States," *Psychology Today*, January 9, 2014, http://www.psychologytoday.com/blog/abcs-child-psychiatry/201401/adhd-medication-rates-across-50-states.
5. Rae Thomas, Sharon Sanders, Jenny Doust, Elaine Beller, and Paul Glasziou, "Prevalence of Attention-Deficit/Hyperactivity Disorder: A Systematic Review and Meta-Analysis," *Pediatrics* 135, no. 4 (2015): e994–e1001.
6. Camille L. Z. Blachowicz and Peter Fisher, *Teaching Vocabulary in All Classrooms* (Upper Saddle River, NJ: Merrill/Prentice Hall, 2002).
7. Lloyd M. Dunn and Leota M. Dunn, *Peabody Picture Vocabulary Test* (Circle Pines, MN: American Guidance Service, 1965).
8. Yongqi Gu and Robert Keith Johnson, "Vocabulary Learning Strategies and Language Learning Outcomes," *Language Learning* 46, no. 4 (1996): 643–79.
9. Judy S. DeLoache, Cynthia Chiong, Kathleen Sherman, Nadia Islam, Mieke Vanderborght, Georgene L. Troseth, Gabrielle A. Strouse, and Katherine O'Doherty, "Do Babies Learn from Baby Media?," *Psychological Science* 21, no. 11 (2010): 1570–74, quote on p. 1570.
10. Ibid.
11. Georgene L. Troseth, Megan M. Saylor, and Allison H. Archer, "Young Children's Use of video as a Source of Socially Relevant Information," *Child Development* 77, no. 3 (2006): 786–99.
12. Carole Napier, "How Use of Screen Media Affects the Emotional Development of Infants," *Primary Health Care* 24, no. 2 (2014): 18–25.
13. Neal Halfon, Amy Houtrow, Kandyce Larson, and Paul W. Newacheck, "The Changing Landscape of Disability in Childhood," *The Future of Children* 22, no. 1 (2012): 13–42.
14. Candace Cortiella, *The State of Learning Disabilities* (New York: National Center for Learning Disabilities, 2011).
15. "Literacy," The World Factbook, Central Intelligence Agency, https://www.cia.gov/library/publications/the-world-factbook/fields/2103.html.
16. Organisation for Economic Co-operation and Development, *Students with Disabilities, Learning Difficulties and Disadvantages: Policies, Statistics and Indicators, 2007 Edition* (Organisation for Economic Co-operation and Development, 2008).
17. Lynn Hughes, "Letter to the Editor: How We Diagnose and Treat A.D.H.D.," *New York Times*, March 5, 2014, http://www.nytimes.com/2014/03/05/opinion/how-we-diagnose-and-treat-adhd.html?_r=0.
18. Craig J. Newschaffer, Matthew D. Falb, and James G. Gurney, "National Autism Prevalence Trends from United States Special Education Data," *Pediatrics* 115, no. 3 (2005): e277–e282.
19. Richard P. Smith, "Boredom: A Review," *Human Factors: The Journal of the Human Factors and Ergonomics Society* 23, no. 3 (1981): 329–40.

20. Annetta Weber, Chantal Fussler, J. F. O'Hanlon, R. Gierer, and E. Grandjean, "Psychophysiological Effects of Repetitive Tasks," *Ergonomics* 23, no. 11 (1980): 1033–46.

21. William L. Mikulas and Stephen J. Vodanovich, "The Essence of Boredom," *Psychological Record* 43, no. 1 (1993): 3–12.

22. Lannie Kanevsky and Tacey Keighley, "To Produce or Not to Produce? Understanding Boredom and the Honor in Underachievement," *Roeper Review* 26, no. 1 (2003): 20–28, quotes on p. 24.

23. Stewart Shipp, "The Brain Circuitry of Attention," *Trends in Cognitive Sciences* 8, no. 5 (2004): 223–30.

24. Michael Rutter, "Incidence of Autism Spectrum Disorders: Changes over Time and Their Meaning," *Acta Paediatrica* 94, no. 1 (2005): 2–15.

25. Salynn Boyles, "CDC: Autism Rates Higher than Thought: But More Aggressive Diagnosis May Explain Increase in Cases," WebMD Health News, December 31, 2002, http://www.webmd.com/mental-health/news/20021231/cdc-autism-rates-higher-than-thought.

26. "Data and Statistics," Autism Spectrum Disorder, Centers for Disease Control and Prevention, http://www.cdc.gov/ncbddd/autism/data.html.

27. Ibid.

28. Maureen W. Lovett, Susan L. Borden, Teresa DeLuca, Léa Lacerenza, Nancy J. Benson, and Demaris Brackstone, "Treating the Core Deficits of Developmental Dyslexia: Evidence of Transfer of Learning after Phonologically- and Strategy-Based Reading Training Programs," *Developmental Psychology* 30, no. 6 (1994): 805–22.

29. Donald L. Compton, Amanda C. Miller, Amy M. Elleman, and Laura M. Steacy, "Have We Forsaken Reading Theory in the Name of 'Quick Fix' Interventions for Children with Reading Disability?," *Scientific Studies of Reading* 18, no. 1 (2014): 55–73.

30. Ibid.

31. M. Scheiman, S. Cotter, M. Rouse, G. L. Mitchell, M. Kulp, J. Cooper, and E. Borsting, "Randomised Clinical Trial of the Effectiveness of Base-In Prism Reading Glasses versus Placebo Reading Glasses for Symptomatic Convergence Insufficiency in Children," *British Journal of Ophthalmology* 89, no. 10 (2005): 1318–23, quote on p. 1318.

32. Cecilia Elena Rouse and Alan B. Krueger, "Putting Computerized Instruction to the Test: A Randomized Evaluation of a 'Scientifically Based' Reading Program," *Economics of Education Review* 23, no. 4 (2004): 323–38, quote on p. 323.

33. "How It Works," Interactive Metronome, http://www.interactivemetronome.com/index.php/what-is-imhome/how-it-works.html. Accessed February 11, 2015.

34. Ibid.

35. See, for example, Sigmund Eldevik, Richard P. Hastings, J. Carl Hughes, Erik Jahr, Svein Eikeseth, and Scott Cross, "Meta-Analysis of Early Intensive Behavioral Intervention for Children with Autism," *Journal of Clinical Child & Adolescent Psychology* 38, no. 3 (2009): 439–50.

36. "Patients Who Can Benefit," Interactive Metronome, http://www.interactivemetronome.com/index.php/what-is-imhome/patients-who-can-benefit.html.

37. Lakshmi Gandhi, "A History Of 'Snake Oil Salesmen,'" Code Switch, NPR, August 26, 2013, http://www.npr.org/blogs/codeswitch/2013/08/26/215761377/a-history-of-snake-oil-salesmen.

38. Elizabeth A. Harris, "Sharp Rise in Occupational Therapy Cases at New York's Schools," *New York Times*, February 17, 2015, http://www.nytimes.com/2015/02/18/nyregion/new-york-city-schools-see-a-sharp-increase-in-occupational-therapy-cases.html.

39. Michelle Zimmer, Larry Desch, Lawrence D. Rosen, Michelle L. Bailey, David Becker, Timothy P. Culbert, Hilary McClafferty, et al., "Sensory Integration Therapies for Children with Developmental and Behavioral Disorders," *Pediatrics* 129, no. 6 (2012): 1186–89, quote on page 1186.

40. Ibid.

41. Jennifer Stephenson and Mark Carter, "The Use of Weighted Vests with Children with Autism Spectrum Disorders and Other Disabilities," *Journal of Autism and Developmental Disorders* 39, no. 1 (2009): 105–14, quote on p. 105.

42. Andrew J. Wakefield, Simon H. Murch, Andrew Anthony, John Linnell, D. M. Casson, Mohsin Malik, Mark Berelowitz, et al., "Ileal-Lymphoid-Nodular Hyperplasia,

Non-Specific Colitis, and Pervasive Developmental Disorder in Children," *The Lancet* 351, no. 9103 (1998): 637–41.

43. Melly Alazraki, "The Autism Vaccine Fraud: Dr. Wakefield's Costly Lie to Society," DailyFinance, January 12, 2011, http://www.dailyfinance.com/2011/01/12/autism-vaccine-fraud-wakefield-cost-money-deaths/.

44. Clare Dyer, "Lancet Retracts Wakefield's MMR Paper," *British Medical Journal* 340 (2010): c696.

45. Fiona Godlee, Jane Smith, and Harvey Marcovitch, "Wakefield's Article Linking MMR Vaccine and Autism Was Fraudulent," *British Medical Journal* 342 (2011).

46. Stephen M. Camarata, *Late-Talking Children: A Symptom or a Stage?* (Cambridge, MA: MIT Press, 2014).

47. Robert L. Koegel, Daniel Openden, and Lynn Kern Koegel, "A Systematic Desensitization Paradigm to Treat Hypersensitivity to Auditory Stimuli in Children with Autism in Family Contexts," *Research and Practice for Persons with Severe Disabilities* 29, no. 2 (2004): 122–34.

48. George J. DuPaul, Tanya L. Eckert, and Brigid Vilardo, "The Effects of School-Based Interventions for Attention Deficit Hyperactivity Disorder: A Meta-Analysis 1996–2010," *School Psychology Review* 41, no. 4 (2012): 387–412. Russell A. Barkley, ed., *Attention-Deficit Hyperactivity Disorder: A Handbook for Diagnosis and Treatment* (New York: Guilford Publications, 2014).

49. Ibid.

50. Mark D. Rapport, Sarah A. Orban, Michael J. Kofler, and Lauren M. Friedman, "Do Programs Designed to Train Working Memory, Other Executive Functions, and Attention Benefit Children with ADHD? A Meta-Analytic Review of Cognitive, Academic, and Behavioral Outcomes," *Clinical Psychology Review* 33, no. 8 (2013): 1237–52, quote on p. 1237.

51. DuPaul, Eckert, and Vilardo, "The Effects of School-Based Interventions for Attention Deficit Hyperactivity Disorder," 387–412.

52. Sheila Wolfendale, ed. *Parent Partnership Services for Special Educational Needs: Celebrations and Challenges* (New York: Routledge, 2013). Laura Lee McIntyre, "Parent Training Interventions to Reduce Challenging Behaviour in Children with Intellectual and Developmental Disabilities," *International Review of Research in Developmental Disabilities* 44, no. 1 (2013): 245–79.

Chapter 10: Follow Your Intuition to Enjoy the Journey

1. Pamela Kilian, *Barbara Bush: Matriarch of a Dynasty* (New York: Macmillan, 2003), 50.

index